THE UNIVERSE IS TALKING TO YOU

Messages in the Numbers

BY ALANA FAIRCHILD

This re-designed edition printed 2026.
Copyright © 2015 Alana Fairchild

All rights reserved. Except for personal use, no part of this book may be reproduced, in whole or in part, without written permission from the publisher. This book is for spiritual and emotional guidance only and is not a substitute for medical advice or treatment. The author's views, within and beyond this publication, do not necessarily reflect those of the publisher. We respectfully request that this content not be used to train AI-generative models or machine learning systems without the publisher's written consent.

Published by Blue Angel Publishing®
10 Trafford Court, Wheelers Hill
Victoria, Australia 3150

info@blueangelonline.com
www.blueangelonline.com

Edited by Tanya Graham

Designed by Gemma Christensen

Blue Angel is a registered trademark of Blue Angel Gallery Pty Ltd.

ISBN: 978-1-922574-59-6

Designed in Australia. Printed in China with soy-based inks.

DEDICATION

This book is dedicated to those people who see 11.11 on their alarm clock or mobile phone and wonder *could this be trying to tell me something?*

And to those who have pondered a problem and then wondered *is there anyone out there who cares?* A big YES to both questions.

This book is for you.

ABOUT ALANA FAIRCHILD

An artist of a different kind, Alana Fairchild is a visionary powerhouse with a gift for soul-stirring communications. With a loving sense of humour and considerable knowledge across a broad range of metaphysical topics, Alana weaves magic into the world to uplift, vitalise and comfort the heart. She is a rare and nourishing channel who stimulates spiritual awakening and healing through her very presence. Alana's energy is a consciousness catalyst for transformation with a gentleness, purity and potency that sets her apart.

Alana's insights articulate a spirituality that is creative and personally empowering, valuing freedom and self-responsibility. Alana has devoted her life to creating unique works that resonate deeply with the soul and ignite the subtle fire of Spirit within, to inspire and spiritually equip human beings to reach most sacred and blessed fruition.

To explore Alana's special offerings, including online programs, unique in-person experiences and more, you are warmly welcomed to visit www.alanafairchild.com.

CONTENTS

THE UNIVERSE IS TALKING TO YOU   7

NUMBER ONE   21

NUMBER TWO   59

NUMBER THREE   85

NUMBER FOUR   113

NUMBER FIVE   143

NUMBER SIX   161

NUMBER SEVEN   187

NUMBER EIGHT   209

NUMBER NINE   231

ZERO   252

Afterword   256

THE UNIVERSE IS TALKING TO YOU

The Universe is a powerful, intelligent and creative field. Much of what goes on within it may appear random to us, from the perspective of our relatively small, human lives. It is so incredibly vast that it's hard to imagine that we are an important part of it. Yet, within its intelligence lie creative solutions for any difficulty you could possibly encounter.

Included in that intelligence, is a benevolent streak of compassion. The Universe is not, contrary to the beliefs of some, entertained by your struggles in life, chuckling away with perverse humour at your misfortunes. The Universe is rather more like the greatest cheerleader ever, urging you on to the right path, encouraging you to make the most fearless and loving choices, guiding you towards your ultimate destiny, which is to live all of your being, that being far greater than one would typically imagine.

In short, the Universe wants to help you! If that means it's necessary to give you signs through the clock on your mobile phone, computer or alarm, or through the number plate on the car in front of you, then so be it. There are messages in the numbers. Those are the messages that the Universe wants to get through to you – to help you grow and live a happier, more connected and fulfilling life. Are you ready to hear them? It's easy! Let this user-friendly guidebook help you interpret the messages in the numbers and start reading the signs that are meant for you.

Although I was raised in a Catholic household with Christian traditions such as going to church and praying to God, Jesus and Mother Mary, that household was very open-minded, unusually so perhaps, about other religions and spiritual practices. I was extremely lucky and grateful to have been raised in such a relatively free and tolerant family. Supported by that childhood openness, I have since explored and embraced the heart of a variety of religious and spiritual practices and consider myself to belong to neither one in particular, and yet somehow to all of them. I suppose because underneath all genuine religious tradition and spiritual discipline, there feels to me to be a similar vein – which is to connect with the Divine.

There is a reason that I mention religion first up, in a book that is not actually religious at all. Numbers are a universal, and by that I mean neutral, language. That is part of their power and accuracy. They can cut through overly complex interpretations and fearful belief systems, delivering clear, simple messages. However, our various religious and cultural tendencies can impose filters of beliefs or associations upon them without us being aware of it at first. That isn't bad. We are entitled to choose what we want to believe in. It's part of our free will and our spiritual development to take responsibility for our beliefs as we grow, choosing what to release and what to adopt, according to the truths of our hearts. The only difficulty is, if we choose beliefs that are based in fear, making some things bad and other things good, we can unintentionally block the messages of assistance and kindness that life wants to bring to us, in order to assist us on the path.

If we view life with suspicion and fear, we can end up turning our back on opportunities that may have seemed to be challenging and yet held within them the seeds of our future liberation. So in working with this book, it's good to know right from the beginning, that you might feel challenged to let go of some of your fear about life, and your need to control things, and instead be asked to open up and begin to relate to the messages in the numbers from a place of trust, believing that the Universe genuinely loves you and wants to help you live your life in the best way for you.

Even though living our life in the 'best way' will often mean very different things for different people, there is one aspect of it that we all have in common. That is, when we live in that way, the 'best way' for us, it is a win-win situation. The greater scheme of life benefits when we are true to ourselves because we are trusting in the grander divine design. We weren't made to be something or someone else. We were made to be ourselves, to discover the divinity or the brilliance or the love, within.

No matter what your religious or spiritual background, or even lack thereof, if you can come from a more trusting place, and be prepared to let go of your fears, one at a time, you'll receive much clearer and stronger messages in the numbers. The numbers are here to help you heal and to learn to trust and feel safe and guided in life. There's nothing to fear in them at all.

It can take a while to really learn and trust in this. Some numbers, depending on your particular religious or cultural background might instinctively and powerfully be viewed with fear or suspicion, even without you realising it at first. The number pattern 666 comes to mind in Western, particularly Christian, culture, and in Eastern culture the number 4 is sometimes viewed as being 'unlucky'.

I confess it took me some time, with my Christian upbringing and childhood association of the number pattern 666 with Satan, to stop viewing the number 6 as a vibration that had negative connotations. That persisted for a time, even when my own belief system had grown so that I no longer saw the devil as an external entity, but rather as a way to describe the tendency towards evil, to move against life and love, that lay within every one of us and had to be brought to conscious awareness so that we could choose to live from our hearts as much as we possibly could.

If that could take some time and effort on my part to release, even with me being aware of the process and having moved beyond my old belief systems of fear of the devil which were part of my childhood religious conditioning, then imagine how stubborn such a fear could be in someone who wasn't aware that there was any other way to think about such numbers! Well, I wanted to make an offering that could free people from fear and open them up to the love in the numbers, if only because I have found it so very helpful in my own life, and believe many others will too.

Fear and negative associations can be very persistent though, even if we are trying to consciously work beyond them, to move into a more loving, peaceful and trusting way of being in the world. To this day, I still see spiritual teachings from some very well known teachers that suggest that the presence of a number 6 indicates excessive materialism. To me, that sort of teaching is still tainted by a fear of the material world, as though it were a distraction to the spiritual path rather than a means through which the spiritual path can be attained. You'll see in the chapter on the number 6 that my understanding of the number 6 energy and the material world that it does relate to (amongst other things, like love and feminine energy and abundance levels that are not only physical, but also emotional) is not fear-based or judgmental at all. Perhaps, like me, you will go from being fearful or uncertain of the 6 energy and instead learn to really love it and feel happy and excited when 6 energy comes to you through messages in the numbers.

That journey from fear to happiness begins as we become aware that our cultural or religious conditioning is just programming of belief systems based on a mass consensus, rather than some higher truth. Sadly, mass opinion is typically based on a lowest common denominator of fear rather than an empowered expression of free intelligence. It takes people who are willing to release fear and receive more of what the Universe is offering us, which is great abundance in all its forms, to rock the status quo and bring through ideas that are far more helpful and conducive to living a good, full and happy life. Working with messages in the numbers is about taking that journey – daring to believe in a different sort of life to what you may have been taught when you were little. So, that life is hard and must always be a struggle is only one belief. Sure, there are going to be moments like that in our lives, but there are entire other ways to live, that involve trust and surrender and that actually get us to where we would like to be with so much more ease and grace. The messages in the numbers are about that other way of life. They help us learn how to live that way and to enjoy the journey of life more, allowing us to feel more supported and guided. I am sure you will agree with me that there are definitely times in life when some genuine, helpful guidance wouldn't go astray!

I don't personally believe that there are lucky or unlucky numbers. Except that I understand if you won the lottery with certain numbers, you might disagree with me! Fair enough. Essentially though, number vibrations are neutral. We might have a reaction towards them, but that is our own 'stuff' coming up. We might have positive associations from past experiences or social conditioning, as well as negative ones. Learning to accept a neutral message and release our fear, and turning that message into something helpful and constructive is one fun way to begin to heal our relationship to the Universe. We can move from an anxious and fearful relationship, into something more playful and trusting.

I think you'll find out for yourself, just as I did, that working with numbers is a type of play. Once you get into this way of thinking, you'll find yourself smiling and laughing a lot as the Universe talks with you day in, day out, guiding you, encouraging you, letting you know how to proceed – all through the many encounters that we have with numbers on a daily basis. It helps to bring the Divine to life, and to our lives, in a very real, palpable way. It's like a running Universal commentary on how our life is unfolding, on what is happening and on the particular energies that are with us, helping us. That in itself can be so healing.

This is what *Messages in the Numbers* is all about. The Universe wants to help you. It wants you to understand that it is alive, and it knows you, and loves you. It wants to assist you to become all that you can be, to lead a fulfilling life and grow spiritually. Every living being benefits when you do this. It isn't about being selfish. If you have cultural or family conditioning, perhaps particularly in Eastern or some European cultures, that says putting yourself first is wrong then you might struggle with this idea. In that case, the messages that come with the 1 vibration might challenge you for a little while, and that's fine – it's just part of your own journey this lifetime. Equally you might find the messages of that vibration finally giving you permission to honour yourself as an individual to be most liberating and welcome. Even though we will have our 'off days' from time to time, through the messages in the numbers we can become bright, happy human beings that feel loved and connected to life – just what our planet needs! Learning to receive the messages in the numbers helps us to feel loved and supported by life, naturally, genuinely, and more often.

My experience is that the Universe has a powerful and benevolent nature, and that when we ask for help, it is freely and abundantly given. Usually instantly, though it might take us a while to realise we are being given an answer to our prayer or question of course, and that's OK. Numbers are a way that the Divine helps us with clear guidance. Simply by 'tuning in' to the frequency of a number, we can receive a kind of energetic alignment, like a mini energy-balance or a jolt of spiritual vitamins to help bring us back to our centre again.

Whether the Divine for you is a God in the sky or a Goddess in the Earth, or a higher intelligence in your own mind or heart, or angels or the Divine Mother or a vast Universal mind, or even if you aren't really sure about the Divine at all, it doesn't matter. You don't have to be 'really into spirituality' to read this book and play with its material. Anyone can benefit from *Messages in the Numbers,* which is essentially about helpful communication to support you on your life journey. Even if you aren't sure that you believe in a higher being, you can still receive the messages in the numbers – think of it as luck, if you prefer, or as being tuned into the natural flow of energy and life, as serendipity, 'signs' and synchronicity. No matter what your particular spiritual philosophy, or lack thereof, the material in this book is written to help you on your path, equally, for one thing that all human beings on a path in life have in common is a heart. The numbers serve love – the language of the heart.

If you do have a strong spiritual belief system, that's fine too. Believing in a higher being–in whatever form sits with your personal beliefs– communicating with you in a loving, reassuring and often funny way, can bring great inner peace and a feeling of real and palpable closeness to the Divine that can be very startling at times and deeply fulfilling too. When so many humans are struggling to deal with change, the pace of which only seems to be accelerating on this planet, or dealing with financial challenges that breed anxiety, being able to connect with numbers in a loving way can be enough to release the stress, relax, and trust, so that solutions become more readily accessible.

If you had a wise, powerful and extremely helpful friend who wanted to assist you in your life, you would more than likely make time to listen to them as you would surely trust that it would benefit you greatly. *Messages in the Numbers* offers ways to tune in and listen to the greatest friend you have already – the Divine.

So don't dismiss the number patterns or repeating numbers that you see on your mobile phone, your alarm clock, your computer screen, or on the number plates of the cars as you drive by. Modern technology comes with gifts and challenges. Staying balanced and grounded in the world can be a challenge with constant mental stimulation and distraction available. A great gift of modern technology, however, is that the language of numbers as sacred communication becomes more accessible to us, more obvious to us because we have so many more chances to see them. Who would have thought your mobile phone could bring you closer to God?

This book can be used intuitively, just by reading the particular chapter of a number that you feel drawn to, perhaps because you keep seeing it everywhere, or because you just feel you want to read it, without knowing exactly why. That is fine. That is your intuition speaking. Just go with it.

The healing suggestions that are included at the end of each chapter are to help you easily and effectively tap into the healing power or energy of the number vibration, so that you can receive the guidance not only on a mental level, but actually allow it to help your body to heal at a deeper level too. If you have ever been stressed out and stepped into nature and felt your body and mind begin to relax, then you've already had an experience of a healing at an energetic level. It can be very effective and helpful. It might seem really strange to do those little healing processes – you might wonder if they are doing anything at all, especially if you tend to be a more intellectual rather than intuitive personality. If you feel that way, it's completely normal and understandable. The healing processes have been designed to work beneath the conscious mind, encouraging the healing wisdom of each number to enter into your subconscious mind, and into the cells of your body. If you have ever tried to do something consciously and with a clear intention, only to end up doing something else—perhaps the exact opposite, such as starting a new diet by eating a cheesecake!—then you will have had first-hand experience of the power of the subconscious mind. It is useful to work with the conscious mind too, of course, with explanations and stories, to help us change the way we consciously relate to life for the better. Working with the subconscious mind through the healing processes allows the wisdom and healing of the numbers to anchor within you, supporting the changes in your conscious mind, and allowing you to not have to fight so much to bring about a happier way of being. It can just happen more easily and naturally. That being said, if the healing process feels right for you, do it, but if you don't feel like it at a given time, that's fine too. Trust yourself.

How do I know if I am seeing numbers as a sign, or just seeing numbers?

In my view, there is no difference. If you are consciously recognising a number or number pattern rather than blandly ignoring it or hardly registering it, it's a message for you. It doesn't matter if you see it once or several times in one day, whether you dream about it, or end up doodling the number on a notepad in the midst of a telephone conversation with someone.

What distinguishes it as a sign is that you feel something; a nudge, an inner knowing, even just a questioning about whether or not it could be a sign. That's enough. You don't need trumpets blaring and the hand of heaven to reach down and graffiti "11.11" on the road with a big cosmic spray can before you, or set the sky alight with 11 shooting stars whilst 11 angels blast 11 horns through the ethers! Though if something along those lines happens, then, ah, yes, that would be a message too.

How do I know that I am seeing genuine guidance and not a 'fluke' or just what I want to see?

Good question! If the above paragraph isn't enough of an answer for you, then I will add this information for your benefit.

Genuine guidance repeats itself over time and it does it when we are not expecting it. Staring at your phone and waiting for 444 to appear is not the same as switching it on and seeing it, or randomly checking for a message and seeing that it is 4.44pm when you do so ... Do you sense the difference? One is sought, one is given. Guidance is given. So, ask for guidance and then let go. Don't try to hold on to it when it is given – there is so much forthcoming on a daily basis as we open up to it.

That can be easier said than done, but in time and with trust, we come to learn that messages come to us without any effort on our part. Once we have asked, we have to surrender and be open to receive it randomly, and when it does come through that way, it is easier to 'believe' because we weren't trying to make it happen. I have lost count of the number of times I have–without conscious thought–just leaned over and checked the time on my phone for 'some reason that I don't know,' only to find a clear number message there for me. Frequently 444 or 11.44, but it could be anything really. I am always grateful. I have a little smile or a quiet thank you and I go about my day.

Another way that I get messages in numbers is in paid parking tickets – the ones you purchase at a machine and display on the front dashboard of the car. I often get number patterns that are a mixture of the current date, the amount paid and the time of expiry – something that is completely 'random' and based on the amount of change I have in my wallet at the time. There will often be a consistent pattern in one day with several different tickets. I believe this happens more often for me, than perhaps others (at first) because I am so open to it. Even I have my moments where I think, "Wow, I can't believe that!" but of course I do really believe in it – enough to write a book about it to help others find assistance too. Like any form of loving guidance, the more we open to messages in the numbers, the more the Universe realises, "Hey, this is the way to get through to her!" and on those messages flow in greater quantity. It is never too much though. If you become frightened by how real the Divine becomes to you, it will pull back a little. It loves you and wants you to know how connected you are to all of life. It doesn't want to freak you out!

So in short, you'll know it's guidance because it will be consistent and unexpected. It will make you laugh, cry, or gasp and wonder how that can be. You'll start to notice it more and more as you open to it, get in the 'zone' and realise that the Universe does actually know you and want to talk to you, and help you in your life.

As for flukes, or accidents, I don't believe in them. You can, of course, but for me, there are too many coincidences that end up being evidence of a greater hand at work – even if it is only years later that we see the evidence of the plan unfolding. So I have given up any belief in randomness as being anything more than the great divine plan unfolding – it's just that we may not quite see the bigger picture at the time and mistake it for an accident, a fluke or an expression of chaos.

And as for whether you want to see it or not? Sometimes we get guidance that we want to hear, and other times we don't want to hear a particular message, maybe because it asks us to grow and we aren't sure that we are ready for that. It has been my experience, just as an aside, that even when we aren't sure that we are ready for something, when the messages and nudges come for us to do so, we are more ready than we might easily acknowledge. The numbers are wise in that way. They bring us what we need, even if we aren't convinced of the guidance at first.

Either way, whether easily accepted or not, we know when it's guidance; deep in our hearts, we just know. We need to learn to trust ourselves on that. It takes some time, but we can learn how to do so. Working and playing with numbers will help us do this.

A Note ◆ The Tarot

I will refer to the Tarot (pronounced tarrow) in this book at times to help pass on the wisdom of the numbers. The reason that I do this is that the Tarot is a non-religious, self-help system that is based on playing cards, which in turn, are based on numbers. Tarot dates back at least to the 15th century, and spiritual seekers have been using it to find guidance ever since. Tarot might be perceived by some as an entertaining or scary tool for fortunetelling, but the deeper use of the Tarot serves to help us understand ourselves and the life path before us through the use of numbers and images, empowering us to make intelligent and loving choices so we can grow, successfully fulfilling our life purpose, instead of living a fearful, controlled existence in defence against life.

Now if you don't feel comfortable with the Tarot, that is perfectly OK. You may choose to read about the number messages or images that I describe from the Tarot (usually a paragraph only in each chapter), or just skip over that paragraph altogether. Whatever you choose is just fine.

Please do know however that the Tarot is not evil and you are not being asked to believe in anything just by reading about it. The images and meanings in the Tarot help give a visual symbol of the energy of a number, which as I mentioned in the introduction earlier on, is actually neutral. My intention to include this information is two-fold – I absolutely love the Tarot and so I wanted to share it and it is also how I began learning about numbers and their messages.

A Note ◆ Life Path Numbers

Your Life Path number is a number that is based on the digits in your birth date. It is a number that is especially about your gifts and lessons this lifetime. When you work out your life path number, which I will show you how to do in a moment (it's easy!), you can then read the chapter for that number and this will help you receive some extra guidance on your life path. It doesn't mean other numbers won't relate to you, of course. I believe that we have all the energies of the Universe within us and all the numbers are relevant to us at particular times in our lives. Your life path number is more like a special course of study that you are supposed to be taking this lifetime, a set of particular qualities that you naturally have and are here to develop and utilise to live your most fulfilling life. In reading the chapter that relates to your life path number, you can receive a particular message in the numbers for you – a theme or point of focus to help you grow into your whole and most amazing self this lifetime.

You can work out your life path number by adding up all the numbers of your birthday as though it was a sum. For example, my birth date is 15 July 1974. So the sum is: $1 + 5 + 7 + 1 + 9 + 7 + 4 = 34$. Then you add those two numbers until you get a single digit: $3 + 4 = 7$, so 7 is my life path number.

When I receive number messages that contain 3 and 4 in combination and especially a 7, I know that there is special guidance there for me about my life purpose and path, as well as the other messages associated with those numbers.

So, if you don't already know it, you can work out your own life path number by adding up the individual digits of your birth date as I did in the example above. Keep adding the end numbers as though they were a simple sum until you get to a single digit – that number is your life path number. There is one exception here – if at any point in the summing of your digits, you end up with a repeating number such as 11, 22 or 33 and so on, then don't keeping adding those any further (11 stays as 11, it does not become 2, for example). These are known as 'master numbers' and they are not reduced to a single digit. Just read the section that relates to 11, 22 and 33, or 44 and so on, in this book and that will be your guidance for your life path.

A Note ◆ Sacred Geometry Mandalas

In this book, at the end of each chapter, there is a sacred geometry image; a mandala that holds the frequency of the number we explore in the chapter.

Sacred geometry is the study of the energetic form beneath all of creation – the invisible, mathematical blueprint upon which nature manifests herself. The patterns repeated in so many natural forms from seashells, to entire galaxies, to human DNA and flight formations of birds, the artistry of a snowflake and the elements of the periodic table, all have an underlying template. The same geometric patterns reveal themselves as the basic patterning underneath all of life. This is why they are known as sacred; they are the foundation of life itself.

The term sacred geometry, for the purposes of this book, refers to the shapes and proportions created by the numbers when translated from a concept into a visual representation. This visual representation then symbolises far broader concepts – an example being the energy of the number 4 being 'encoded' in the shape of a square with four points.

Each geometric shape holds certain qualities; to continue the example of the number 4 and the square, the qualities ascribed can include stability, foundation and a representation of an integration of heaven and earth creating wholeness (as some spiritual traditions hold that a human being has four bodies – physical, emotional, mental and spiritual, each one represented as a point of the square, in perfect balance and equilibrium with each other). These qualities are the basis for the messages in the numbers that are expanded upon and expressed in each chapter.

When these sacred geometry shapes, and their associated proportions, are repeated, patterns are generated, which can then become a mandala. Mandalas are visual designs and symbols that have been used in various spiritual traditions, including Buddhism and Hinduism, as well as in the Jungian psychological approach, as ways to focus attention, enter into sacred space, open up altered states of awareness and promote a sense of wellbeing, wholeness and healing.

A mandala is a powerful symbolic tool, representing the nature of the universe, of balance, of wholeness, and also in this book, of the energies or 'qualities' of the numbers. Mandalas represent completion and yet also, paradoxically, of continuation, of a repeating cycle.

When we look at the sacred geometry mandalas in this book, we are taking in all that they contain – and that is an energy of life, of creativity, of raw power and of the entire universe! As extraordinary as it seems to the left-brain, perhaps, which governs our more logical and intellectual mind, the right-brain, which is capable of abstract thought and intuitive synthesis, can draw in the visual medicine of these mandalas, the energy, wisdom and power that is encoded within them, and through that process, receive healing.

If you are uncertain if that is possible, just think of what happens when you gaze at a sunset, how it can affect you beyond logic. This might be all the more noticeable if you tend towards a developed right-brain (with an appreciation for and capacity to moved by music, art, emotion, feeling, dreams, intuition and the like). When we gaze at these mandalas, we are gazing at nature too – just stripped back to her bare bones, which are beautiful in their own way.

If you are not particularly right-brained, being more of a left-brain intellectual type, working with these images will still benefit you. You may not feel the subtle effect as consciously as a right-brain type who is energetically sensitive, but the healing power works on you just the same. We are all made up of the same 'stuff' or substance, coming from the same raw materials of creation, no matter whether we tend towards artistry or logic or are blessed with a healthy integration of both.

Sacred geometry may *seem* to affect us differently – perhaps being an emotional, feeling experience for a right-brain type and an interesting but more detached viewing experience for a left-brain type, but fundamentally, it will heal us at a deeper level in the same way because at that deeper level, beyond our particular ways of responding to life, we are all an expression of life force and sacred geometry gives us access to more of that life force.

Right-brain dominant individuals and left-brain dominant individuals are actually perceiving the very same reality – even though sometimes it may seem as though they are 'worlds apart' due to the difference in how they experience life and express themselves. I am not a mathematician, and certainly–despite my law degree which required a hefty amount of left-brain intellectual development–I am naturally more at home in the right-brain territory of non-rational, intuitive worlds. Yet I chose each mandala for the relevant chapter in this book. I did so based on which mandalas felt like they held the energy of each particular number. I just looked at the work of the artist, felt which image resonated with me as holding the number in question, and then chose that one. The selection process took mere seconds to complete. When the artist, who obviously is rather more mathematically-inclined, expressed his pleasure and agreement at my choices, and even explained the rather complicated reasoning behind my intuitive choice of the image for the chapter on zero, I realised that yes, we are all perceiving the one reality, just via rather different methods.

So in working with these images, as superficial as the practice of gazing at them may seem, we are actually tapping into the raw power of life itself. Whether you are a right- or left-brain sort of person, you'd probably agree, this is a rather efficient way to experience healing. If you are very left-brain oriented and you aren't sure about the concept of healing at all, but perhaps are just curious to learn more about the numbers, my suggestion for you is to treat the healing processes at the end of each chapter as an experiment. Perhaps try them even if you are uncertain about their value. See what happens. Treat it as a way to further your education on the numbers in a different way.

I included this brief discussion on the right- and left-brain qualities as I have the sense that readers of this book will not all be right-brain dominant, as can be the case with much of the material in the 'new age' writing field, but may actually be more left-brain oriented, or even more likely, be blessed with qualities of right- and left-brain orientation that have been well integrated.

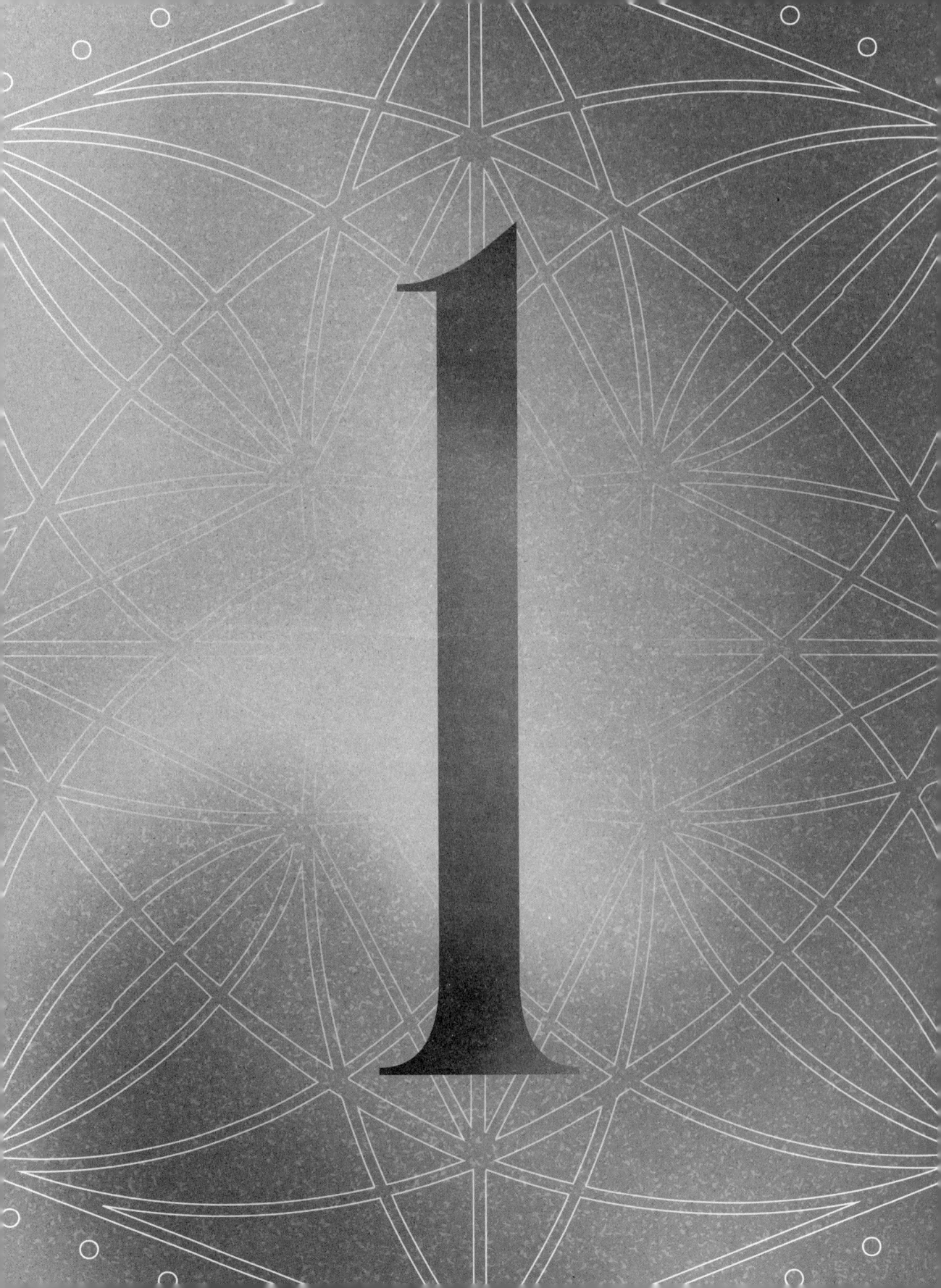

CHAPTER ONE

The meaning of 1 is new energy. It is the first in a sequence of numbers and indicates that something is starting now or is just about to begin. It is a hopeful number because of that – it holds the energy of new life and freshness, and clean slates. When a 1 arises, there is always a message that we can start afresh at any time we choose and there is no better time than now! If you struggle with feeling guilty or ashamed of the past, or if you are critical of yourself for not having done something, the 1 is an opportunity to let the past be the past, to put it behind you now and to move on with a different attitude and renewed determination. Give yourself a break and choose not to shame or judge yourself or another anymore. Let it go and gain all that energy back into the present moment instead, so it can fuel the new start upon you. This is a new chapter, a new day, says the 1, and it's time to put your energy into what is beginning, not what is ending. Be present, look ahead with vision or inspiration, leave the past in the past, and you'll move towards your goals most rapidly.

When a 1 pops up, it is a sign that it's time to take action, to get things moving through your physical world activities. It's not about thinking and planning and assessing, it is about doing. It is not a number that sits around and twiddles its thumbs, so to speak. If you are contemplating taking action, then this is a confirmation to do it. If you are thinking of applying for a new job, or enrolling in new training for a different career, or accepting an offer that is different to what you have known in the past, then the 1 is encouraging of all of that. If you are thinking of going to social gatherings that you wouldn't normally go to, and introducing yourself to people, even if that feels a bit challenging for you (and it is, for most people) then go ahead and do it.

At the same time, it's good to know that the 1 also indicates that you might feel a need to go it alone for a while, and that you'll have some time focused perhaps more on yourself than others, and if you feel that in your heart, that's just fine. Accept the guidance. It doesn't mean you always be alone or any such thing! It just means you need some 'you' time. Perhaps that is because you have had a lot of socialising or are coming out of a relationship breakup, or simply that you just need to check in with yourself. Perhaps you have been getting caught up in the belief systems, opinions or ways of doing things that other people think are 'right' and though they may be 'right' for them, they may not be 'right' for you at all. You might need to check in with what is best for you, what feels truthful for you, what inspires you. That isn't selfish, that is growing into who you are so that you can share yourself genuinely and authentically with others when the time to do so also feels right for you.

Despite the push of the 1 to get things moving, it also indicates a need for patience. You know that expression, "Rome wasn't build in a day"? That is a message the 1 vibration brings. It says, "Hey, don't worry about getting everything done today!" It is literally about taking one step at a time. It guides us to recognise that every journey, project, dream, is attained with all the little steps that we take from the moment of first inception through to completion. Without each of those steps, as time consuming and even tedious as they can be after the initial thrill of something new wears off, they are still essential to the end result. The 1 asks you to look for the new, even in the familiar, to keep your perspective fresh. If you have ever learned something new about someone that you had known a long time, and were shocked and began to see them differently (for better or worse!) then you'll know that the 1 energy of freshness and keeping things interesting can pop up anywhere. We just need to remain open to it. So the 1 says, don't get stuck in routine – walk a different route today or look at someone in the eyes today and really see what's going on. Don't just plod through life, day in, day out, as if it's boring. Then you can feel some inspiration and new ideas, fresh energy and the healing of the 1 coming into your life. Whilst you are at it, be patient, and do what you can do today. Don't worry about the bigger picture because that will take care of itself as you take the steps you can each day (though sometimes at the beginning of a new life stage or project, we'll have a vision or a sense of what the end result could be, and that's fine too of course).

If you are anything like me, this might be your least favourite part of the message! I much prefer to get things finished as soon as possible, but sometimes of course it's reassuring to feel that you don't have to do everything at once. If you have a more impatient nature, you'll perhaps find waiting for results something that isn't much fun. When a 1 is appearing, you'll gain more results in the long term by taking it one step at a time and not trying to accomplish everything overnight. Know that this doesn't mean your results have to take a long time in coming. Sometimes a step-by-step approach that seems slower at first is actually faster in the long term because you don't miss out on essential parts of the process and therefore avoid the time consuming process of going back and fixing something that could have been done correctly in the first instance, with a bit more patience and attention. I am certainly prone to falling into that trap if I am not aware. The 1, when it appears to me, is a particular message to not only believe in where I am heading and to take steps towards it, but also to know that it's OK not to rush headlong into my destiny, but to live it each day as best as I can, doing what is before me that I can do, and dropping everything else. The 1 will likely have similar guidance for you too.

There is excitement when a 1 appears, because it usually comes when we are about to take a big leap of some description. That leap might be into an entirely new belief system, relationship, way of being in the world, change in our work, the country we live in, or an internal leap that takes us from fear to trust and in doing so, opens us up to countless more adventures, and greater love and opportunity to play and succeed in life! This is especially the case when a 1 is partnered with a 9 or a 0 (you'll see more about that in number patterns that I'll outline below). If that's the case, the beginning that you are embarking on is a very significant one. It's not just an ordinary beginning, so to speak, it's the start of something that will turn out to be important for you on your life path in a broader manner, even if you cannot quite fathom how that could be at this time. Fortunately with a 1 message, it doesn't really matter if what is beginning is going to be the most important development in our lives or a simple change, the guidance is the same – just take the next step. Do it! It's time.

In the Tarot, which is a wisdom teaching system based on numbers, and originally derived from playing cards, the 1 vibration belongs to the magician. Even if you aren't interested in Tarot, you have probably come across the magician as an archetypal figure in films or books. Certainly the popular *Harry Potter* series of books and films brought that to life for many people would perhaps not have otherwise thought much about the fantastic dreamy worlds of magic and magicians, wizards, sorcerers and so forth.

The magician is quite a powerful symbol and it helps us understand another aspect of the message of the 1 and how it can help us.

The magician within the 1 asks us to set a clear intention because from that, life flows and events take place. I had a client share a simple story with me about this once. He was out for a walk a new city that he had moved to, still finding his way around, and he had the thought that he would like to go bike riding. He meandered along and, just a few seconds later, he found he had 'accidentally' come across a stall that rented bicycles. He was quite amazed. When he had some further clear thoughts, with the 'answer' manifesting rather quickly and in surprising ways, he began to believe it was more than mere coincidence.

It wasn't a surprise to me, however. He always seemed to me to be something of a magician, though I couldn't exactly explain why, and I knew he didn't think of himself in that way at all, it was just a feeling that I had about him. When he intended something, it happened and as he grew spiritually through inner emotional healing and learning to trust in life, that process just became more swift and clear.

We all have this magician power within us, says the 1, we just have to remember to practice using it! Sometimes we might be fearful of this power, especially if we have been taught (as is often the case in religious households, for example) that power is only for the Divine and not something we should be dabbling in. Yet, even if we learned this, we might also be able to come to believe that the Divine exists within us and is expressing itself in that creative power, so we can relax a bit, trust in its goodness and not be afraid of it.

The magician in you is being acknowledged when 1 makes an appearance. It is the Universe reminding you that you have more power than you might realise; the power to set clear intentions which will evoke a response from life. It isn't about controlling life – that would be rather like the tail of the dog attempting to control the dog. It is more about participating consciously in your life, realising that although you cannot force events to happen in a particular way (or even if you believe that you can, perhaps acknowledging that it is wiser to let a greater wisdom that includes all of life, and not just your own life, work out what will suit the greatest good in the best way possible), you can still contribute greatly to your desired outcome through your actions.

So the guiding message of the 1, and of the magician, is to become as clear as possible about your intentions, about what you would like to create in your life, and then ask yourself if you have set priorities and are taking steps–even only small daily steps–that are in alignment with that intention. The 1 tells us that we have the magician energy in us. Not in some sense of jumping on stage in a cape and performing all manner of optical illusory tricks (though if that is for you, go for it!). It is more in the sense that we are co-creators of our life experience with the universal energy. It is so easy to forget this, but the 1 energy is a reminder to go back to the building blocks of our power to create – what intention are we cultivating and what actions are we taking to support it?

The 1 generally pushes us to get clarity, to let go of the extraneous or distracting elements in our lives (which can be very hard at times!) and to focus on what is essential in this moment so we can be most successful in bringing that intention or dream into our reality. Singular focus – without getting caught up with distraction – is one of the hallmarks of very productive people. The 1 can help us if we have a tendency to think of too many ideas at once, or too many possibilities and end up feeling paralysed with indecision over all of the options available to us. Many highly creative people can suffer with this tendency. I often have done. I can look at those people who have one task and just work on that task with much envy at times! I often have to make a choice to deal with what I can deal with in any given moment, understanding that for me, the multiple and varied is my nature, but I still have to learn how to be singular in focus to complete each of the many and varied projects that I have cooking in my life.

When the 1 appears, we will also be given a message that it's time to make a decision. Sometimes if we are having trouble setting clear intentions, it's because at a deeper level we are yet to really decide upon what we want. It can be hard to choose what we really want if we are yet to give ourselves the time and space to contemplate how we feel and what matters to us personally. We might even need to decide if we are willing to give ourselves permission to receive what we'd really like, or to accept that our dream is possible, to decide that it is worth taking a risk and going ahead. Or we might have to decide to let go of an old belief or dream, an old view of ourselves as unworthy or less-than, or as needing to be perfect, in order to decide to really allow ourselves to be happy and fulfilled in our lives now.

Whilst some intentions can be set–and manifested–with little effort, if we have a personal issue clouding our belief in a particular idea even being possible, then setting an intention to manifest it might only happen after we've done some inner work. It's nearly impossible to set a clear intention to create something if we don't know what we want or what has genuine meaning for us. If we feel we don't really have any life goals, and the 1 is making an appearance for us, the Universe might be giving us a nudge along that path, to decide for ourselves what matters so that we can set some intentions and enjoy the experience of manifesting our will in a loving way in our lives. I say loving, because what really matters to us comes from our heart's urging. It might have little to do with what we were taught was supposed to mean something for us.

In my angst about career, which existed throughout most of my young life because I was raised in a culture that believed in practicality and that what my heart wanted–which was to sing, to share spiritual light, to perform and be up on stage–wasn't practical or any way to make a living, I learned a valuable lesson that relates to the message of the 1. Whilst those that I turned to for advice in my teens suggested most strongly that I complete a law degree, in truth I did so only through sheer determination, because I hated it, but believed that I must finish it. Perhaps this was useful for my increased sense of self-esteem when I completed it, more than anything else. Perhaps it was important because it gave people who came to see me for spiritual guidance something that they could relate to–my law degree–which marked me as a sensible and educated person and therefore someone who could be more trusted, even whilst she was sometimes expressing rather unconventional ideas. But truthfully if that part of my life hadn't happened, I expect I would still be in a similar place, living a similar life, certainly heading in exactly the same direction, just through a slightly different route. Perhaps I would have had happier experiences during those five or so years, rather than the depression that came from honouring the advice of others rather than what I really was interested in for myself, which was what I eventually ended up doing anyway. The message of the 1 is clear in that set of circumstances. What do you want? What moves you? What is inspiring to you? What would you like to have begin in your life? What will you decide? What will you choose for yourself now?

Sometimes it isn't even really about the 'right' or 'best' decision, but just about making a choice: then life can flow. It's a bit like unblocking stuck or stagnant energy, and in that flow we can then make another choice or set a new intention, when we don't feel so stuck or confused. This is what eventually happened for me with law. I did my studies, and graduated, but the choice point about letting go of law in favour of my heart interest in spirituality as a vocation kept coming up again and again. It did so until I finally took the leap to honour who I truly was, rather than who I thought

I had to be in order to be successful in the eyes of those who I believed, in their own way, wanted the best for me, but didn't really know what I needed. Only I could know that. In time I made the choice to pass on some apparently coveted job offers in the legal profession to become a spiritual teacher, which was far more fitting for who I was and what my skills were. Naturally I encountered some resistance from those around me, I might add, but the message of the 1 is not about our choices being easy so much as them being truthful and authentic. Though I also learned that being truthful and authentic is far easier in the long term.

The guiding message in a 1 is also therefore about individuality. Some people have been raised to believe that this means selfishness or self-centredness, but it is not so. Individuality means that you know who you are and don't try to change yourself to suit the fears or expectations of another. This sort of person is very healing and helpful for other people to be around because they have learned to break free of the, "I'll like you or love you if you change to be what I want you to be," pattern. Being around these sorts of people helps us learn how to be ourselves too.

This means that we can choose to live a life that suits us, make choices that feel right for us, and learn to allow others to 'live and let live' as they so choose as well. The result is that there are less power struggles and disharmony within us, and in our relationships with others, and more truthful, authentic decisions being made. Everyone benefits from this increase in harmony. There is a spiritual teaching that goes along the lines of this – when there is peace within, there is peace in the home, when there is peace in the home, there is peace in the village, when there is peace in the villages, there is peace in the country, when there is peace in the countries there is peace in the world. The 1 brings us that message of great attainment, great spiritual possibilities, that all start with a single choice, a singular intention, a solitary decision, a first step taken.

Far from being selfish, learning to honour our individuality and be who we truly are actually benefits Mother Nature too. So much environmental damage is caused by over-consumption and dissociation from the body and from the realities of life, through trying to deal with unhappiness and chronic disappointment. People who feel that they are not allowed to be themselves and to live their life according to their own truths will suffer emotionally and often try to medicate themselves with all sorts of new toys and gadgets to ameliorate their pain. It doesn't work for long and soon enough, more is required. As this pattern continues, the earth and our environment suffer. Yet when permission to be truthful is claimed, as in the healthy individuality supported by the appearance of the 1, those coping mechanisms are not required nearly so much. Acceptance and presence in life increases, relationships improve, interaction increases, tolerance and compassion for others and their own authentic path increases and we become less fearful and more loving of each other. So, far from being all about 'me', the 1 vibration is actually about creating a healthier 'me' for a healthier 'we'.

1 IN COMBINATION WITH OTHER NUMBERS

If the 1 is partnered with another number, so you are seeing 12, 13, 14 and so on, then you'll have even more specific messages about which parts of your life are going through a new cycle in some way.

You can simply apply the above general guidance and messages of the 1, with particular focus on those parts that feel most relevant or appropriate for you, and add in the information that is included below.

1 with 1
(e.g. 11.11, 111, 11, 1/11, 1/1)

This is a big energy! There were many spiritual gatherings by people who loved working with number energies on 11th November 2011, because of the 11.11 frequency on that day (11.11 on 11.11.11). You can still tap into the 11.11 energy even though that date has passed. There is always an 11th of November in your future! And at other times, the energy will come to you through the channels I spoke about in the introduction – the time on your mobile phone, alarm clock and so forth. But back to 11.11.11 for a moment. I remember holding a spiritual class on that day to bring in the frequency of the 11.11 energy which is all about new beginnings on the biggest, most Universal and grand level possible – where dreams can become reality and the darkness of the past can be peacefully surrendered and released. That class was one of the wildest and most powerful groups I had ever run. It felt like an enormous wild horse had galloped out of the sky and straight through the circle that had gathered in my lounge room! I had never felt like I had lost control of the reins, so to speak, when teaching before, but I did that evening! It was rather sobering to be exposed to so much power of that Universal 1 energy at once. I realised I could only ever allow, with some attempt at holding the space, such a strong energy to flow through my work, but that I had an icicle's chance in hell of ever controlling such energy. I was rather grateful and excited by the experience once I got over my shock at its intensity. I certainly never underestimated the power of 11.11 again! Many people in that group, who had linked up to the event by internet (the wonders of technology again!) from Sydney, Western Australia, Queensland and even a couple of places in Europe, had powerful experiences of new beginnings from that evening.

For many years now, I have had people asking me, often people who have no particular interest in spirituality by the way, what it means if they keep seeing 11.11 on their alarm clock or phone. Even before my experience in 2011 with this energy, to me 11.11 has always represented a big cosmic alarm or wake up call to those seeing it. Even people who don't have formal beliefs in spirituality, as I do, seem to sense something is happening. 11.11 is a powerful sign from the Divine saying that you are not only starting a new cycle, but it is a highly spiritual one in the sense that it relates directly to your life path and fulfilment of your potential this lifetime.

Now that might mean different things to different people. It could look very different from one person to the next. For one person, it might mean starting work as a healer, for another it might mean finally writing that book they've been thinking about for ten years. For someone else it might mean leaving a job, family and country to go travelling and for someone else it might mean that there are no particular external life changes to be made at all, and yet on the inside, it's like a switch has flicked on and nothing really feels the same anymore. At the very least it is a sign to progress on your path, to take steps that you feel in your heart to take, because the Universe is working with you on those steps to bring about something that is genuinely important for your life journey.

A friend of mine was organising a barbeque recently, and I wanted to go. I was looking forward to it actually, I felt really heart-centred about it and couldn't wait. I knew that there would be all sorts of old friends from various spiritual groups I had been involved in who would be present and that my friend's new partner, whom I felt some sort of psychic connection with (even though I had never met nor spoken with the man previously, nor had any idea if he knew anything of me!) was going to be there and I really wanted to meet him too!

Then on the day, I was struggling with some pretty heavy emotional stuff. It was not long after I had left a five-year relationship and my heart was more free, but also still processing a lot of grief and sadness about the way things had gone.

I still intended to go to that barbeque, but I needed to have a little rest first, I thought. I snuggled on my bed and felt so cosy and nice, and started to drift off. I didn't set my alarm because I thought it would just be a short rest. I underestimated how much I needed to sleep though, because soon enough I was in a deep, dreaming slumber. I remember thinking vaguely, that this must be what it feels like to fall asleep in snow – that you know you shouldn't but its just so nice that you cannot help it. Well obviously a rather less dramatic version of that! Anyway as I drifted more deeply into sleep, without a thought about having to get up, suddenly one loud, piercing beep sounded and I fumbled to grab my mobile phone, thinking that I must have set an alarm for myself without realising it. As I picked up the phone to switch off the alarm, I saw the time, 1.11, and realised that I had no alarm set at all. Even if I had, I would never have chosen that high-pitched shrieking sound anyway!

As I flirted with the notion of falling asleep again, just for a little while, another single loud blaring shriek erupted and I felt as though the sound catapulted me upright! I certainly ended my nap and got myself quickly to the picnic. There I had some important experiences and new connections were made, including with the new partner of my friend who commented that he had watched a video of me on *YouTube* and felt some sort of presence and realness in me, and that as he saw me walking towards the barbeque he felt it again. We spoke of love and surrender and music and creative projects and it was great. I loved seeing my beautiful friend so happy with a lovely man who was on a spiritual path just as she was, living in such a trusting and open way. I was so glad that they had found each other. It affirmed my faith in the possibilities of relationship when my own heart was feeling quite broken.

When I got home later that evening, I realised that it was the low battery alert in the smoke alarm that had been causing the beeping. Well, that and the fact that the Universe was using it as an alarm clock to get me moving.

11.11 is probably the most powerful 1 message that you can receive. It also functions like a type of cosmic seat belt. When you see it, the Universe is saying to you, "OK, there are some changes going on, sometimes there will be upheaval, but you are going to be OK! Don't fight it. Go with it. It's going to work out because it's all part of the greater divine plan happening now! It just needs to happen so here we go! Wooohoooo!"

There are certain patterns that I see when I am going through big changes. 11.11 and 1 partnered with 4, or just 4s on their own (which I will describe in the section about the number 4 below) are some of the most consistent. For me, any numbers in communication with me means that the Divine is close, but there is something about 11.11 that means the Divine is right up in your face, staring you right in the eyes and telling you to pay attention to what is going on for you right now, or what is just about to start, because it's going to be important whether you understand why at that moment or not.

At a time when I was going through the major relationship breakup that I mentioned above, I also needed to move out of the house that we shared. I choose to move into a completely new area, rather far away from my old life, which would involve me starting completely afresh. I felt that this was the right thing to do, but I was also a bit tentative. Part of me thought it was probably going to be the most supportive decision I could make for my own wellbeing, a clean break from the relationship and the area in which we had lived together. I considered–for a very short time–moving in with someone else instead of living on my own. That other person was still very involved in 'my old life' and I intuitively felt that perhaps such circumstances would have made it more complicated and difficult for me to let go of my old life.

During the short time in which we were looking at places together, I noticed that I was often receiving text messages about various real estate options with the time stamp of 11.11. It would happen more often than not. I would also see 11.11 on my alarm clock, my stopwatch if I had set a timer for meditation or relaxation, on my mobile phone and my computer screen at least once a day as well. I could be driving and look up and see a digital clock face on an office tower blinking back at me. 11.11.

Eventually I realised two things. Firstly, I had to get clear with my intention – what did I want to create for myself? I realised I needed a completely fresh start if I was going to be supporting myself in really clearing and releasing the emotional pain involved in the break up and leaving my old life behind.

So that would mean cutting ties with people from that old life, and that meant not going ahead with the idle idea of moving in with that friend. I also realised that after four years of living with a person that I had found very difficult to live with on a number of levels, I would love to have my own space again! So I moved out, trusting my gut, and all the 11.11 signs that came my way, and moved on my own, to an entirely new area where I had no previous associations, and began building my life from the beginning all over again. It was a difficult decision but I felt supported by the numbers and to be honest, after making the move, I was so relieved that I had chosen to trust the numbers and my own intentions and do what was right for me. It truly was a new beginning, a step back into believing in my independence again and a realisation that I needed to tend to my own healing process now, to shed the last painful vestiges of that relationship and focus on what I wanted to create for my future, as well as being more happy and free and peaceful in the present moment – which even amongst the process of deeply painful grief at times, I somehow was!

The other anecdote I want to share with you about the 1 vibration as it manifests in multiple 1s relates to a reading that I had with a spiritual mentor that I wanted to work with who is based in the United Kingdom. It was some years back, but it was at a time when I needed some clarity in my life on many levels. Well, she certainly delivered that! She saw images of things that I had only just begun dreaming of, and offered me insights into an entirely new life journey that was opening up for me. Now part of that was good timing – we connected at the right time and it just happened. Part of it was certainly her wonderful skill and loving heart and my openness to receive what she was offering. The other part of it was the Universe giving me a big, fat nudge.

At the end of the session, which was meant to be one hour in duration, I kept trying to end the call, being aware of the time and knowing that as a healer myself, sometimes other appointments get backed up if you don't stick to your designated appointment time. However my mentor just kept speaking. She would pause, as if waiting for something, and only then add another comment. So we kept talking for some time after the hour. Eventually it just ended quickly and easily. I was very grateful for the session and used it as a guide to help me find my way through some challenging life situations–including the relationship breakup I mentioned above–for years following. There were things that she mentioned that certainly were dreams held close in my heart, but which I hardly dared to dream were possible. Yet she seemed certain. I decided to have faith and at least do my part to set intention and cooperate with the Universe in bringing as much as possible of my heart's desire to life. It was a session that pushed me to make choices and to take my dreams even more seriously than I already was – seriously enough to act upon them with discipline, focus and self-belief.

The reason I wanted to share this with you is that the time stamp, indicating the exact duration of the session, was one hour, eleven minutes and eleven seconds. 1.11.11. The Universe, it seems, likes to have the last word.

1 with 2
(e.g. 11.12. 11.22. 12.11. 12.12)

Now if you've been in a stagnant cycle or relationship situation that just seems to be dragging on and on, and not really changing much, and you have had enough, then the appearance of the 1 might feel like absolute salvation! It is telling you that it's time for a new start. It might be happening by your own actions, such as going to counselling, or breaking up, or setting new boundaries or taking some time for yourself instead of excessively focusing on the relationship, or you might feel like it is happening to you as an external force or event, such as an affair discovered, or a death, divorce or job offer that breaks up the partnership, but no matter what it looks like, the 1 and 2 indicate change is going to happen either way.

If you are noticing a 1 paired with a 2, then that change is not only about current relationships. It often brings a message of a new relationship starting now or in the near future. It can also indicate a new healthier and more loving cycle in your current relationship too of course. This number combination is about a new way of looking at partnership and a new way of relating to each other, in current and new connections with others.

Take chances, the 1 says here, be open to others. Make new connections. Introduce yourself. The focus will be more on one-to-one relationships than about larger groups though. The 2 energy is about one-on-one connection, and the 1 is about you. This number combination is encouraging you to find your own truth about what a relationship is and to act on that in whatever way feels right to you. It can also be a sign to maintain your independence even in relationship with another, to check in with how much you are giving in the relationship, and taking the wishes of another into account, and how much you are honouring your own needs for independence and assertiveness too.

There will be increasing focus on partnerships when these numbers appear in pattern together—be they romantic or business partnerships—and you'll be encouraged to not only work on taking your own individual steps, but to also be open to connecting with others. 1 paired with 2 is about synergy of relationship, about being able to accomplish more with the added energy of others.

If you are interested in psychology then you will probably have heard of the masculine and feminine energies. These are not only biological features, in the field of psychology they are also energies that exist within us. So men will have an internal feminine energy as well as the masculine energy of their body and cultural conditioning and women will have an internal masculine energy, as well as the feminine energy of their body and cultural conditioning.

The feminine energy in women and men is about how we connect, and the extent to which we are able to receive and to sustain ourselves through relationship and intimacy. If a man or woman has a well-developed and mature feminine energy, they will be able to do this quite well. They will find it natural or easy to give and receive emotionally in relationship, they'll often feel love, tenderness, affection and connection with others, and others with them. If they didn't have the greatest role models in this feminine energy, or for whatever reason, it just doesn't come naturally to them, then they might find that part of their life journey this lifetime is learning how to access that feminine energy within and develop it. They might need to practice getting in touch with their feelings, for example, and learning how to express them in one-on-one connections with others. With numbers, the feminine energy relates to the number 2, the number of partnership.

The masculine energy is more about individuality and accomplishment, action and leadership. It is about self rather than the other. When well-developed in men and women, the masculine energy is the part of us that can set boundaries, allowing us to have a sense of self and still feel like we exist as an individual even when we are in a close and loving relationship with another. If we feel like our sense of self gets lost in relationship or that we have to always choose either our own independence or a relationship, but can't seem to sustain both, it's an indication that our masculine energy is still maturing and developing, learning how to stay clear even whilst the feminine energy of connection might be strong in us. In terms of numbers, the masculine energy is the 1.

When you encounter number patterns that feature 1 in balance with a 2 (such as 12.12, 12) or slightly more prominent than the 2 (such as 11.12, or 12.11), it is a signal that you need to work on your own sense of self in relationship, on setting boundaries and balancing your own needs with the needs of the relationship. You might also see these numbers and realise that you have been too focused on your own journey or your own needs and you actually need to give more to your partner, bringing the two back into balance (especially if there are more 1s than 2s in your pattern). Or perhaps you are being shown that your partner is rather self-focused and you need to think about whether your own needs for feminine connection–whether you are a man or a woman–are being met within the relationship. We'll look at the slightly different meaning of patterns of 1s and 2s when the 2s are more prominent in more detail in the next chapter, but from this discussion you can probably already guess that it relates to developing your feminine energy and being more receptive and giving in relationship with others.

With all messages in the numbers, trust what you feel in the moment. Your first instincts–especially with any 1 numbers–will usually be right.

The other message that comes with a 1 and 2 in combination is to allow your new starts at independence to be supported by others. That might sound like a strange paradox, but healthy relationships can help boost your self-esteem which can contribute greatly to your ability to trust yourself to make your own decisions, and to your belief in yourself and your own worthiness so that you can do your part in bringing your dreams to life in the world. Look to cultivate relationships that nurture independence and connection, and allow that to support you–and the other parties in the relationships–to achieve your individual ambitions and dreams in life.

1 with 3
(e.g. 13, 11.13, 11.33, 13.11, 13.13)

Of course we'll look at the 3 vibration in more detail in its own chapter, but for now all you need to know is that a 1 partnered with a 3 is about creative awakening, new steps in your creativity, and sometimes about creativity on a biological level with pregnancy or a new child coming into your life in other ways such as adoption, or perhaps through work in some way such as a new student, patient or client. This connection is important enough for the Universe to bring it to your attention.

1 with a 3 is particularly urging you to become aware of sustaining your individuality in group situations, whether that be with a family – such as new parents learning to find a way to not become subsumed into the role of parent and being able to still have a sense of self too. That can be tricky, to say the least. Or perhaps you are learning to work with others on a creative

or professional endeavour. You are being guided to do the balancing act of communication and creative work with others whilst still honouring your own voice. You may also get a message from this number combination to do creative work that is solitary in practice–in short, do what you can on your own–and that is part of your creative path, at least for this time. If you have been waiting for others to come along and work with you, the latter guidance is telling you to get the ball rolling on your own, so to speak, and the energy of your project can attract the right people later on. It takes a lot of courage and self-belief to initiate a project on your own, with faith that the help that you need will come at the right time. Yet if you are receiving that message, then you have within you exactly what you need, and it will be the right step for you. You must trust in your own potential whenever a 3 enters into a number message. You are far more capable of giving birth to something–a book, a job, a way of life, a new body, a song, an empire–than you may realise right now. But the Universe knows your potential! It's just reminding you with the 3 that it is there, and with the 1, to believe and act upon it.

How do you know which interpretation of the numbers is for you? It is a matter of listening to your heart and sensing what feels like the most truthful message for you. Keep in mind that this is not always the easiest message to receive, nor necessarily the one you really wished you would receive, but it is most likely that in time you will come to recognise and appreciate the wisdom in it, if you choose to follow that guidance.

The 3 and 1 can also mean that within creative work, you need to acknowledge yourself and what you are bringing to the table. It doesn't mean becoming egotistical about what you are offering (that is hardly going to be helpful guidance, and genuine higher guidance is always helpful). It does mean that you may need to assert your creative input or not underestimate how much of your own energy is going into group projects.

I remember partnering up with a girl called Felicity in a primary school project. I was very young and I don't remember what the project was. What I do recall is how angry I was at the time because it seemed to me that she wasn't pulling her weight, which I could recognise even at that tender age. I felt like I was doing all the work and she was taking half of the credit for doing less than her fair share. It was an early experience of a 1-and-3 energy – a need to balance the individual right to respect and acknowledgement in a creative endeavour with another. It is something that a lot of creative people will struggle with at times and if this particular number pattern is something that feels difficult for someone, they are likely to be the sort of person who either prefers to work on their own or with others only when the boundaries, roles and responsibilities are clearly defined.

The appearance of a 1 with 3 also indicates that it is time to start new creative and/or small group enterprises, if you are thinking about it, and that there is the 'right energy' for those things to come together at this time. Timing being so important in creative work, this pattern of numbers is a positive sign. 3 being the combination of 1 plus 2 make it a number of birth and this is likely to manifest as a new idea that comes through – one that is relatively mature, rather than half-baked, and worth acting on. It is a great encouraging vibration for new creative endeavours and there is a sense of good timing, and the capacity to attract the right people to that new idea or venture in accordance with that timing.

The 3 vibration is also linked with loving beings known as the Ascended Masters in the Western Mystery spiritual tradition. We will explore these beings and their role in chapter three however it is important to mention now that if you are open to the idea of loving spiritual beings who offer invisible, but palpable, help and guidance, then the appearance of the 3 with any number indicates that they are with you. Of course it is my belief that they are with us even if we don't particularly believe in them, but you might feel very differently and that is OK too. If you don't like the idea of Ascended Masters and their loving spiritual guidance, then just let this part of this chapter go and focus on the parts that you do relate to or find more helpful.

A discussion of the 1 and 3 pattern couldn't be complete without discussing number 13!

Long considered to be an unlucky number in many cultures, I remember feeling quite spooked as a little girl riding in an elevator on my first trip to the Gold Coast for a family holiday. As I counted the numbers of the floors, as we scooted up rather quickly to whatever floor our rooms were on, I noticed that there was no number 13, which I found really spooky indeed. I kept imagining an invisible floor where dead people went and that it was very real, even though it apparently didn't exist according to the numbers on the elevator. I had a very Gothic imagination as a child, as you can probably see. Anyway, when I asked why there was no 13th floor, I was told that it was because it was considered by so many people to be an unlucky number. Apart from my gothic imaginings, I also responded to that statement by thinking it was rather silly, because the 13th floor would still exist, it would just be INVISIBLE! Actually in truth, there still would be a 13th floor, it would just be marked as 14 on the elevator and room numbers.

Anyway, not being one to just accept things as they are–sometimes to my detriment if I try to make a proverbial sow's ear into a silk purse–I wasn't convinced by the belief that 13 was so unlucky. Many years later I knew why I harboured such suspicion, discovering some wonderful wisdom and messages in the number 13.

The number 13 is associated with the goddess and the Divine Feminine, and the 13 lunar months in a year. 13 is the number of the Christ with his 12 disciples. It is a powerful spiritual number! Friday the 13th is often considered most unlucky, but when we dig a little deeper, the reasons are quite surprising. Friday was named after the goddess Venus and the number associated with her was 13, so Friday the 13th came to be a day of rituals involving various levels of freedom and some might say debauched behaviour! The powers-that-sought-to-be at the time didn't really like that; quite possibly because they couldn't control people if they were celebrating and happy, rather than fearful and anxious. So Friday the 13th, and the wild goddess energy associated with it, was soon labelled as something to be eschewed rather than celebrated. The body became seen as sinful and dirty, sexuality was judged and human beings took up residence more in their heads than their bodies, resulting in emotional suppression, which led to ill health and imbalanced lifestyles. Claiming Friday the 13th as being unlucky has caused some unnecessary difficulties for humanity.

Fortunately for us, and unfortunately for the powers-that-would-still-like-to-be, the tide is turning and humanity is realising that we need a connection to the body and to the Divine Feminine world of feeling and playfulness to have any sort of wellbeing. So in a way, we are reclaiming our 'Friday the 13th' energy. As I write that sentence I notice that my computer clock reads 13.13. I think that's a sign that now is the time to reclaim this completely and utterly. And also to care for my own body and have a lunch break.

1 with 4
(e.g. 11.44, 11.41, 14.11, 14.14)

I mentioned above that 1 and 4 are number combinations that come to me when I am in particular need of guidance or support during big steps on my life path. During the relationship breakup and relocation that I mentioned earlier on in this chapter, I was taking risks and leaps that were unexpected. Whilst I didn't mind doing that, and even bearing the discomfort of change, I also wanted to know that if I was going to all that effort and bearing all the pain involved, I was at least taking the best step forward on my life journey.

My idea of prayer is pretty simple. It involves me 'talking in my heart' with the Divine, usually saying something along the lines of, "Hey God / Angels / Mother Mary / Divine Mother / Mother Earth, I need some help with this, thanks so much" or simply sending a feeling from my heart out to the Universe – like an emotional email straight to the Divine. People worry about how to speak to the Divine, thinking that there must be some etiquette or method to use, but you can speak however you like. I choose to be open, honest, respectful and most of all, just myself! It is my experience that the Divine knows and loves us unconditionally already, so there's nothing to hide and we can just relax and communicate freely. Anyway, during that time of change in my life, I asked the angels to help me know if the steps that I was taking were the best ones for me to take.

They responded in many ways, one of which was through the time stamp of 444 very often. I'll talk about that more in Chapter Four obviously, but for now I can say that I had a lot of 11.14 and 14.11 and 11.41 popping up on my phone and computer during that time. The combination of 1s and 4s let me know that my initiation, my action to leave, to move out on my own, to find somewhere completely new to live, was the foundation of my new life cycle (with 4 being about setting foundations and 1 about starting anew) and that it was guided and protected by the angels that I loved and who I knew loved me and helped me everyday (the 4 also symbolises the angelic kingdom for those of us who have beliefs tending in that direction).

I felt so reassured and that sense of acknowledgement that my choices were in alignment with my divine path helped me to make an emotionally painful transition in my life. Whenever I see combinations of 1 and 4 I know that the Universe is giving me–and whoever else receives those numbers in combination–a particular message. It is saying that the changes that are happening are for the best, that the decisions and choices being made, or soon to be made, are helping lay the foundations for future fulfilment. We are being given particular guidance that the Universe is bearing witness to our life changes or decisions and more than that, supports them and is encouraging us to continue and stick with our change or decision until that becomes grounded into a new reality. To that end, the angelic kingdom and Mother Earth herself (both symbolised by the 4) are supporting us with assistance and opportunities (right people, right circumstances) on the way. It is a beautiful message to receive. As you can imagine perhaps, at the time, I found a lot of hope and comfort in those number patterns.

1 with 5
(e.g. 15.15, 15.11, 11.15, 11.55, 11.51, 11/5)

This is another combination that I have seen a lot of at particular times in my life, typically at the onset of great change, as 1 indicates the new beginning and 5 indicates shifting energies of change. 11.55 catches my eye more often than I would perhaps like! Just now as I am writing this, the time stamp on my computer is 13.55! Bringing new beginnings, the power of the three for creativity and the energy of the 5 for change. Numbers can combine in patterns greater than two – but for ease of learning translation, we are mostly sticking to single or twin number patterns in this book. Once we get the gist of that, we can become more open to combinations of three or four numbers or more without getting confused. I do tend to find however, that the messages in the numbers are simple and direct, more often than not and that a single or double number message can be the most powerful.

Now the message of 11.55 probably sounds harmless enough. So why would I not like this all the time, you may wonder. That is because the 1 and 5 vibration together is a bit of a wild ride! Sometimes it's just fantastic but at other times you may just want to chill out in the comfort of what you know for a while and rest your well-travelled spirit. But the 1 and 5 combination is a call out to new adventure. And soon! That combination of numbers brings an energy that is a bit like driving wildly down a highway that you don't know, to a destination you don't know, from a place you don't know, with a person you don't know – and with no doors on the car! It could be exciting and fascinating or downright terrifying. You just never know with a 1 and 5 combination. At the very least it is unlikely to be boring.

Of course at a deeper level, there isn't anything to fear with change. It is essentially a movement into alignment with the universal flow of life, and that universal flow in turn moves us deeper into fulfilment. However it's all a matter of perspective – especially when the change is starting and you don't feel much in control of it perhaps. Then it can be like you are happily swimming about in a pond and all of a sudden you are scooped out, gasping and confused, before being tossed into a large ocean. Now of course, that is happening because you (a) are certainly able to swim in that large ocean and (b) will get used to it and (c) will have much more fun there, meeting more fish and discovering new territories – but you might not know any of that at the onset of the change. All you know is that there is chaos! We can know that when the 1 and 5 strike together, the change will be great, but it is about taking us into something new that will benefit us. Sometimes we don't realise how suffocating or regressive a situation is in our lives until we are nudged, forced or guided out of it by various life circumstances.

To me, when I see this combination of 1 and 5, I do feel a sort of relief though, especially if I am in a situation that I am not particularly enjoying, because it does indicate that things are going to be shaken up, dramatically enough that a significant new beginning will come from all that cosmic stirring. The excitement of that is often enough to rally my spirit to yet another adventure as I embrace more change in my life. Ironically perhaps, I can do this because I know that all that change tends to lead me into a life that brings me more inner peace too. If you are getting not only a 1 and 5 but also a 6, those changes are leading you into more love in your life, and if you have a 1 and 5 with a 9, the message about greater peace and alignment with your spiritual path is particularly strong for you too.

1 with 6
(e.g. 11.16, 16.16, 16.11)

Seeing 1 with 6 can bring a message of romantic love. It is often about a new level of love, a deepening of commitment or some kind of new relationship coming into your life – or new romance being breathed into a current connection. If you haven't fallen in love yet, this number pattern suggests that you will – it might be with a person or with a life path or passionate interest, but whatever it is, it will be stirring your heart at a deep level and it will trigger the beginning of a new phase in your life.

The energy of 1 is not only about new starts, but also about assertiveness and not being afraid to stand on your own. This doesn't mean that you always have to be alone, of course! But sometimes we have to break with what others expect of us, for example, to follow what is true for us, what feels right for us. Then we can attract other more like-minded people to us. The 6 is about attraction and when combined with a 1 it indicates that we will draw to us our 'tribe'; the group of people that are 'right' for us. The combination of the two numbers together shows that you might need to take some independent or assertive steps in order to attract love into your life. Sometimes receiving what we want has just as much to do with what we are willing to let go of, as it does with what we are willing to open up to receive. It might seem counter-intuitive to separate out from a relationship or connection or group of friends in order to attract more like-minded and loving people in your life, yet if you are putting your energy and focus into something that isn't nourishing to you, then you are better to withdraw it and move on, finding that which you can put your heart and soul into that does nourish you. It is a better investment of your emotional energy.

The 1 and 6 let you know that if you are thinking about doing this, or have already started to do so, continue with it; the love *will* come into it, you just need to take those first steps. I remember a time in my life when I was 'forced' by circumstances to take a 1 and 6 step. I didn't want to do so. I was comfortable where I was. I was a bit obsessed (or a lot obsessed) with going to the local gym. I had made groups of friends there, and because I worked on my own most of the time, it was my social outlet too. However spending time with that particular group of people, whilst I enjoyed it for some years, eventually became unhealthy for me.

The Universe was urging me to find a better way to care for my health and wellbeing. You might think that going to the gym could only be good, and certainly I did, but although I was getting extremely fit, I was damaging my health. I was over-training and constantly exhausted when I wasn't exercising. I would respond to that with even more exercise to feel good again, but it would be a short high followed by a long energy drop. I developed chronic fatigue syndrome, adrenal exhaustion and goodness knows what else and although on the surface I looked fit and healthy, though also tired, as though I hadn't had enough sleep, I found that I couldn't even find the stamina to leave the house for more than an hour or so without becoming exhausted. Everything became a physical effort, even just bringing groceries upstairs, which would confuse me, because I had been running on a treadmill not an hour earlier and feeling on a high.

My poor body was run down and there was no consciousness in that group of friends that could support me in healing that problem. All they knew was what I knew then – more exercise meant being thinner and fitter.

Eventually circumstances conspired and I had to stop training with that group. It was very hard for me to let it go, even though I could feel that life was telling me to do so. I felt socially isolated without them, I desperately missed the thrill of running up and down super-high sand dunes, going for long runs and being super-fit. I missed the adrenaline rush and yet my body didn't want it anymore. I nearly passed out once or twice and although when I went to the doctor he told me that I was so healthy I would outlive him and quite possibly continue on forever, I knew something wasn't right. I went to see a Chinese medicine expert and acupuncturist who assessed me and within about a minute told me what my symptoms were. I hadn't told him a thing! He could tell from what was happening in my energy field. He gave me advice to put my energy in my feet and ground myself, which I eventually learned how to do, and I also learned from him that rest was really important. Psychologically this process was painful because I didn't want to give up my old exercise addiction and I put on weight almost immediately which I couldn't lose again for many years and so I felt uncomfortable in my body for that reason too.

It took nearly ten years of exploration, experimentation and self-healing for me to eventually give up my obsessive and abusive attitude towards my body and become more reasonable in how I approached my health and wellbeing. I learned how to strengthen my body and gain fitness with a more moderate approach, working with my body rather than punishing it with exercise that exhausted it. I learned how to eat without dieting or bingeing (that eating pattern being something that tied in with my gruelling fitness regime and very difficult for me to break). I learned how to care for my body in a more loving way. In that process, I reconnected with my love of dance and met entirely new groups of people who were more interested in listening to their bodies and living their heart truths than fitting in with a clique in a gym. The process involved struggles and challenges to let go of the old way of being, and I felt loss, yet through the process, the more I let go, the more love I experienced and the happier I eventually became. That was the 1 and 6. I had to trust in my heart (the 6) and take independent steps in breaking away from my gym group, even though they didn't understand why I was doing it. I had to bear the feelings of intense frustration that I couldn't train in the way that I had done, thereby gaining the acceptance and admiration of those around me for doing so, if I wanted to be truly healthy. I had to give all that up and learn to love myself instead. Eventually as I healed my relationship with myself, I attracted healthier relationships into my life too.

The 1 and the 6 together ask us to balance our individuality with our social groups, to realise that we are meant to have both connection and accord with others, but also our own truths. The guidance of the 1 and 6 is to be yourself, especially in your connections with others!

I know a man with a lot of 1 energy. He is surrounded by a close-knit group of friends and family that never seem move beyond ten kilometres of each other! Since their early school days and now into their forties, this group is like a tribe and nothing seems to shake their devotion and bonding to each other. However this man is apart from the tribe in a way. Although he is a loved member of the group, his life hasn't followed the same pattern of marriage and children by a certain age as the others' have. Perhaps that will come later for him, or perhaps it is just not for him this lifetime. Either way, he will do it (or not) in his own time. He likes to do things his own way. He thinks about life rather differently to the rest of his 'tribe,' though he won't always admit it. He is an individual who likes to go his own way, but wants and needs many stable and long term relationships around him in order to feel safe, secure and happy. He is a blend of the 1 energy and the 6.

A 1 and 6 number pattern is also bringing you a message about new beginnings in your connection to self-love, and in particular to the feminine in your life. This can mean a healing in your ability to have relationships. We can often doubt ourselves and our ability to have functional loving relationships if we have gone through some difficult relationship issues in the past. However far from being perfect, those that have confidence in relationships are those that are willing to grow and love themselves enough to believe that they are worthy of love from another, and have something of worth to offer another too.

The 1 and 6 suggest that we let go of the past and give ourselves permission to start afresh in our relationships – romantic, or just generally, and particularly in our connections to women. It also suggests that we not be afraid to be independent in our relationships, especially with women. Sometimes women are taught to bond unhealthily, not through encouraging the best in each other, but through subtly undermining each other or feeling better when another isn't as successful as they are, for example. This is often unconscious at first, but if we can become aware of unhealthy patterns in our relationships, friendships and other connections, we can set new intentions to do things differently, for the greater benefit of ourselves and everyone else! The 1 and 6 let us know that we don't have to sacrifice ourselves, martyr ourselves, or give up our independence in order to love another, nor do we have to lose our opinions, intentions or plans in life. We can open up to become more, rather than less, through loving relationship with others. If you think this is great but have no idea how to make it real in your own relationships, the easiest thing to do is to pray or ask for help. You can do this by saying, "Through unconditional love, I ask for help in ..." That's it! It's simple to do, yet surprisingly we often forget to ask for help unless reminded.

The message prefiguring a changing way of relating is not just with others but also to your own body, as in the example I shared with you above. This message applies whether you are male or female, but this will often affect women most deeply because the 6 represents the goddess energy and when it appears women are being called to explore their feminine energy. Many women and men are confused about what feminine energy is. Many women have learned that they have to become more masculine to be successful in the business world, for example, pushing and fighting for their voice to be heard.

However there are ways to work with your feminine energy so that success can come to you, and it's not through the rather unimaginative and unoriginal use of your sexual appeal to manipulate others and assume some sort of power or control over them through their desire for your body! Feminine energy exists in men and in women. It is accepting, open, receptive and intuitive. It is about living from the heart rather than strictly from logic. It is a highly magnetic and attractive energy. It is about drawing to you what is needed rather than having to go out to battle for it. This is not passive, however. We build up feminine energy for it to become powerful. We cultivate it through practice. If you have ever noticed that when you relax and stop thinking or worrying about something, the situation begins to change and flow, then you have already had an experience of cultivating feminine energy and reaping the benefits. When the 1 and 6 appear, if you have any issue with yourself or another or work or anything at all really, the message is to adopt a different, more feminine approach. Don't try to figure it all out logically. Come from the heart. Surrender it. Build up your energy by relaxing and attracting a solution to you through faith. Then act on that.

Learning to accept feminine energy is also about giving yourself permission to learn to love and relate to your body in your own way. The story that I shared with you above is an example of that, but it might also mean rejecting social dictates about your body or even what your family has taught you, if that doesn't feel helpful for you. This can take a while. You might have to wean yourself off women's magazines or any media or groups that perpetuate body fascism. Sometimes this even exists in yoga schools that are supposedly about loving the body. It is really about trusting your gut and seeing how you feel in different places. Some yoga schools will transform your body, but through love and kindness. Others will leave you feeling as though you aren't good enough. Trust yourself. When the 1 and 6 are coming to you, you are being told that you are to leave behind any self-hate and embrace self-love; that is what will bring you happiness and fulfilment.

The combination of 1 and 6 will also indicate new chapters opening up for you financially because the 6 energy relates to abundance (so does the 8, in a slightly different way, which we will look at in a moment). When you are opening up to this combination of the 1 and 6 energies, you will be asked to look at your perception of your worthiness to receive from life. It has always been my understanding that we are like cups and the Divine is like an endlessly pouring bottle of the most delicious heavenly nectar you could imagine. There is always more being offered than could fill even the largest cup. The question is not whether or not the abundance exists, but more simply whether it can be received. The 1 and the 6 ask us to contemplate this and open up to receiving, just for ourselves. If we are used to sharing everything that comes to us with another, never really having been permitted through childhood, for example, to have some 'me' time or truly personal belongings, then we might struggle to receive without guilt or shame as adults. We might look around at the unhealthy sense of entitlement that exists in modern culture, where people just expect others to serve them, that all their wants be instantly gratified or their egos constantly fed, even whilst their actions cause harm rather than benefit those around them, and want nothing to do with it! It might be so disgusting to us that we would rather go without than run the risk of being anything like that. Fair enough, but remember that role-modelling healthy and genuine self-worth and demonstrating an ability to receive can help destabilise the indulgent immaturity and narcissism that many mistake for 'self-worth' these days. There is a world of difference between receiving and taking without thought. The 1 and 6 are urging us to receive.

1 with 7
(e.g. 17.17, 11.17, 17.11, 7.11)

This is a very powerful message that indicates a new start in a philosophy or belief system that is going to lead to your spiritual awakening and a willingness to break with tradition in order to walk one's own path. You have either recently been thinking differently or discovered a new philosophy or spiritual tradition, and are being encouraged to continue with it, or that will soon take place for you and it will be very helpful on your life journey.

In a way this is a rebellious number combination. It wasn't until a new friend recently reacted negatively to the term 'rebel', describing that 'phase' in her life as destructive that I realised not everyone shared my very positive association with the term rebel! I think a rebellious streak is a wonderful character trait, provided that you use it to help you live constructively rather than simply reacting against any rule just for the sake of it. With that in mind, the 1 and 7 are the numbers that bring a message of constructive rebellion. The message is that breaking with what you have been told or taught because you are thinking for yourself is a good move for you now. Trust yourself! Trust in your intuition. Trust in what you know within your own being. Trust in you!

A conscious use of the 1 and 7 energy can be inspiring and educating. I remember as a young teenager just starting out in high school, I used to ask all sorts of questions of my teachers that I am guessing they thought I shouldn't be asking, but I believed in the free and uncensored exchange of knowledge and if I wanted to know something, I would ask! And if I were given an answer that I thought was inadequate, I would say so! Now I don't think I was particularly precocious, perhaps the educational system was rather limited, but no matter. What is relevant is that the 1 and the 7 were there and flowing out of my mouth. I have always been one to challenge authority that doesn't seem to be based on genuine merit but just on having a particular job for example. If someone has a position of authority that they exercise with care and integrity and wisdom, you can be sure I'll be a fan. However when exposed to people who are using their positions of authority to bolster their own power drive or without much thought, care or wisdom, I do tend to ask questions and rock the boat. Or I just leave it well alone and live my life according to my own intuition. Either approach is in alignment with 1 and 7. If you don't fit in, don't try to. If you see things differently, that's part of your wisdom. If you want to go beyond what you have been taught, now is the time to do it. Question everything! Assert your right to challenge authority. You don't have to do so in a disrespectful way, but you certainly have the right to consider for yourself what is real, what is worthy of your belief, your time and your energy and you can shrug off whatever nonsense the media is peddling your way any time you choose! Be a rebel with heart! Think for yourself! Those are the messages of this number combination.

Now that probably sounds great, but I'll share a story that a friend of mine told me once, just so you know what the 1 and 7 is *not* meant to be!

My friend was learning to scuba dive. She was partnered up with a young man and they were to do the next part of the scuba diving course together. Part of the training was to learn how to handle an emergency situation if one of the tanks ran out of oxygen. By using the correct hand signals and gestures (presumably not waving one's arms madly about with a look of stricken panic on your face!), you could indicating to your partner that your oxygen had run out, and that you needed to share theirs so that you could both resurface, with enough air, to deal with the faulty tank back at the surface of the water.

So my friend and her diving buddy went underwater and began the next phase of the training. As they descended deeper, my friend began to make the hand gestures to her diving partner, indicating that she needed to share some of his air. This wasn't only part of the training exercise for her. It turned out that her air supply was actually running low.

When she made the relevant gestures to her partner, rather than responding to her by extending his spare mouthpiece to her, as they had been instructed to do before the dive, her diving buddy had a somewhat unexpected response. He shook his head and refused to hand over the mouthpiece so that she could breathe in some of his air supply! Being rather extraordinarily calm under pressure (something I appreciated about her when we were in law school together, nothing really seemed to rattle her), she repeated the action requesting to share his oxygen supply. Again he denied her. Becoming concerned, she quit the exercise and rather swiftly ascended back up to the surface to deal with her situation herself. She's absolutely fine, by the way. I thought I mention that last bit because even though she was sitting in front of me when she told me that story, I still freaked out on her behalf!

Now both people had a 1 and 7 vibration happening here. My friend dealt with it in her typical manner – cool, calm and collected. If something isn't going to plan, change course and deal with it, even if it means breaking the rules of the game. The young man later confessed that the reason he denied her was because he was dealing with co-dependency issues and didn't want to re-enact his wounding in that moment – a most stupendous blend of nobility and stupidity if ever I heard of one (and I've had quite a few of those moments myself to compare it to). He was trying to work with the energy of 1 and 7 but he was misguided. He didn't yet know the difference between rebellion against an unhealthy relationship dynamic based on his right to exist as an independent person being threatened and abandoning someone whom he had consciously agreed to support in a healthy context.

So what does this mean for you? If you are seeing a 1 and 7 in combination you'll need to really listen to yourself. In practical terms, that might mean not following the family tradition of choosing a particular lifestyle or field of work. Or it might mean that you leave certain friendships behind because they don't allow you to really be who you are, perhaps requiring that you always wear a sort of 'mask' over your true self to make others comfortable or that you play a role to fit in with the crowd. The 1 and 7 are a sign that you need to take some steps to find your own way, your own truth. It can be scary, exciting and liberating all at once. It is essentially about you having permission from the Universe to find your own freedom. You deserve it, you are entitled to it, you just have to trust yourself to work it out for yourself – and perhaps you will have connected with a spiritual philosophy or teaching that will help you with that process. Or soon will.

When we are under the influence of the 1 and 7 combined energy, it can also mean a period of being cast into solitude for a while – either consciously by choice because it feels like what we need, or through circumstances beyond our control where our ability or opportunity to connect with others is restricted for a time. The purpose behind this is to help us take some time out to check in with our own truths and intentions, so that we can take action on them. It can just be a bit tricky to hear our own opinions if those around us are constantly blurting out theirs! We'll learn much more about the inner truth and intuition of the 7 vibration in Chapter Seven of course, but for now it's good to know that a 1 and 7 ask us to trust in our own path, even if (perhaps especially if) that is different to the paths of others around us.

1 with 8
(e.g. 18.18, 18.11, 11.18, 1.18, 8.11)

If you are seeing 1 popping up in number patterns such as those described in this chapter, or simply noticing 1s more often than not, then you are being given permission and guidance from the Universe to deal with your life choices from a more individualistic and assertive position. Sometimes this actually benefits the group. It might mean that the group or relationship that you are separating out from actually needs your leadership or assertiveness in order to grow.

If a 1 is coming to you with an 8, then leadership is definitely highlighted. 1 is already leadership-oriented in that it is certainly guiding you to step forward, step out, be bold and initiate action. It can be wise to sit and wait for signs sometimes. At other times however, we will feel a spontaneous push from within to get up, to get moving, to just do something that we might have been worrying about for some time. The appearance of the 1 says, "Enough is enough! Let's go! Let's move! It's time!"

When you combine that with an 8, which has a vibration not only of leadership, but of authority, it is a powerful combination for any type of leadership and responsibility. It suggests a time of new opportunities for you to develop and express yourself. If you have been working in the same field for a while, these numbers herald a time when you can expect more recognition of the skill and expertise that you have developed. You might have to give yourself permission to step into that role. If you are doubting your abilities or yourself in some way, the 1 and 8 remind you that you are more ready and deserving than you are giving yourself credit for, so step forward and claim your destiny.

If you were considering applying for a new position or grant, for example, and these numbers were coming up, then it would be a message to reach for a new level of honour and responsibility, acknowledgement and leadership, because that could benefit the others in your field and take you further on your own life journey.

If you are not looking at employment development and these numbers are arising for you, you might want to consider going further with your work, to find ways to step into positions of more authority. If you find that whole idea a bit challenging, then you might want to do the healing process for the eight vibration in Chapter Eight as well as the healing process for Chapter One below, just to move things along!

Remember that the 1 vibration is the stick upon which the carrot dangles, urging us forward with the promise of something we want. If we fail to be motivated by that, eventually it goes from stick with carrot to just plain stick, as the Universe gives us a whack from behind in the form of some life circumstance or other changing beyond our control and forcing us to change too. With all divine signs and messages, a good rule of practice is to take it seriously enough to really act when you feel guided to do so.

If you have been doing some personal work around learning to feel more empowered and responsible in your life, then the 1 and 8 are confirming that your efforts are paying off and to keep going with it.

This combination of numbers also indicates a new start on a financial level or in any area of abundance and empowerment. It indicates a fresh start and that your intentions around money, wealth and/or power can come to fruition, but you must give them a kick-start with action too! Take steps towards what you want to manifest. This number combination is promising great new strides in those areas. You are being asked to believe!

If you feel as though you have been struggling with an issue for some time, the appearance of the 1 and 8 also indicates that a time of mastery (the 8) is approaching you soon. Sometimes this mastery or resolution of an issue, where we finally get a handle on something that perhaps we never imagined we could, comes when we least expect it, right at the moment when everything seems to be such a mess – suddenly we are somehow blessed with an ability to sort it out once and for all and we are free. This sort of healing does happen. I have experienced it myself. I did have to work towards it and I learned a lot of patience in the process. When it came however, it was so absolutely wonderful, so great to feel that I had passed a test–finally, after nearly 30 years of struggle–and I could let go of that old struggle and enjoy a new turn on the spiral of my life in a happier place within myself and in how I was living in the world. You might already be in the first stages of that when the 1 and 8 appear and you are being given confirmation of this by the Universe. It's validation that it isn't a lucky fluke that you are where you are in your life; you have earned it, and likely another 'promotion' of sorts is on its way to you soon.

1 with 9
(e.g. 9.11, 11.19, 19.19)

This is the big, powerful combination that says something is starting, and it has to do with your spiritual path and life purpose. It will probably also mean something that has to be surrendered or released altogether from your life. It isn't a small message, this one, it is very much about important endings and beginnings.

Sometimes this will mean leaving people behind and that can be very sad. However life is naturally ebb and flow, winter and summer, death and rebirth. This is how growth happens and life can continue. Life wouldn't last long if it was always summertime. That doesn't make it easier, but it does help us to accept the message of the 1 which is about the beginning of something new. That will typically involve the ending of something else – especially so if you have a 9 popping up in your patterning.

You might have a clear sense of what that is going to look like as these big changes happen, or it might be really surprising to you even when it starts to happen. You can be sure though that whatever is ending because something else is beginning, it is meant to be and if you can trust in that, as sad as it might be to lose someone or something that you have valued, it will be easier and quicker to go through the process.

The solitude of a 1 might be required during this time – to go it alone, so to speak, for a while at least. This sort of solitude, especially combined with a 9, tends to be short-lived though. It is like the time alone that we have when we venture to a new country, start a new job or training course, or move to a new town, and we have that period where we feel like the 'newbie', not having really found our feet yet or settled into a group of friends.

We will settle in eventually of course, but if we are worrying about not having found our 'groove' yet, we are being told not to – the 1 is letting us know that we are just going through a natural phase. Sometimes personal comfort (like having a secure place within a group of well known friends) needs to be sacrificed for growth. If those friendships or that work situation was becoming stifling to us, not allowing us to do what we needed to do in our life, then the 1 energy would be telling us to step back a little, or a lot, and make our move. Perhaps we can reconnect with those people later on, or we'll attract new connections. Either way, the message of the 1 is the same – forge ahead.

The 9 in that combination brings the message that we are not to be reluctant or afraid to let people, situations or attachments go. It is the time to do it. It is the time to surrender completely into a new life.

The message of the 1 and the 9 together is also about compassion and spiritual wisdom (the 9) and how that can bring about new beginnings (the 1) if we allow it. I want to share a story with you that illustrates this message.

I was speaking at a spiritual festival, explaining how intelligent the number patterns are and how they reveal guidance when one woman asked if she could share her story. She had been due to travel to New York only recently. She kept seeing 9.11 everywhere before she was due to leave. It made her a little concerned about her trip, to put it mildly. She thought of the pain that still surrounded the experience of the World Trade Center twin towers being destroyed on September 11 all those years previously. Her first reaction was panic! Call 911! Then she made a connection with the 9 and 1 (and an additional 1!) more consciously. There had been much panic around the destruction that took place on September 11 in New York. It was understandable, but not conducive to long term healing if it remained that way. What was needed was a different energy of 911. This wise woman realised that instead of this panic that was building within her about her trip, a change was needed. She had a spiritual path, and a strong sense of connection with the Universe and she chose, instead of plugging into this energy of further panic, to surrender into spiritual wisdom, compassion and fresh new starts. She realised how the ending of the 9 was applied to the two 1s (that could rather poetically be said to represent the twin towers and also the joint energy of new beginnings needed at a universal and human level) and that it was time to take that event to a place of healing. The real way to deal with an emergency is to call on the Divine and allow ourselves and the Divine to become the dual action, the two 1s, that make a choice based in wisdom. Her choice in that case was to not respond with fear. It was to respond to the call of 911 energetically as indicating that there was a need for compassion, to redefine that energy and claim it afresh. I was so moved by her story and the wisdom she claimed out of it, that I instantly asked her permission to share it in this book, which she generously gave.

The 9 and 1 message of taking something and claiming it afresh, with a wiser attitude can be applied in all areas of our lives. It is the same approach that is needed in any situation where we would have once responded negatively, with fear or resistance, perhaps. We are being given an opportunity to rise above that, to make different choices. When the 9 and the 1 are together, we have a great spiritual power for a new beginning at our disposal, no matter what our spiritual beliefs may be. We can tap into that power through our surrender and our compassion, which can allow for us to release fear, hate and unforgiveness, and just let the past be complete, moving on afresh with hope in our hearts and understanding in our minds.

If you have had a time in your spiritual journey where you have broken with the past, suffered from religious or spiritual abuse in some way, or been deluded or conned, then this number pattern also comes with a particular message for you. You are loved. You are worthy of spiritual healing that is truthful and from the heart and all that other stuff can be put behind you now. It is time for you to start afresh with God, the Universe, the Angels, whatever your spiritual beliefs may be, and to know that all is forgiven and forgivable, so that you can be free to take the next step on your own personal spiritual journey.

1 with 0
(e.g. 10.00, 11.00, 11.10, 10.11, 10.10)

In the Tarot, there is a card called the Ace of Wands. The card often features a big hand holding a large wand in an upright position. It sort of looks like a big cosmic 'thumbs up' or 'yes'. That is the energy of the 1. It's a bit like the Universe saying, "Take this step," in whatever area is of relevance to you at the time.

When you add the 0 to that 1, or to any number, it's like the Divine adding its own personal stamp to the number. It amplifies everything. So it's not just a 1, it's a big, fat, super-charged 1, with extra emphasis! So 10 instead of just 1 means divinely ordained beginnings and not just a yes, but a big divine yes!

Whatever you are considering beginning or have just begun, this number pattern is encouraging you in the greatest way possible to do it, or continue with it, to set it in motion, because it is in alignment with the divine flow of life and that is like riding the biggest, most incredible wave ever – it can move us so much farther than we could move ourselves using only our own steam or effort. You are being given the seal of approval of the Universe and will be assisted in whatever is starting for you now.

Healing Process

If you are getting lots of 1s or relate to any aspect of this chapter and want to bring in more 1 energy into your life, use the healing process below to stimulate and integrate the 1 vibration. If you are struggling with any of the messages above, this healing process will help you cut through resistance or doubt and just absorb the healing guidance at a deeper level. It sounds easy and it is!

You'll need a pen or pencil to write with. You'll also need a piece of paper with the circle and point image copied from below, if you don't want to write in this book.

Start by thinking about what you want to start afresh – is it a new level in relationship, in your work, a new project or attitude for health? Generally a new cycle in your life?

When you have an idea, come up with one or two words that sum it up. If you can't think of anything, that is fine, just choose a word that sums up what you would like to bring more of into your life – love, abundance, peace, health …

Write that word or those words as close to the centre point in the middle of the circle as possible, either in this book or on your separate piece of paper.

Put down your pen. Gaze at the circle, focusing first on the outside circle and then after a little while on the point in the centre. You can be aware of your word or words, near the centre point, but just focus on the point.

When you are ready, gently place your left index or pointer finger in between your eyebrows and rest your right index or pointer finger upon the point in the centre of the circle.

Say aloud, "From all that is, I now focus into the one."

Close your eyes and imagine all the energy flowing from behind your left fingertip, from inside of your head, through your left arm, into your body, down along your right arm and into the point on the piece of paper.

Stay there and breathe normally. Stay focused but don't strain! If you find your mind wandering, simply add a little more pressure to one or both of your fingertips.

After several breaths, simply remove your fingers from the paper and your forehead and open your eyes. Gaze at the mandala image for the 1 vibration included at the end of this chapter. Simply gaze and imagine you can absorb it in through your eyes as you relax.

Rest for a moment and close your eyes. Imagining that a visual impression has been made in your deepest mind.

Then simply open your eyes again when you are ready and you have completed your process for the 1 vibration!

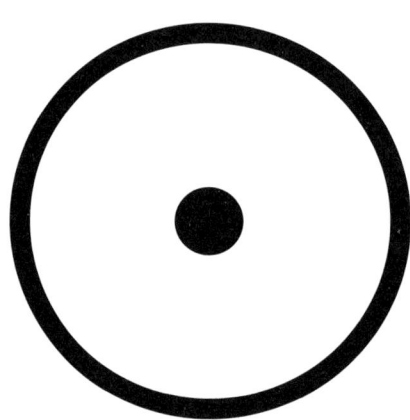

CHAPTER TWO

The 2 message is about connection, intimacy, romantic partnership and all forms of one-on-one relating including friendship, business partnership, therapeutic relationship and of course, marriage. The 2 speaks of union and joining together. This is usually going to refer to people, but it can also relate to the bringing together of two ideas or approaches, philosophies, styles of music, two different worlds, or even businesses, families, nations or other groups. It is about relationship and relating in all ways that involve two people or parties.

The 2 is also about exploring and balancing sometimes opposing roles or demands. That might be the different roles that you have in your personal relationships – lover and mother, for example, or businessman and husband, or daughter and spiritual healer, or even responsible friend and wild free spirit. It might also relate to the demands that these competing roles place on your time and energy. The 2 is about balance, so it isn't actually about choosing one over the other. The message of a 2 is about finding a way to include and balance, to manage and integrate more than one role, task or career, for example. You are not to feel bad about this–selfish or unfocused– it is actually part of your legitimate life experience right now and you are meant to be exploring it.

When the 2 makes an appearance, it is telling you that you do not need to 'go it alone', so to speak. You are going to have help, or you have help already available to you (and perhaps you need to ask for it or become more open to receiving it). You are meant to have an ally (or two!) on your path, and that might be in a variety of ways, and with the 2, you are guided to accept that. This doesn't mean that you are weak or less independent than you would be if a 1 were appearing. It simply means that the way to fulfilment for you now, to success, is through letting yourself benefit from your relationships, even if it is just through moral support.

The 2 alerts you to current or future partnerships in business, love and friendship that can change your life considerably. If you are noticing many 2 numbers or patterns, then generally speaking, you'll want to pay attention to relationship. Even if you think that there isn't a relationship or relationship matter that is particularly important, if you are noticing 2s then the message is that whether you see it now or not, relationship is a significant matter for your life path, or very soon will be. Now this could relate to relationships that are already in existence in your life. However if you have been asking the Universe for relationship healing, or in your heart are desiring more true friendships or an intimate romantic relationship, for example, or even a supportive business partner, agent or publisher, as another example, then the appearance of the 2 is a signal from the Universe that your wish is possible and is being sorted out. Remember that the form of the solution may or may not look exactly like you expect, but it will be what is most needed. The 2 can also bring confirmation, if you have just met someone, that there is an opportunity to explore intimacy in that connection, or that you are going to work with someone you have just met in a way that is helpful, or that there is someone who is just coming into your life who will be significant.

It can also indicate, when in combination with other numbers that we will explore below, that there is a chance for you to do some particular relationship healing within yourself, and through that, your life and levels of happiness, wellbeing and fulfilment can improve.

Now there will be some of us that are more than happy to put time and energy into our relationships because we understand their value. Those of us who have well developed feminine wisdom in our hearts will enjoy and value our relationships, rather than seeing those in our lives as being at our disposal, to meet our various needs. We will feel quite comfortable with the messages that the 2 brings and very open to connection, play, romance, sharing, intimacy and unity with another.

There will of course be others of us that find all that a bit challenging. Perhaps we are more aligned with the solitude of the 7 or independence of the 1, or even the constantly moving energy of the 5, or the detached compassion of the 9, and intimate personal relationships are not the first and foremost things on our mind. In those cases, receiving the message of 2 might be awkward or uncomfortable for us. If that is happening, however, we can be sure that the Universe is calling us to explore this other side of our personality with which we are perhaps rather less familiar. We might have to learn sensitivity or how to set boundaries with others. We might need to express our feelings when we are much more comfortable with keeping them bottled up so that we can avoid feeling vulnerable. We might also discover that we are 'better' at relationships than we realised, and through letting go of old wounds about distrust or being let down, we can actually be nurtured and nourished by relationships, even if we experience hurt feelings in connection with others sometimes.

Whether our response to messages from the 2 is "yippee!" or "oh no!" we can be sure that there is more to be gained by joining forces in one-on-one connections with others at this time, so don't try to slog your life away on your own! Allow yourself to be helped. Yes, that may bring up issues of trust (especially if that 2 combines with a 7, which we will see below in the section on other numbers combined with a 2) but that will be part of what opens you up to let go of past hurts and receive more in this moment, as well as opening you up to a different future.

Remember too that one of the most profound connections you can have is with the source of life and part of the message in the 2 is to allow yourself to be nourished by connection. So what does this mean? It means don't forget to ask for help every day and allow yourself to receive that help! On a practical level, this looks like you praying or speaking to the Divine (whatever you imagine that to be – God, Goddess, your own spirit being, or if you aren't sure what the Divine is, then you can just use this prayer, "If there is any being that loves me unconditionally, then please help me today! Thanks!" Then the receiving part is saying yes to opportunities and assistance that come to you. That last part probably sounds really easy, but I can tell you from personal experience that it is much easier to just keep going the way we are going, not accepting any help that is offered. Sometimes we don't even realise we are turning away assistance because we are so in the habit of being 'strong' and getting on with things on our own. Learning to let others help us can be the start of really putting the messages of the 2 into action. We might feel confronted about even needing help, or we might be able to accept it with gratitude without feeling guilty or ashamed. Whatever our response, it is part of our journey, and we can choose to have compassion where it is needed and continue on our journey to exploring relationship, knowing that the Universe is giving us confirmation with the messages of the 2, that this is indeed meant to be.

2 WITH OTHER NUMBERS

The 2 partnered with other numbers is giving us messages about relationship healing, about new partnerships or connections that are coming into our lives and we need to be open, ready or aware to benefit from those relationship developments.

2 with 1

(e.g. 22.11, 2.12, 2.21, 22.21, 22.12, 221, 21)

The 2 with a 1 is an exciting balance of masculine and feminine energies. This can mean that a new romantic partnership is about to begin, that a new start in a relationship that already exists is coming into being, and also it can mean that a new level of healthier balance between independence and intimacy is taking place. It can also indicate that there will need to be a gentle pulling back on independence for a time—not giving it up completely—but being willing to not be a lone wolf either. That independent streak in you needs to be balanced in connection with another.

It might also be that you find the independent side less comfortable than the relationship side, in which case, you would need to tilt the scales in the other direction, to not fall into relationship so deeply that you lose yourself in the process. You might be learning how to be yourself in solitude and in connection. This is the Universe saying to you, "Hey, you can have your relationships, just remember to have a relationship with yourself as well!"

Any pairing of a 1 and 2 energy is about the balance between individuality and independence, having your own life and interests separate from the relationship *being balanced with* the connection and quality time, common interests and mutual affection of the relationship in question.

If it is not a romantic relationship that is most pressing upon you at the time you are seeing 2 and 1 in combination then the message still applies, but just with a slightly different quality. So if it is a business partnership that is on your mind, or that you are wishing for, then the 1 and 2 are talking about new beginnings in that area of your life, but also about balancing your own business input and independence along with being open to what you can share and receive from the partnership.

If you were asking a question of the Universe, say something along the lines of, 'Can this new business partner be trusted?' and you kept seeing 2 and 1 in response – perhaps whenever you were thinking of that question and happened to glance at a clock on your computer or mobile phone for example, then the sign would likely be that the new partner was bringing something of value to the partnership but perhaps they would also be looking out for their own independent interests too. That doesn't necessarily mean that a business partnership couldn't work, but it might be worth further investigating – perhaps if that partner will still be running a business of their own or if they have very clear individual opinions about what they want to bring to the business in question. It might be a cause to delve a bit deeper to manage your expectations of the partnership. It might be that in further investigations you actually like what you find, or you might not be so enthusiastic, either way, through the journey, you learn something that is helpful.

If you were thinking about whether or not you were being a good enough parent to your child, a different kind of one-on-one pairing as an example, and you received the 2 and 1 message, then the guidance would be that it's OK to balance connection with your child with your own identity outside that of being a parent. The guidance could be that the child might need to see that you are a separate person in your own right too, that this is part of how you can be a good role model for them, showing them that a loving parent can have interests and passions of their own, as one example.

I mentioned in the previous chapter that I was given many 1s when leaving a relationship recently. I also received numerous 2s and 1s together and my sense of this was confirmation that my leaving was not only about a more general change in my life, but about new relationship patterns being born. What I found is that as soon as I left, I began naturally relating to myself and to others very differently. It was quite a surprise to me, but as soon as I was out of the old relationship dynamic, it just happened. I could be naturally more empowered and free, respectful and respected, expressive and receptive–all qualities that are associated with a blend of the 1 and 2 energies–in all of my relationships. It certainly was a new beginning of more conscious relating for me and I very much enjoyed it. As I gaze at my computer clock at this moment, I notice 12.01 and then a click into 12.02 – a nice synchronicity that reminds me that I am still on that journey, and for the most part, enjoying it.

2 with 2
(e.g. 222, 22, 22.22, 2.22)

The message of repeating 2 is a powerful indicator of a connection that is in some way going to be profound or align you with your life journey in a significant way, perhaps through giving you help or assistance, or teaching you a valuable and extremely beneficial life lesson.

If you believe in soul mates, in the concept of relationship between two people that stems from a powerful spiritual rapport and results in a profound connection of mind, body and soul, then you will already have a sense of the quality of multiple 2 patterns. It is the quality of connection so profound and purposeful that it feels as though it were divinely orchestrated or inspired. The repeating 2 reminds us that there are profound soul connections that are taking place in our life or that will take place in time. They will have the feeling of destiny about them. Those people that you know you are just meant to meet, whether they stay in your life forever or just for a time, are an example of the multiple 2 message at work. Sometimes you'll have an indirect connection with someone–not even meet them in person at all–but perhaps just hear them speak, or read a book that they have written, or just hear a story about them through someone else, and at some deep level they'll touch your heart and soul. The sort of connection that a repeating 2 indicates is not a superficial one. It is deep, meaningful and aligns you in some way more fully with your destiny. Having a destiny doesn't mean you don't have choice or free will of course, it means that there is a greater potential in you, something that you can become, a bit like a seed that can flourish into a certain type of beautiful plant. Repeating 2s indicate that you are going to nurtured (even if the relationships might sometimes be challenging, the result of them will be to nurture you further on your life path) in the garden of life by some very effective gardeners! You will be assisted to attain your potential.

The multiple 2 vibration is also associated with spiritual guides. If your belief system is open to this, then you'll understand that these are the guides that love you unconditionally and are something like your personal cheerleading team and group of spiritual strategists (with the best view and therefore the broadest and most helpful and inclusive perspective) combined. Their job is to help you on your path, by giving you signs and nudges, so that you can get through the tricky bits of life and flourish into fulfilment, growing as you go. My belief is that everyone has this team of guidance, suitable for their own temperament and purpose this lifetime, whether that person is aware of them or believes in them or not. But of course, you might disagree with me on that, and that's just fine.

For those of you who are open to the notion of spiritual guidance, the 2 in repeat brings you a particular message. If you are going through a tough time in your life or even a time of great joy, and you are seeing multiple 2s, it's a 'direct hit' from your spiritual guidance, saying, "Hey, we're here with you, this is covered, don't worry about it, it's going to work out according to a higher plan, and we're coaching you through it – so keep asking for our help so that we can continue to assist you!"

Because we live in a free will zone as human beings, we have to ask for help. That means dispensing with wounded notions that there are others who are more worthy of help than you, and so you shouldn't be greedy and ask for too much assistance, or that there are other more important tasks for spiritual beings to attend to than whatever is on your mind at the moment. I have been working consciously with spiritual guidance my entire life–so around forty years now–and I still had a moment only yesterday where I was asking my guides to help me with some really mundane matters and I got rather embarrassed about it, worrying that I was being inappropriate in asking them, something that I never normally would feel. When usual situations like that take place and I am writing, I know that I am meant to be including it in the project I am working on, so I am including it here now.

I said to them (I was at home alone, with the cat and my houseplants for company, so I didn't mind having the conversation aloud), "I am sure you have far more important matters to attend to than this, I am sorry to ask you to help me on something so insignificant. I feel a bit ashamed for doing so actually."

You know what they said in return? I should add here, that I do 'hear' my guidance, sometimes as a voice, but more often as an inner flow of thought, like seeing, hearing and feeling the conversational flow but it is inside my mind, clear to me but not audible to another. I have had that ability my entire life. I feel extremely blessed by it as their messages for me and for the people that I help through my work have been very loving and wise. Anyway, in response to my moment of embarrassment, they said, "We want to support you on your journey to write your books and do your other work to help people. You can do this more easily when you aren't bothered by trivial matters that drain your energy and cause you to worry, so let us help you even with those. We want you to be happy and fulfil your life destiny. There's no need to apologise for anything you ask us to help you with. We want to help you."

I was so touched and felt very loved. That is what the messages of the multiple 2 feel like. Absolute, unconditional accord between two beings. Even when one of those beings is perhaps spiritual and the other is human. If you have had a being who has passed over, for example a loved one from your family or even a beloved pet who has passed on, and you want to know if they are alright, and you are seeing multiple 2s then that is a signal direct from the spiritual worlds to let you know that everything is working according to a higher plan and not to worry, it's OK.

Of course even if you don't see that number, they are still going to be OK because even our death is in harmony with our greater life path and plan, and all beings who leave their body to continue on with their spiritual journey are loved and supported after passing. We live in a very loving Universe at a spiritual level, even though at a physical level that can be hard to believe at times. But if you are noticing repeating 2s then it's because you are ready to understand this at a higher level. That is the deeper spiritual meaning of the repeating 2 pattern, it is a confirmation of the divine plan, carried out with absolute and unconditional love and support for the spiritual essence of all beings. We can feel reassured and comforted by this. It is real and it is loving.

So if things in your life are running rather amok, and you are wondering what on earth is going on and are concerned that all the wheels are falling off your moving vehicle (!), multiple 2 messages are a reminder from the Universe to breathe! It's OK! It might seem like chaos, but you can't get any rainbows with a little rain, so just go with what is happening – there is a far bigger purpose underneath it all, even if you can't understand it consciously at the time. It is safe to trust in what is happening. The wisdom in it will eventually reveal itself.

2 with 3
(e.g. 2.23, 22.33, 22.23, 23, 3.22, 23.22, 2/3)

The 2 combined with a 3 is about new life that flows from relationship. It can literally mean pregnancy but also, more symbolically, a creative gestation process whereby some joining together leads to new life. That could be a merging of ideas, leading to a new modality, philosophy or approach to something, or of two businesses or talents that integrate into an entirely new business, or of two people that come together in partnership and give birth to something – a project, idea or community, for example.

If you are an artist or writer, and you are feeling creatively blocked, then this number combination is telling you that you can benefit from working with others for a time, and/or to be patient because you are 'incubating' or 'carrying' your idea and it just isn't quite time for it to be born but it will be soon, and it will be something new. In the interim, you might need to be stimulated by an 'external' force, whether that be another person, an art exhibit or some time in connection with your loved ones.

2 with a 3 indicates relationships or partnerships that will be creative in some way. So earlier when we used the example of contemplating a new business partnership, this sort of number patterning will give an indication that the partnership is likely to bring in new creative energy. If it came in response to you thinking about a romantic partnership, it might be that the relationship in question would stimulate your own creative processes – perhaps biologically through bringing a child forth in that union, or even through providing the inspiration you need to create on other levels such as through your art or business pursuits.

I feel to make a note here about age. Sometimes a number patterning will have a very specific message to you. So say that you were asking a question and you kept getting one number repeating, say a 23, rather than noticing your clock at 2.23, 3.22 and 22.23. The latter is a pattern of 2 with 3. If you kept noticing 23 on its own, it might be just a message including all the above, but it could also mean that there is something important that happened around the age of 23 for you – or will happen at that age for a person that you are thinking about. Even though number messages are clear, we still need to trust our intuition about them and feel for what the message is for us. As we do this, we don't need to worry about 'getting it wrong'. The Universe will keep showing you the communication–sometimes in various ways–until you get the loving message loud and clear.

2 with 4
(e.g. 22.24, 22.44, 24.22, 24, 2.24, 4.22, 22/4, 2/4)

The 2 and 4 combine with messages of partnership, relationship and stability.

In relation to the business partner example, it would suggest that the partnership will become a foundation upon which the business can grow. If in response to a relationship question, it speaks to the quality of stability and long-term commitment in the relationship, and is an indication that it can be built into something solid, reliable, substantial.

A 2 and 4 in combination bring messages of developing intimacy which leads to a sense of substance within a relationship upon which we can rely. If there have been issues in your relationships of profound rejection and abandonment (and that will apply to many people) then noticing the 2 and 4 vibration suggests that the Universe is giving you a message that you are going to be able to heal these wounds through your life experiences. Sometimes that looks like having a repeat of those experiences! At least at first. But the purpose of the experience is to help you put the ghosts of the past to rest. You were hurt, but you got through it. You are still here. You don't have to deny your pain but you don't have to let it dictate how your present or future will be. To experience the partnership stability that is promised by the 2 and 4 in combination, you might need to do some inner work around letting go of past disappointments and apparent failures. Relationships can be tricky at the best of times. Even if one has ended, even if it didn't end nicely or with a sense of closure at the time, we don't have to chalk it up to a failure. Anything can become a useful experience through which we grew if we are willing to take responsibility and learn something of ourselves through the processing of that particular life experience. The 2 and 4 are suggesting to you that you are learning something through your relationship experiences. You can take that learning and let it become the basis upon which you build a foundation for a healthier or more fulfilling relationship in the present moment and in the future.

Sometimes with a 2 and a 4 we can expect another to ride in (on a white horse, perhaps?) and offer us the emotional stability and commitment that we crave. That can happen, of course, but often we need to do some work on ourselves too! When the 2 and 4 are combined in a number pattern, we are being urged to ask ourselves if we are really ready to receive emotional stability and commitment in our lives. Are we committed to our own emotional wellbeing for example? Are we taking care of our own emotional needs by writing in our journal, or honouring our emotions by expressing them in some other way – through conversation, through dance or art, or through listening to music and allowing ourselves to really feel? Are we expressing that in our closest partnership or relationships? The 2 and 4 combination speaks to us of needing to ground our emotional energies and get in touch with the feelings in our bodies as consciously as we can. This will heal the relationship we have with ourselves, helping us to know what we feel and why more easily, and therefore be more present, articulate and truthful with our partner, or future partner.

That is all helpful not only for attracting a similarly emotionally respectful and grounded relationship into our lives, or improving the emotional consciousness of the relationships we already have, but it is also helpful for our physical and emotional wellbeing, which are intimately connected. When the 2 and 4 turn up, you can be sure that you are being offered chances to develop an awareness of how your body and emotions affect each other. Our physical health will virtually always improve as we tend to our emotional wellbeing, and our physical wellbeing and immunity can become quite depleted if we are not tending to our emotional health. As you explore that, you have a chance to make some real changes in how you relate to yourself so that you feel more loved, safe and secure within yourself. That makes it easier to open up and trust others, thereby inviting relationship into your life more deeply too.

When the 2 and 4 combine in a number message, you'll know that the Universe is wanting to bring you more concrete channels for your emotional fulfilment. If you have always had a lot of emotional energy, or a big desire for connection with others, but have never really found relationships that were personally fulfilling for you, or never found a method to express your emotions and release them (perhaps through art or music) then the 2 and the 4 are letting you know that better circumstances and situations for you are coming! Be open to trying new ways of grounding your feelings. Don't be afraid to express them in physical ways. Don't give up on people, either. You might not have had luck in attracting those that could 'go the distance,' or to the depths with you in the past, but if you are willing to be more open and to continue to run the risk of rejection and share yourself with others, you will whittle out those relationships that aren't suitable for you and be more capable to consciously choose the one that is right for you now.

The 4 relates to the physical world, and making things real and solid. You might want to look at how committed you are to your need for intimacy and to sharing and expressing your feelings by checking out what actions you are taking to support yourself. Are you picking up the phone and initiating conversation? Are you socialising enough? Are you socialising with the sort of people that you really want to connect with and who really want to connect with you? If not, ask for help from the Universe by saying, "Through unconditional love, may I be helped with … Thank you!", then follow up on what comes through in the days, weeks and months following.

The message of the 2 and 4 is about bringing your intimacy and relationship needs to life, about receiving commitment and taking those needs seriously enough to invest your attention and time in them. Doing this work for ourselves can attract a far more healing and pleasurable experience of that intimacy and commitment from others towards us, and us towards them, too.

If you have been dabbling in more superficial or fast flings (and the 2 and 5 might also be coming up to bring that to your attention!) then the 2 and 4 bring a message that you might want to think about settling down in a more responsible and committed loving relationship, not because you have to but because it will be good for you, leading you into more happiness and fulfilment. If you are receiving 1 and 2, or 7 and 2 patterns as well as the 2 and 4, then you are also being given messages that you can expect to be able to maintain your freedom and independence even in a committed, stable and loving relationship. You might need to hear that if you are fearful that commitment means lack of independence or freedom, which doesn't have to be the case at all.

2 with 5
(e.g. 2.25, 22.55, 22.25, 5.22, 25)

2 and 5 as a message speaks of change and sometimes quite abrupt change at that, in your relationships or relating patterns and habits.

Have you ever had a moment where someone said or did something–it might not even have been a dramatic statement or action–and it was enough to give you a sudden shock of clarity? Suddenly you saw that person or their behaviour rather differently? Perhaps you saw yourself and how you were behaving in the relationship rather differently as well. It was enough to jolt you into a new awareness. You might have changed your own attitude into something more mature or cut the relationship off, seeing it clearly for what it was and realising that it wasn't healthy or respectful.

Sometimes this number pattern will reveal that your partner–or friend or business associate or colleague–is trying to change their behaviour or is going through a big change in their life and that this will be an influence in your relationship with that person. You can either attempt to flow with it, or resist it, but change is going to take place either way. Often the less we resist and the more we attempt to work consciously with what is happening–perhaps becoming more flexible or tolerant in some way, or setting stronger boundaries in other ways–the more depth and closeness can come from that change. Certainly this is the case when the 2 and 5 combine. It may even be you that is going through such a change in relationship.

You may find that long term relationship dynamics or patterns suddenly change when these numbers are coming up for you. Relationships may take on a second wind, a fresh lease of energy and become more important to you and supportive during change. It could be due to an apparently external event, such as retirement or a life circumstance that causes a big change for one of the partners. Or it could be through inner work whereby a person grows more mature and changes their expectations and requirements for what is acceptable to them in their relationships.

Allowing yourself to be supported by those that are close to you, by nurturing partnerships during big life changes is another message with the 2 and 5 in combination. It is not only about relationships changing but about relationships supporting change in other areas of your life. It can mean that a relationship is (or soon will) ask you to adapt and grow, to change along with it, or that a current relationship will be able to grow along with you. It might indicate that the tension a current relationship is undergoing is as a result of growth and change in the two parties. Depending on the other numbers that appear together with the 2 and 5, such as a 4 or 6, that might translate into deeper commitment, or in the case of additional 5s, it might mean that the future of that particular connection is undecided at the moment or not capable of transitioning into something more long-lasting or stable. Either way, your relationships are likely to be getting a shake-up and that's part of what will help all involved to mature and grow.

Again it is a matter of sitting with what feels most truthful and relevant for you, trusting your heart and knowing that the Universe will continue to deliver the message until it becomes clear and helpful for you.

2 with 6
(e.g. 2.26. 6.22. 26)

The combination of 2 and 6 is probably the most romantic number combination possible!

We know that the 2 speaks of intimacy, connection and relationship, and the 6 speaks of love, of the Goddess, and together – well, there is a deep, soulful loving connection in relationship that you are being asked to recognise or open to receive.

What to do if you are not in a loving relationship when you are being zapped by 2s and 6s? First of all, be happy! They are a lovely combination to receive. Then ask yourself if you can find a way to celebrate and be grateful for the love you already have in your life – whether that is just within you, or between you and a beautiful pet or even a houseplant! Any living thing can emanate a quality of love, we just have to be willing to receive it and give it in return through our behaviour towards that creature, choosing to be caring or responsive to their needs.

From there, take the hint that these numbers are giving you, and ask the Universe to help you open your heart and connect with a loving partnership, if you are willing to do this, because it's highly likely you are getting these numbers coming to you because that loving partnership is on its way in and you are just not quite ready yet. Best to get on to that immediately! Love is too precious to be allowed to slip on by when we just weren't paying attention. The Universe will help you ensure that this doesn't happen to you. Just ask for help, through unconditional love, to be open to soulful, loving relationship, and you'll be just fine.

Also if the thought of loving partnership scares you, don't be too hard on yourself. Love can be the greatest adventure and it is rarely without its hurtful moments. Two human beings connected in great passion can enhance each other's lives dramatically, but they can also cause pain, intentionally or not, at times and accepting that is part of accepting a human relationship into your life. Perhaps past experiences have left you feeling uncertain about how much of that you want to open yourself up to again. However, in receiving this number combination, there is guidance that there is a relationship developing or soon to come to you that is worth facing your fears for. Don't give up on yourself, on others, or on love.

If we are already in relationship, the combination of the 2 and the 6 also reminds us to seek out romance. That might mean making some time to get a babysitter and going on a date with our spouse, for example. It might mean celebrating love in some way together – taking note of an anniversary, or sharing a special gift or letter, or just doing something sweet (another quality of the 6 vibration is sweetness from the heart) for your loved one.

The 6 also brings a message of abundance coming to you and it is possible that there will be a shift in your financial wellbeing due to the arrival of a partner or through a partnership in some way, even if that partnership is not a marriage but a business arrangement. The latter might have less of the romance aspect of the 6 and more of the prosperous vibration – either way it can be a beneficial number pattern bringing more love and money into your life.

2 with 7
(e.g. 2.27, 7.22, 27)

The 2 combined with a 7 is a special relationship combination and indicates a relationship with a spiritual or educational focus. That could be a relationship with a teacher, or a kindred spirit whom you feel just 'gets you' at a deeper level, and allows you to grow personally through your connection to each other.

It may also indicate a relationship or a relationship situation that can help you heal your issues with trusting and valuing your own intuition and insight. If you have learned to distrust your own inner voice, perhaps through childhood experiences where others reacted fearfully to what you intuitively knew, accusing you of making it up or finding out through some other means, then you might have learned to regard your own natural intuition with suspicion or fear about how others would respond to it. Having access to our intuition is such a valuable resource for living life well and avoiding at least some unnecessary pain and suffering (we can frequently spare ourselves a lot of trouble by listening to our own inner counsel and wisdom). It is worth facing old anxiety and fear about our intuitive abilities and learning step by step to trust ourselves again, especially if we acknowledge that living in distrust of our own inner wisdom is not how we actually want to live anymore!

If you can relate to all that, then this combination brings you good news. You are in a situation, or soon will be, where you can undo that damage and learn to trust your instincts again. Don't be fooled however. Sometimes those opportunities come from a loving, supportive friendship that nurtures your insight and helps it grow in that positive fashion. But sometimes healing will happen through a relationship where the other person doubts you, reinforcing the old pattern in you until something snaps inside and you decide you've had enough and you are going to listen to your own inner voice anyway!

The presence of this number combination also indicates a time when you will really need to trust your own intuition about any matter that involves another person in a one-on-one connection with you, or about any relationship of another (perhaps a friend or family member) that has been on your mind. Perhaps your friend has a relationship issue going on and wants advice and you are not certain to what extent you should get involved. Or perhaps a family member is having an issue with their spouse or child and you are not sure if you are best to intervene or if that would just be interference. Or in your own relationship with another, you might feel that you are at a crossroads or decision-making point, or that there is a pattern of behaviour that you would like to resolve in a different way if you are to proceed in relationship with each other.

The point of the 7 in combination with the 2 is that you are being guided to trust yourself and find your own truth in the situation; to be guided by your own intuition. You are not necessarily being asked to withdraw from the other person to sort it out in solitude, although you may need a little of that to find your own thoughts and feelings if you are the sort of person who is easily persuaded or influenced by another. Eventually however you are encouraged to share your intuition in your relationship, to let that intuition guide you in your relating to others, and if you have a big decision to make – such as whether to stay together or to leave a relationship behind, the guidance in this number combination is to trust yourself, without doubt, and follow your intuitive nudge.

If you aren't sure what your intuition is telling you, ask for help! You can do this simply by saying silently in your mind, or aloud (perhaps whilst standing in your home or garden, rather than walking down a public street), "Through unconditional love, I ask for help with ..." and then just express the matter that is bothering you as clearly and simply as you can.

Then pay attention to other numbers that come to you to sort through the clues, as well as trusting your own gut instincts on what you feel in the moments, days and weeks following your request for assistance. All such requests are answered, without exception. Sometimes we just need patience to receive the answer though. Sometimes with the 2 and 7 in combination, it will be the words of another that actually confirms our intuitive insights and gives us the extra confidence we need to trust ourselves.

Recently I had a session with a client that had this happen in an unusual way. She wrote an email to an ex-boyfriend who she had put on something of a pedestal. She wrote a very apologetic email about her behaviour in the relationship, some seven or so years ago, although most objectively, they both contributed to the good parts and the painful parts of their relationship, probably fairly equally. She did this with a view to making peace with him, if there was indeed anything still unresolved between them. It had been many years since there was any contact, so she wasn't exactly sure how he would respond, though given the love that they had once shared, she had hoped that her efforts would be conducive to peace.

The ex-boyfriend's response surprised her, though not me, I have to say, because it was basically consistent with the way he had been with her when they were together. Having not engaged in any sort of personal healing work, it would be unlikely that there would be a huge change in his behaviour. Nonetheless, my client was a little thrown by his passive-aggressive, emotionally manipulative response.

Eventually what came to her, however, was that she needed to stop excessively apologising and realise that they both had their good guy and bad guy moments! Instead of taking his response as a way of compounding her old feelings of badness, she chose instead to flip her attitude (though not her finger, as I probably would have done – she was far more restrained!) and choose to trust herself.

She knew deep down that despite struggling to shake the notion that she was a bad person, she actually wasn't a horrible person at all, and if anything, she tended to take on more guilt and responsibility than was healthy, even to the point of feeling excessively responsible for the feelings of others.

The shock of her ex-boyfriend's response, and his ungenerous behaviour was so dramatically below what she felt she deserved that it jolted her into awareness. She decided, perhaps for the first time in her life, to give herself the benefit of the doubt. Perhaps his reaction was about him, and not about her at all. Perhaps she actually didn't deserve what he was dishing out.

I wanted to squeal with glee. In her sessions, it was so painful to watch her go through the self-criticism and self-doubt despite her intelligence and willingness to do her personal work. To see her have this breakthrough was like watching sunlight burst through thick storm clouds. It was a healing shift in trusting herself instead of placing her sense of self-worth in the emotionally manipulative (though quite likely unconscious) head games that others sought to play with her. She just didn't want any part of it anymore. She had used her own intuitive insight and trust in herself to step out of a relationship pattern with another that was damaging and into a relationship pattern with herself that was healing. This is the 2 and 7 wisdom in full effect. May we all be blessed with such healing inner vision – though perhaps through less painful encounters, if possible!

2 with 8
(e.g. 2.28. 8.22. 28)

The 8 brings power, authority and wealth to the 2. It is somewhat different to the experience of wealth and love of the 2 and 6 together. The message of the 2 combined with an 8 is much more about a powerful presence coming in through relationship.

It might be that a new authority figure is coming into your life, or that you are stepping into a position of authority within your relationships or through a new partnership or work promotion. It might indicate that you are connecting with a colleague who will be of great benefit to your status and career.

If you have been feeling inadequate or disempowered in a relationship, and this number pattern is coming up, then it is indicating that you need to remember that you are not a victim, no matter how the circumstances may appear! You have a power and love within you that cannot be taken from you. Ever! They will always exist within you and no one can own you or control you without your permission. In fact, at the deepest level within, no one can own you or control you ever; there will always be part of you that is pure and intact within your deepest self and there is nothing anyone can do about that, no matter how powerful you may believe them to be.

With the 2 and the 8, you are being asked to become aware of the power dynamics in your relationships and to see if you can become more comfortable with your own sense of power and realise that it is indeed compatible with being in a relationship. The 2 and the 8 together are about being able to reconcile power with connection, and not allow a need to be in control or in authority to prevent one from being intimate and sharing themselves with another.

If you are in a dilemma about whether to give up your career in order to stay at home or be more involved in a parental or relationship role, the 2 and the 8 in combination suggest that this might not be the best way for you. Perhaps you can change how you work in your career to include your relationship focus, but giving up the career focus or responsibilities outside of the relationship might not be the way that you will fulfil yourself this lifetime. It is more about striking a balance.

If you are in a leadership position already, this number combination urges you to remain connected to your troops, so to speak; to not put yourself above or beyond them whilst you strategise in some distant outpost. They need you! Allow yourself to be accessible to them. It is going to be to your benefit ultimately to do so, and it will strengthen your leadership. This is amplified if you also receive the 6 and 8 or 8 and 9 number combinations.

Finally the 2 and the 8 together will be guiding you to consider where responsibilities lie, and how they are divided in your relationships with others. If you are thinking of an issue with your son, for example, and the 2 and 8 comes up, you might want to think about whether or not you are giving him enough responsibility—or even too much for his age— to encourage his sense of masculine pride and responsibility, without it becoming overwhelming which would not be so constructive for him. You might consider if you and a loved one in a romantic partnership are dividing responsibilities fairly – especially if a 7 were thrown into the combination of the 2 and 8. If a 1 were thrown into the 2 and 8 combination, then it would be time to get really truthful about power and responsibility in the relationship and perhaps start afresh. It might also indicate that you are about to connect in some partnership or relationship with a wealthy and powerful free-thinker, or that you need some time on your own to explore your own personal power and intuitive insights, and then to share those in the relationship in a new way.

You see, the messages need to be applied to your own life, based not only on the 'clues' of what is already happening in your world, but based on what you feel within as being truthful for you. Remember that if a choice arises to make an interpretation of a message in a kind and loving translation or a fearful and critical translation, always choose the former. The Universe is benevolent and loving and wants to help you. The Universe doesn't do fear-based messages, those come from a frightened ego and they deserve to be responded to with compassion certainly, but not with respect.

2 with 9
(e.g. 2.29, 29)

This is a loaded combination! It is a karmic number sequence that indicates an important time in a relationship, usually either its end or the ending of a phase within that relationship, opening it up to a new cycle. What I mean by karmic number is that when a 9 appears, there will be some kind of spiritual learning taking place that is important for our personal growth this lifetime. Whatever lessons or challenges are coming up in your relationships when you find 9 in combination with 2, you can be sure that it is really important that you work through it and come to some resolution within yourself, some peace in your own heart about your part in the process, whether the relationship continues on or not. What is the best way to ensure that you gain the learning you are supposed to gain? You ask for help of course! You can say, "Through unconditional love, may I see whatever I am supposed to see here and understand it clearly, for the highest good. Thank you!"

When 2 with a 9 comes up, it is a time when the connection cannot simply continue as it has been. This can be felt as a crisis of commitment where it becomes obvious that a level of relating has been reached and either has to expand and grow and deepen, or the relationship will need to be released altogether.

This can be so sad sometimes! Even though a part of you knows that something has run its course, or that a relationship with another doesn't have the substance, endurance or flexibility to be able to continue to grow along with you (or with the other person), you might still love your partner very much. This is the karmic aspect. Sometimes our personal preferences–that we continue in a particular relationship for example–are subject to a greater plan unfolding. The sacrifices necessary in order for us to stay might be too great to bear – for example, we may not feel able to be ourselves, or to feel happy and authentic in the relationship. Even if we wanted to stay with a person so much that we believed we could bear such an outcome, it would cease to be a relationship and become something more like a prison that would eventually starve us of genuine love, light and life. If we have a destiny to fulfil and certain learning to take place (and of course, we all do) then at times, that's going to mean that something or someone may have to be released in favour of something or someone else.

Now of course, this number message doesn't always mean the ending of a relationship. It might indicate that there is an expansion happening at a deep spiritual level (the 9 bringing a very spiritual and compassionate vibration into the combination) so that the love in the relationship can become increasingly unconditional. Now that is something very special! So this combination can indicate–in any relationship whether romantic or not– that there is a new level of trust and complete acceptance opening up. It can indicate the sort of relationship that can teach one about unconditional love.

I had a relationship like that during my twenties. We were together for nearly six years before we parted ways, when our ability to grow together finally drew to a close. It was a very sad parting and yet we were both able to accept it and move on with our lives, still with love in our heart for each other, each wishing happiness for the other.

During that relationship I learned a lot about how to love someone. My partner at that time in my life was different to anyone I had ever known. He was very pure of heart, and quite defenceless in love. He was open and vulnerable with me emotionally and let me know how he felt about me, about life. I always knew where I stood with him. He was very intuitive and sensitive, and he listened when I spoke. He helped support me emotionally, which I was profoundly grateful for and I felt loved and supported in that relationship in a way that was as close to unconditional love as I had ever experienced. I was in shock and very sad when I finally realised that although there was much unconditional love in that connection, there was a limit to what the relationship was capable of sustaining without breaking, and my growing independence as I matured was one of those things. We tried, but we couldn't work through it. We had reached a different expression of the 2 and 9 number energy that typified our relationship; we had reached the end of our journey together as a couple.

Sometimes the best place to explore unconditional love is within ourselves. Learning to get to know ourselves, even the parts that we are aren't so enamoured with, and appreciating them for what they are–part of how we have responded to life and become the person we are today–can be a good way to respond to the 2 and 9 message. From there, we can attract more unconditional love into our world through the old principle of like attracts like, or the law of attraction.

The final message of the 2 and 9 vibration is to surrender into the relationship and to allow the Universe to bring healing. The best way to do this at first is through prayer or actively declaring to the Universe that you are handing over this relationship for healing. Then we take off our control mechanisms and emotional seat belts and just go with it. It doesn't guarantee that the relationship will last for all eternity, but it does indicate that no matter what happens, there is some valuable learning about love that will take place and it will nourish us spiritually on our life journey too.

2 with 0
(e.g. 2.00, 20, 2.02, 2.20, 0.22)

We have already learnt in the first chapter that a 0 adds a big punch to a number vibration. In combination with a 2 it is a message from the Universe saying that there is a cosmic connection, or some incredibly meaningful relationship learning taking place right now, or there soon will be, so DON'T MISS IT!

It can also mean that there is going to be a sort of divine intervention in your relationship. Sometimes we just really need this – two people might be doing their best but really, they need some more help! I call on the 'relationship angels' in these sorts of situations. As an aside, I also call on the parking angels and the bargain angels in other situations, but for now, let's just focus on the relationship angels. Whether you believe in angels or not, there is nothing wrong with asking for help in a relationship issue that has been troublesome or difficult to resolve.

I had a problem like this in my past relationship. We were fundamentally rather different creatures, and whilst sometimes that worked to our advantage, the more I grew into my own self, the greater the difference between us became. Our differences then seemed to stop working to our advantage, becoming instead a source of struggle and dissatisfaction for both of us. I remember once trying to turn that disadvantage around in a rather arrogant way, which was to try and pull my partner along on his spiritual path by asking him to have empathy for the situation I found myself in at the time. He couldn't though. It would have required something from him that he couldn't give at the time. It wasn't a terrible thing to ask for, it was quite a reasonable request, logically speaking, but at a deeper and more truthful level, it wasn't mature of me to ask something of him that he wasn't able to give emotionally. I was trying to satisfy my desire to stay with him and still grow on my path, rather than accepting that if I were to choose to grow on my path, that might mean that I would have to give him up; to detach and let go of the relationship even if I didn't want to do so at the time.

However, I didn't have that awareness at the moment of asking for empathy from him. It wasn't until he was responding to my request with a lot of anger, quite possibly born of frustration, that I had a moment of '2.0' as it were.

My partner's guidance appeared above his head and said to me, "Don't ask him to give more than what he already is, Alana; he is already pulled to the edge of his limits by just living with you, he is not meant to take further steps on his conscious spiritual journey in the way that you are – his is a different path, let him be."

Rather surprised by their sudden appearance and what they had to say, I suddenly felt contrite as I realised how immature I had unconsciously been, believing that I knew more than his own being about what his spiritual path should be (well, perhaps it was more about what I hoped it could be, so that we could stay together even if I kept growing, but it was misplaced behaviour on my part, nonetheless).

So whilst my partner argued with me, despite appearing somewhat puzzled by me gazing over his head and the sudden change in my energy as all the passion and defensiveness went out of my side of the argument, the Divine had intervened. What happened soon after is that I genuinely apologised and explained what I had just seen and heard, and I let it go. Eventually I had to let the relationship go too, though it took me over a year after that point to do so. I was learning to trust in the 2 and 9 vibration that was coming through for us, and in the 2.0 moment that urged me to accept the reality of what was ending. I also learned, as I mentioned above, that in every ending there is a new beginning too – a new start in relating in a way that made me much happier came from that ending, sad as it was at the time, and in the months of working through the grief that followed the ending.

Healing Process

This healing process is for you if you relate to any of the issues above and want some help to get the healing flowing (in addition to simple requests for help as mentioned above, of course).

It is also for those of you that are seeing lots of 2s around you even if you don't immediately relate to the guidance shared above but you want to receive the help that is coming to you through that 2 vibration, in some other way than what is described in this chapter.

Look at the image below with a soft gaze. Place your right hand over the left half of the mandala and your left hand resting lightly over the right half. Don't cover the image completely, just place your hands on each half, so that it is comfortable for you. This may mean only your fingertips rest on the image. That is fine.

Focus on the portion of the mandala still left in view, in between your hands, in the centre.

Gaze for a few moments and then see, sense or feel that there is life force, energy or a feeling from the mandala rising up into your hands and flowing up your arms, into your heart and then rising up into your brain. You may feel or sense this as a fountain of light flowing if you like. Relax. Breathe in and out. Take your time.

When you are ready, simply uncross your hands and place the right hand on the right half of the mandala and the left hand on the left half. Relax. Gaze at the mandala, the portion that is still in view in the centre being the point of your focus. Imagine, sense or feel the energy, life force or feeling of that mandala rising up into your hands, up through your arms and into your heart, rising up into the centre of your brain. You might like to imagine this is a fountain of light flowing into your body.

When you are ready, simply stand up, shift your weight lightly from one foot to the other and when you feel grounded and present, you are done with your healing process.

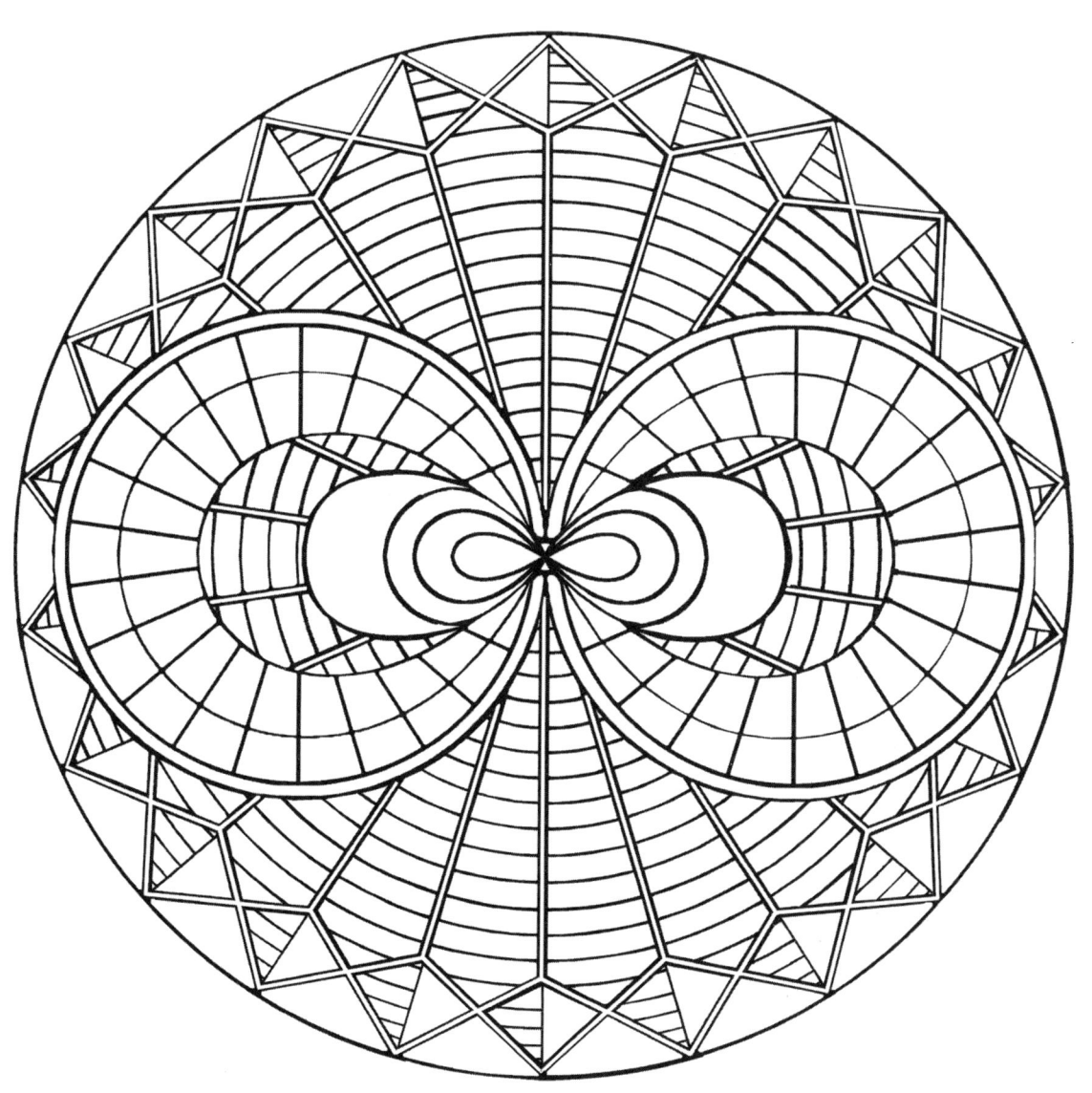

CHAPTER THREE

The 3 brings a playful and healing message of wellbeing and signals new life is beginning now. It speaks of the bringing together of apparently different things and creating harmony so that something new can happen. When the 3 features in a number pattern, that harmony and unity might manifest on the physical, emotional, mental or even spiritual level. Or on all levels coming together so that our physical lives, emotional wellbeing and spirituality can all flow in one coherent direction, for example.

On a physical level, the 3 can indicate a birth. It might be a pregnancy leading to the birth of a biological child, as one example, but it can also be the birth of a new talent, new life phase or new career. If you were considering training for example, and you were noticing 3 as a number message, the likely message for you would be that the training you are considering is instrumental to a new line of work for you, perhaps even a new sense of self, a broader identity and a sense of psychological wellbeing and self-esteem. It might even indicate that you'll meet new friends and have more fun playing too!

Likewise if you were thinking of enrolling in a new class to learn a musical instrument or cooking skill, as another two examples, the 3 would likely be guidance that these decisions will bring you more energy, increase your creative self-expression, offering you a helpful outlet for any stress or excess energy, and give you a chance to bring more of yourself into harmony thereby increasing your wellbeing.

The 3 energy has a message for those of us that feel tired, as though we are lacking in energy. Fatigue does not always mean that we don't have enough energy. Often it doesn't mean that at all. The 3 tells us that fatigue is a sign our energy is just going in directions that aren't conducive to our wellbeing. That might be because we are trying to 'spread ourselves too thin' with too much going out and not enough coming in. It might also be because we are fighting with ourselves (or another) about the course of our lives, or trying to resist something within us, rather than surrendering and letting it happen. With the 3, the message is to take steps in our physical life to attend to our wellbeing and to learn to nurture ourselves.

In the Tarot, the third card is the Empress. She is often depicted as a beautiful pregnant woman in a field of lush grass, with her hand on her belly. She looks serene and at peace with the world. The feeling of wellbeing, creativity, flourishing energy and life are all qualities of the 3.

When women wish to get pregnant, if it is not happening easily for them, a journey often begins as they seek to boost their fertility by understanding the needs of their bodies. They may tend to their connection to their body in a new, more present and caring way, to allow the body to become more fertile – which often happens through adequate rest, adequate exercise and movement, adequate nutrition and hydration, and through letting go of excessive or obsessive thinking (usually about getting pregnant!). When we let go, life can flow. My mother used to say, "A watched pot never boils," which means that once we start something, it's OK to let it go, to put our attention elsewhere for a while and to come back to it when the time is right. The way that I explain this idea to my students is to say that when you are in a restaurant ordering your meal, if you keep the waiter at your table asking him over and over again if he got your order right, if he is really going to take it to the kitchen and tell the chef, you are likely to go very hungry and not get your meal! You have to give it up at some point and let the waiter deliver your order to the chef. In that situation, we usually don't think about it; it's easy to do. We just have to apply that sort of trust and surrender once we send our 'meal request'–from our heart's desire or declaration of intention–to our soul kitchen, where the great chef–our own spiritual essence or the divine creator–gets a-cookin'!

This process of tending to our wellbeing applies to those of us who receive a 3 pattern regularly enough and feel as though our physical wellbeing is in need of a boost. It doesn't only relate to pregnant (or wanting-to-be pregnant) women. When a 3 is present, we need to take care of ourselves. That is always good advice, but at some times in our lives, perhaps during periods of high stress, it will be even more useful. At times we just need the reminder.

The wellbeing of the 3 is about body, but also emotions and mind. The 3 is about unity and harmony. So the 3 is good news for those of us that might be feeling some conflict in our lives – about work and home life, about being a parent and a partner, or between a desire to cut loose and live a wild, free life and yet still tend to our responsibilities with integrity. The 3 tells us that there can be harmony brought to bear even within the most apparently contradictory or opposing forces. The 3 comes from the sum of 1 and 2, which are naturally very different energies.

So the message for creating the unity and harmony we desire is that we don't have to try to be singular in order to be integrated. We don't have to be just one person or have one side to our personality. It is about accepting our differences– within us and with each other–and from that place of absolute acceptance, things can flow more easily, especially when we surrender to allowing creation to happen. Healing, creativity and wellbeing, the hallmarks of the 3, are not things that we can force to occur. They are things that happen naturally when we are in the right frame of mind, doing particular actions that feel supportive and appropriate for us (based on our own truths – what works for us might not suit another and vice versa).

So the 3 teaches us about getting our part of the process in order – how we tend to our health and wellbeing, how we give ourselves opportunities to be emotionally well (perhaps through art, writing in a journal, going to a dance or singing class or group to give ourselves permission to self-express in that way, or through sharing our feelings with those that we trust) and mentally well (through choosing what we watch, read and listen to with discernment and a sense of wanting to nourish ourselves, as well as through being open to changing belief systems that aren't supporting and nurturing us). Then our job is to tend to the things we can tend to, and allow the rest to happen. Just like a pregnancy! We deal with our part, and life happens.

When we are in the midst of wanting creation to happen, or wanting more harmony in our lives, and we are taking the steps to support ourselves physically, emotionally and mentally, as well as asking for spiritual help (always a good idea, with all the numbers, and very easy to do – we simply say aloud or quietly in our own minds, "I call on the assistance of unconditional love, please help me here!"), we become very magnetic to healing, wellbeing and creative flow. The 3 is a number of taking action (the 1) and surrender (the 2) which brings about healing, wellbeing and new life (the 3).

Sometimes we may believe that only special people with particular talent are creative. Certainly there are some that display prodigious talent in particular areas. That is wonderful, yet we have to be careful not to allow that to make us judge our own creativity as 'less than worthy' or refuse to acknowledge its existence. When a 3 appears, the emphasis is on tapping into your own creative energy and allowing that to boost your sense of self-esteem because you are valuing yourself enough to express that part of you. I have seen people who don't believe that they are particularly creative put together a sound system from scratch, fashion a home décor that was absolutely beautiful, create some fierce dance moves or even dress with incredible flair. So creativity can be just as much about how we throw a meal together, how we put together an outfit, or even how we go about solving problems, as it is about more obvious endeavours, like writing a book or painting a picture.

Even so, it has been my experience that there are often vast untapped creative abilities that lie beneath our conscious, day-to-day identity and we often don't even know that they are there until we start to explore that part of ourselves more willingly. I wanted to create music long before I believed that I could.

It took me years to even begin to write any music at all. Several years before I started even attempting to compose, I was working with a therapist on dealing with some childhood issues. She suggested lightly that I write some music and bring it in to my next session with her. It was a perfectly acceptable suggestion and a very safe environment in which to explore whether I had any fledgling talent in that area. I flat out refused! I was terrified. Even when I did eventually build up the courage to write something, it was because my partner at the time (the one who taught me about unconditional love) responded to an issue I was having. I wanted to find someone to write background music for the meditation CDs that I wanted to record. As I spoke with prospective people and was uncharacteristically indecisive, my boyfriend at the time turned to me, and simply said, "Well, why don't *you* write the music?" I was stunned but I took comfort in his belief in me and had a go. I found it was easier than I thought. It was possible! I was shocked.

Eventually I was proud of my music and it ended up on my first meditation CDs which were later picked up and re-released by Blue Angel Publishing. You can still hear that music on the *Radiance, For Love and Light on Earth* and *Mystical Healing* albums. Later on, I wrote another piece of music that features on Blue Angel meditation CD dedicated to Kuan Yin, called *Divine Lotus Mother*. Then all of my meditation music ended up on a relaxation music CD, *Voice of the Soul*. Clearly when I first explored music composition, there was a creative plan hatching that I had no idea about at the time, to nudge me more into sacred healing music. I love that now, of course, but I am glad it happened in stages, one step at a time, conquering one fear at a time, so that by the time I was performing music live on stage with others for healing, I really was ready and didn't suffer from a lot of the anxieties and fears that I saw other performers struggle with when it came to offering music publicly, no matter how talented they were.

I also know that I am not the only one who has untapped creative depths. It is my belief that people are generally more creative than they consciously realise. It takes time, patience, commitment and discipline to explore one's creativity. Sometimes it is more confronting than fun, because we have to face our fears that we aren't good enough, talented enough, or that we will feel silly and ashamed at being shown to be beginners at something when we are not children anymore. Yet if we are willing to move past the barrier of doubt and judgement that blocks us from even trying, and just be creative without having to be perfect or professional, we can then have so much fun!

I have memories of being in my early teens and setting up a mock art studio in the back room of my childhood home. I would blast whatever music I was in love with at the time on the stereo, and paint whatever I felt like painting. I have no idea if any of it was any good. Quite likely it wasn't! Yet I didn't mind one bit. It wasn't being created to be viewed and assessed. It was being created because it felt good to do it, to express something in that way, and in that moment (not so much in the cleaning up afterwards), it made me feel happy.

I am so passionate about this that I have written an oracle deck called Sacred Rebels Oracle, another Blue Angel Publishing release, to help people awaken their creativity, overcome fears and doubts in manifesting their life path, and gain confidence to awaken and practice their creative self-expression.

When the 3 is coming to us, on its own or in combination or repetition, we can be sure that at least part of the message is to nudge us to honour our creativity, to acknowledge that we are creative beings, and to allow ourselves to experience that–in whatever way–as part of our healthy self-esteem, and wellbeing.

3 WITH OTHER NUMBERS

The presence of the 3 with other numbers usually indicates that there is a healing that can take place, a new birth of some description, and/or a more creative approach that can be helpful for you that will show itself soon. The 3 comes with a message from the Universe that it wants you to be well, to create and to experience more harmony and unity in your life. It is also a suggestion to attend to your self-esteem and realise that you are a child of the Universe, no better or less than any other, and deserving of care and respect.

3 with 1
(e.g. 3.13. 3.31. 1.33. 31)

The 3 combined with a 1 can have various straight-forward messages—a new birth is coming to you now—a new child, a new career, a powerful creative inspiration that will set you off on something of an inner journey, and perhaps an external journey too, and bring you into a new level of harmony and wellbeing within yourself.

The 1 and 3 together say 'act now' on the creative urge. Do it. Do your class, take action on that idea, say yes to what is coming your way and don't hesitate. The 1 with the 3 is about the now (or what will come to you very soon) and it is a bold number combination that asks you not to be shy, but to believe in your creative ability, or that you are worthy of having a child or a successful creative career (or whatever it is that is in your heart) and that the actions and guidance you need to bring this about will come to you.

A 3 and 1 in combination also promise that there is a new beginning at hand; it might be a creative 'resuscitation' on a project or dream that you held in your heart but cast aside for one reason or another. The 3 with 1 tells us that new beginnings are possible in our creative endeavours. Even in nature, during the winter, things appear to die. Yet in the spring, somehow new life forms. During the apparent inactivity of winter, the replenishment and restoration that were taking place all along would eventually result in great fertility when the time was right. So the message with the 3 and 1 is also about divine timing, which is another way to say the right timing, so that things can come to life.

If you tend towards impatience (as I do) then you might wish that things were just done right now. However there is a higher intelligence in patience; a lesson some of us will have to learn over time (patiently!). In that learning, I have personally found that there is more trust in life, and the timing of things, when we realise that there is no point scattering great seeds, filled with potential, onto barren ground. It's better to prepare the soil, to wait until it is fertile and then plant the seeds. There's a much better chance of a successful harvest that way. The 3 with the 1 brings with it a call to action, but with a reminder to have patience in the timing of our process, and trust in the next step that will eventually present itself in due course, and in the ultimate results of our actions coming together according to a higher destiny. If you are losing faith because of an apparent delay, don't. The 3 is validation of your creative work, or process of healing change (which is creative work applied to the self), and the 1 is validation of your efforts, your intention, your action. Have faith! This is a particularly strong message for you if you also receive a 3 with a 7, which you can read more about below.

The 3 with 1 asks us to surrender about how and when things happen, and even about all the details. We need to trust that the creation will take place, things will come together, according to a natural creative process, provided that we take the steps that we can take here in the physical world to help the process unfold (without trying to control or force it, because quite simply, that is unnecessary).

3 with 2
(e.g. 3.23. 2.33. 3.32. 32)

The 3 combined with a 2 suggests creative partnership, and also the burgeoning of new life within relationships. That might indicate that a new relationship, perhaps with a manager, an agent, a helpful mentor or an inspiring friend, is going to boost your creative life or bring new creative potentiality to you.

It can also indicate that you can gain creative inspiration and emotional wellbeing by allowing yourself to connect with others in relationship. If you are a person who tends to do things on your own, be that making all your decisions alone or engaging in more solitary creative work, such as writing, design or art in various forms, then this number pattern brings you guidance to connect with others, and allow relationships to bring you energy for your creative work. It might mean that it is best for you to combine your talents with those of another to create something together, or simply to allow your relationships to support your solitary creative process. You'll sense or feel in your heart if this applies to you and if so, in what respect.

Now, sometimes we define creative work far too narrowly, as I mentioned above. Your creative work might be in a more typical artistic sense but it could also, and legitimately, be in broader ways. Your creativity might come out in how you dress or decorate your home, in generating money for donations to a worthy cause, or in creating new belief systems and applying them in your own life, thereby inspiring others to do the same. Creativity is not only putting pen to paper or brush to canvas. At a spiritual level, each of us is creating our life experience every day with our thoughts and responses to what is happening in the world. When the 3 and 2 arise together, we are being asked to notice how relationship affects our creative process. Can it bring more energy to us if we socialise rather than getting too wrapped up in our own inner world, for example? Are there relationships that can inspire us to feel more positive and therefore create a life with more gratitude and peace? Are there people that we spend time with that make us want to write, or paint, or sing? People who are already in touch with their creativity often inspire others to want to do the same. That is part of their gift.

The 3 and 2 suggest that seeking out the company of such people might ignite your own creative passion, even if you aren't exactly sure what that is! Where would you find such people? Drumming circles, free-style poetry nights, fashion shows, art exhibitions, music jams and open mic nights, conscious dance classes. Any big city will have plenty to choose from. If you cannot find such events in your town, and you haven't decided to start your own instead (!) then you can inspire yourself through the wonders of technology, images from art books, reading poetry that you love or exploring music that moves you. There are ways to connect with others that do not only involve physical connection in the same time and place. Such is the wonder of modern life.

Now, of course, the big nudge in a 3 and 2 is also about divine relationship. Are we asking for help with our wellbeing, with what we want to create? Are we surrendering (the 2) into the creative process or healing process, or are we having trouble letting go and trusting because there is rather more change or chaos happening than we feel comfortable with (forgetting perhaps the reminder that to make a cake, one has to crack some eggs!)?

This number combination asks us to trust. We aren't in the creative process alone – the Universe is in it along with us! So even when things appear to be getting worse, this can be necessary before things can get better.

The example that I often share with my students is that of the alcoholic becoming sober. When drunk, even though their life, health and potential would be in great peril, life probably seemed just fine. When sober, things would seem a lot worse. If they were going to stay sober and learn to deal with their life situation, so that things could genuinely change, improve and heal, allowing them to live the life that they really deserve, things would likely seem to be a lot worse than when they were still in the throes of their addiction, because they are confronting and dealing with the realities of their life situation, rather than escaping them. But that is essential for healing.

Once those realities have been dealt with, and the pain of that endured, there is a new sense of fulfilment and wellbeing, and creative potential that will awaken from within them. New potential and abilities can spring to life in a way that is most surprising, pleasantly so.

That happens at the other end of what can be a very long process, however. It takes a lot of courage and often a very deep spirituality of some sort (in the sense of a surrender from a place of love and trust to a higher/greater power of some description) to keep going through that process in order to get to the other side of it, into the new life. The more we can rely upon the sacred partnership of the Universe and perhaps our beloved partner, spouse or best friend (the relationship of the 2), the more rapidly the birth (the 3) can happen.

There will often be many attempts to bear the process, and falls back into the old ways of addiction, using the alcoholic example, before one can truly cross through it to the other side. Whether we be the alcoholic, or stuck in any addiction at all, or we are simply trying to allow for something in our life to heal so that we can be happier within ourselves, then the 3 with the 2 says to us, "Ask for divine help, and then surrender, and the rest will happen naturally, just as nature gives birth to life in spring, after the winter."

If you feel like you are going through a winter of some sort–a time where not much is happening or you cannot see any signs to give you hope that there is anything good going to come of what is going on in your life–the appearance of the 2 and 3 together in any variation brings you hope. Just because you can't see it, or don't understand it, doesn't mean that healing isn't happening! It is! It is the natural way of life. Our job, with the 3 and 2, is to learn to ask for help, and to take whatever other steps are available to us, and then surrender, rather than try to force a resolution. We are being asked to trust that all manifests according to the innate and wise timing of life itself.

3 with 3
(e.g. 33. 333. 3.33)

This is a beautiful vibration. I have written a book based on it called **Crystal Masters 333** because I wanted to share the energies of a beautiful group of spiritual guidance called the Ascended Masters. These are beings that lived as humans–just like you and me–and reached such a level of spiritual evolution that they were able to overcome fear and be completely free and unconditionally loving, and from that place of wisdom, are dedicated to helping the rest of us do the same. The hallmark of an Ascended Master is that they have united body, mind (including the emotional part of the mind) and spirit. They are a living example of harmony and unity. Because of this, they are in harmony with each other. You never hear an Ascended Master squabbling with another master about how to deal with something! They are in accord and alignment with each other, working towards the same passionate purpose, which is to liberate humanity from fear and into love. It might sound fluffy but it's quite a huge task and one that requires great skill. There are all those ego tricks of the mind to get around, so that a human being can harness the courage to step onto a path of trust in life, no longer held back by fear. In taking such a step, we gain an ability to live more in harmony with the greater cycles of life, allowing life's abundant energy to flow through us, which in turn supports us in living a fulfilling life.

That is the energy of the Ascended Masters. If you are noticing multiple 3s, something deep within you is about to click. You may or may not be conscious of it, but it is the energy of the Ascended Masters reaching for you and letting you know that you are loved, that you don't have to be afraid of anything and it's OK to just live your life from your heart and be bold in that. You don't have to hide yourself away or make yourself small. Just be who and what you are – and if you need help with any part of that process, ask them to help you! When you see 333, the Ascended Masters are telling you, "We want to help you – so ask us and we'll do it!"

To do this, simply say, "I ask for help from the Ascended Masters who love me unconditionally. Please help me! Thanks."

I absolutely encourage you to make this simple request on a daily basis. It is easy to do and the Masters want you to accept their help, because they want all beings to be happy and free. If you don't ask, it's like having a problem that can be resolved and a whole team of experts patiently waiting for your call, but you never pick up the phone to ask for their help. It's a waste.

Sometimes people worry that they shouldn't call on guides, especially Ascended Masters and angels (whom we will meet in the next chapter) because they think that if they ask for help, they might be depriving someone else with greater need from receiving the help that they need too. Whilst that is a kind thought, it is not correct. It comes from fear that is based on a belief in separation and limitation. What actually happens when we ask for help from an Ascended Master, or angel, or Mother Earth or any unconditionally loving being that fits in with our belief system—even if it is so broad as to simply be 'the Universe'—is that energy starts to flow. The beings of unconditional love actually gain energy from helping people. It is like the electricity of love becomes more powerful when people open to it, and so those of us that are energised by love can do our work even more thoroughly when it is permitted to flow. The light of it becomes brighter because more of it is flowing, which makes it more obvious to more people. Everyone wins.

The presence of repeating 3s encourages us to ask for help, even if we think we can manage on our own. In asking for help, we invite the love and light to flow and become more powerful, shifting us from fear (including doubt, uncertainty, anger, helplessness and hate) into love (including trust, surrender, inner peace and compassion). Please note that there is no judgement in the spiritual worlds. Hate and fear are just energies. They are lower frequency energies that do not generate the same healing response in our body, mind and soul as love does, for example, but we are entitled to choose to go on that path if we wish. The Ascended Masters will help you find a more loving path, because that is their job, but it is always up to you to choose if you want their help or not. Personally, I would always recommend it, but I do also absolutely accept that each one of us has a path to take and we have to choose that for ourselves.

It's important to know that we can ask for assistance in unconditional love from the Ascended Masters at any time. Even in those times when we might be in great fear, depression, feeling tremendous hate or terror for some reason or other, we can be helped to move more quickly through such challenging experiences, and onto the path of love by simply asking for help from these beings.

When you see repeating 3s you can be sure that you are being reminded by the Masters to ask for help. They also ask me to say here that some of you will be wondering if, when you see that number, you can ask for help on behalf of another being. Of course you can! However it is best to do so in the way I will now explain because, even though you feel that you want to help, and you might think you know what is best for that other person, you might not understand that their struggle is helping them grow somehow.

The Ascended Masters have a better view however. It's a little bit like rather than being down in the trenches, they have ringside seats with a broader perspective. They can see that perhaps the darkness that we think is terrible is actually helping a person to let go so that they can receive the grace that is just around the corner for them, and will help them take leaps and bounds in their spiritual journey in the years following, which they would have missed out on if they weren't broken into surrender at this point. It might sound tough, but that doesn't mean that it's not love. If you knew that you had to exercise a bit harder, which meant more sweat and puffing now, but no heart attack later, you'd probably say, "Ah well, OK, it's worth the pain now."

If it was up to us, we might just want that sweating, huffing and puffing body to be able to sit on the lounge, oblivious to the trouble that approach would cause later. The Ascended Masters would see it more clearly however. Does that mean that they wouldn't step in to help? Of course they would still help, but instead of giving that body encouragement to sit on the lounge instead of exercising, they would support the person to feel motivated to get moving and happy in their choice to exercise. They would offer support to that person so that they could carry out their discipline. The beings of unconditional love do not seek to change your path for you when it needs to be a certain way for your learning, but they will help you walk your path more easily when it is challenging.

Now you might just think well, why couldn't the Masters just tell that person what the consequence of their choosing not to exercise would be? But quite likely, at some level, that person already knows. How many people actually go through heart attacks and still find it hard to change their diet and lifestyle even though they have had a first-hand experience of what will happen if they do not? Knowing something at an intellectual level is not enough. The energy of the 3 is about wellbeing that is more total, that involves the mind but also the body and the emotions. This process is about finding enough love for ourselves to make better choices, and nurturing a spiritual connection can support us in being able to make physical choices that support our wellbeing too. Most of us are over-educated to the point of confusion with conflicting reports about what is good for us. What we need is support to connect to our own bodies and experiment with what works for us to feel well. We also need spiritual support and encouragement to apply that knowledge in our lives. This is the message of the repeating 3. It is about more than knowledge; it is about living the wellness so that we feel better. Of course we'll have our off-days and that's fine. The message of the repeating 3 is about understanding that wellness is not about a temporary diet or the bingeing that inevitably and eventually follows as the body tries to rebalance itself after starvation. Nor is it about a punishing exercise program. Wellness is a process of getting to know ourselves and what works for us. It's a journey, and when we ask for help we can take that journey more effectively.

Remember too that the Ascended Masters are humans that have evolved through many different religious and spiritual traditions to come to a place of oneness. They want you to walk the path, religious or otherwise, that is going to suit you and your growth. One is not better than the other; it is not about what is right and what is wrong – to an Ascended Master there is no such thing. There is only what will serve the growth of each one of us, so that we can surrender fear and learn to live a more loving life. Anything else, any other opinion, is just ego getting up to its tricks of making things complicated when they don't need to be!

The multiple 3 energy also relates to the concept of the holy trinity, which is a triple aspect of divinity that is found in Christianity (with the Father, the Son and the Holy Spirit), in the pagan Goddess traditions (with the three-fold Divine seen as being feminine in nature, and expressing itself as the Maiden, Mother and Crone) and in the Vedic tradition of ancient India (with the three-fold face of the Divine Masculine said to be Brahma – Vishnu – Shiva). In the Western Mystery Tradition there are said to be three fundamental building blocks behind all of creation – love-wisdom, power and creative intelligence.

When multiple 3s arise, you are getting a big 'hello' from the Divine in all of its forms. The Universe is asking you to witness whatever is happening in your life, whether there seems to be heavenly intervention behind it or in it or not, and to accept that it's a face of the Divine. It might be the face of love, the face of death (through which new life flows) or an incomprehensible face. That is all just fine. It is all part of the multiple 3 signature and when it arises, you are being given a message. Things are happening in your life. They are helping you come to more wholeness and wellness, so even if you don't understand it right now, ask for help (using the method shown above) and just go with it.

3 with 4
(e.g. 3.34, 4.33, 34)

The 3 and 4 vibration together bring a message to ground your creative work, to set structures, and to find a way to become more methodical. Your creative genius might need to be reigned in! As a practical example, let us say that you want to write a book. You have been thinking about it for a long time. You might have lots of ideas scattered about. You need to bring some order into your chaos. You can do this on several levels. The 4 brings the qualities of time and space and earth. So that means you might schedule time to do your creative work. At that time, each day, you sit down for half an hour or however long you can schedule, and you write. You paint. You draft ideas. You sort out your notes. You organise your chapters or your book plan. You set aside a physical space into which you go to paint. It might be a separate room if you are fortunate enough to have that space, or it might be a corner of a room where you place your easel and your paints, or your sketch book and swatches or your crystals and your jewellery-making kit or whatever are the tools of your creative work.

Now what if you aren't an artist in that sense? Then the 3 and 4 will be talking to you about setting aside time for your wellbeing in other ways too. That might involve scheduling some rest and relaxation time! And making sure that you take it! No jumping up to check emails every five minutes. That's often easier said than done in our technologically infused culture. The 4 with the 3 says that we need to put into place some physical structure, method and time so that we can tend to our wellbeing of body, emotions and mind – and our spirit. Even if you are an artist as well, this message will likely still apply to you as artistic temperaments are often more in need of rebalancing than any other type, being so naturally open and receptive to all sorts of energies, and therefore more prone to falling out of balance.

Setting time aside for wellbeing might be time to meditate, time to relax, time to exercise. The 4 also relates to structure, which we will see in the next chapter. For now, in combination with the 3, the structure aspect will be about finding a method through which your wellness can grow, or you can come into harmony with yourself.

So if you are a grab-the-bull-by-the-horns sort of person, sometimes known as a type A personality, who is always running at a million miles an hour, then your balance and harmony, your wellness, might come through finding a method to calm yourself and restore your energies so that you don't burn out. You might find that running calms you, or you might need yoga or relaxation. Or a combination of these, at different times. I met a yoga teacher recently. I asked him why he became a yoga teacher. He said it was because he was addicted to adrenaline-pumping sports like motorcycle racing, or some such thing, and he needed it to balance himself! Not the typical motivation for a yoga teacher, perhaps, but a pretty good instinct you must admit, and a good example of how the 3 and 4 in combination bring about a grounded wellbeing. You might find that dancing or swimming calms you. Or long walks in nature. You will have to experiment with what works for you and your particular type of body and mind, for each of us will have our own particular temperament to attend to and our own combination of rest and activity that suits us, and even that can change over time.

If you are a more calm person who would quite happily curl up in bed with DVDs or a book and stay there for weeks on end, the prospect of which might sound like heaven to you, but like hell to a more naturally restless person, then your balance might be making time to go out for walks in nature, or to swim at the beach or to stimulate your mind and get some fresh energy pumping through you by socialising with people. Again the 3 and 4 urge you to experiment with what works for you, what suits you.

The 3 and the 4 together is a powerful number combination that calls us to find balance through very practical, physical-world ways, which leads to increased wellbeing. Probably my favourite part of the 3 and 4 guidance is that we are to make time for play. Play brings us a chance to regenerate, to heal, to gain energy.

When I was doing some inner work and this message came up, I realised that I didn't really know how to play. Somewhere between the naturally playful childhood years and the seriousness of academic pressures of law school during my late teens and into my twenties, I had forgotten how to play and wasn't inspired by the methods that others seemed to use, namely getting drunk or taking drugs. It took me a while to figure out what the best combination of activities for play would be for me – sometimes that play could be more mature in the context of intimate relationship, sometimes it could involve me curling up with a box of colouring pencils and a colouring-in book, dancing around my lounge room or a night club, or feeding ducks in a park and laughing at their antics. Often it involved music, singing, drumming or dancing in some form or other, and hanging out with friends, or meeting new people.

Depending on how I feel at the time, my play will involve dressing up in something that makes me feel beautiful, going out to an event or gathering and mixing with friends or meeting new people at social gatherings, spending precious time with my best friend or even staying at home, with a book and my big fluffy orange cat, with nice music playing softly and incense burning, whilst I just luxuriate in my own little world for a while.

Play is not necessarily about being loud or busy. It is about what would feel instinctive and restorative at any given time. Sometimes we just don't know how to do this. It took me years to learn how to play again. It involved me learning to listen to my body, to trust my own signals for what I needed (and not get caught up in the 'fear of missing out' and trying to do everything) and to love myself enough to attend to my needs for play.

I didn't even realise for many years that play was a need. My cat taught me that when he would demand attention and I didn't know what it was for – he had food, water, clean litter and the door open to go outside. He had been stroked, patted, brushed. So what was it that he wanted? He wanted stimulation, he wanted me to play with him. When I did that, he would finally be quiet and go to sleep and allow me to keep working. It was rather an education. If you relate to this topic and want more help, I have an entire chapter dedicated to it in a book that I wrote about taking a personal healing journey called *Crystal Angels 444*.

3 with 5
(e.g. 3.35, 5.33, 35, 3/05)

The 3 with a 5 is never going to be boring! The message of 5 is powerful change and the 3 is creativity and wellbeing, so put them together and we can expect some big changes in how we create and in our understanding and experience of our wellness.

Now if we are trusting and curious about how that change might manifest itself, and willing to 'roll with it' we'll find that the 3 and 5 combination will take us into some great new understandings and help us break out of unhealthy patterns and develop some trust at the same time. If we are going to be at peace during change, we have to have trust; otherwise we'll only know stress. Some stress is helpful of course; without it, we'd be dead. But if it is only stress, or excessive chronic stress, then it's not beneficial and we're also likely to lose faith in the fundamental goodness of life. The 3 and 5 vibration comes to us as a gift. It is a time when life is going to happen and we'll be moved by it. There is a hidden gift in there for us. Two gifts actually.

The first is the change itself – that we'll benefit from a new discovery about how to be well. It might be that we find ourselves in our first yoga class, or eating our first vegetarian meal, or eating more protein and feeling much better for it. Or it could be that we swap our high intensity fitness regime for something more moderate or vice versa. We might move house to a new area and find a whole new lifestyle opens up because the general attitude in that area is more relaxed and health-oriented for example. We might find that we push ourselves less and become fitter and more well because we are no longer over-training. Or that we gain levels of fitness and wellbeing that we didn't know were possible because we start exercising in a different way. Or eating in a different way. Or dealing with our emotions in a different way, or all of the above!

The second gift is the trust that we gain in this process. It is emotionally healing to successfully move through a change in our lives. It helps us realise that we will be OK even when that which we hoped would always remain the same, perhaps only because it was known or comfortable, actually changes. This helps us trust in further changes yet to come. It becomes a positive spiral of spiritual growth where we learn over time that it is OK to let go and allow change to happen and that we can benefit from this by learning something and applying that learning to our lives as the change process happens.

When the 3 and 5 are coming to you, you are being given notice that there is change in your midst, and it is going to affect your creativity, your wellbeing and the way that you experience harmony in your life. So be open! When the Universe brings us change it is because there is another higher turn on the spiral of life available to us. What that means is that we have passed our current lessons and are preparing for new ones. It might be a bit unsteady at first, as we learn to master the changes, but we'll become even more skilled, confident and capable, as we go through that next batch of lessons. Rather than fearing the advent of change, we can actually be proud that we must at some level be ready for it! Having outgrown what is, we are ready for something more. It doesn't mean it will be an easy adjustment, but nor does it mean that it has to feel very challenging either. When we trust, the easy parts of the change process become effortless and the challenging parts become easier.

On a practical level, the 3 and 5 bring us an opportunity to shake things up, change habits and behave differently. If you have ever found that you can behave in a completely different way with different groups of people, or when travelling in other countries, then you'll understand how powerful change can be for our personal growth and wellbeing. I remember seeing this with my older brother when I was in my early twenties. Quiet and introspective at home, you'd barely get a word out of him. Put him with his friends at University and suddenly he was writing music, singing on stage and playing guitar. I was stunned! Yet they were both him. Just in different environments. I am a bit the same. Hand me a microphone for a wild dance and drumming event and you probably wouldn't recognise the same me behind a microphone for a spiritual healing gathering, where my more gentle and nurturing (as opposed to wild and free) side comes out. They are both me; just different aspects in different situations. It is actually very liberating to be able to express the different facets of oneself and to not be locked into one persona. The 3 and 5 are inviting you to explore and express yourself in different ways, in different environments and with different people. You may find after you get over the shock that you might not always be just the 'same old you,' but the same old you with a wicked sense of humour, or a willingness to dance like no one's watching, that you feel more well, happy and content than ever before. And more willing to take further adventures, thereby embracing the 3 and 5 at a deeper level. You have Universal permission to do so! You may as well enjoy it.

3 with 6
(e.g. 36. 3.36. 6.33)

The 3 with a 6 brings us the energy of love and wellbeing in relationship with others, though particularly in romantic connections.

If you have been through a time of being single or feeling separated from love, the message is to open your heart and allow love in because it can bring so much healing into your life now. That love is likely to be through romantic love and partnership, but it doesn't have to be. It could be the heart-opening love of a child, or even through a creative birth that truly changes you and opens your heart to a new passionate purpose. The 6 is generally about human love that brings us deeper into experiencing all the wonder of what human relationship can be. With the 3 it brings us a message that there will be more wellbeing for us, a sense of more balance and integration in our lives through loving relationship.

The combination of 6 and 3 also brings us a message that exploring our creativity, through a new class or greater dedication to our art, can help improve our love life! It might be literal in the sense of meeting the love of your life or enjoying flirtations through exploring your creativity in a class, for example. However when we are switched on and inspired by our life, we become more magnetic to people generally. Our creative journey can take us into more wellness, more expressiveness, more sensuality and openness within ourselves that can bring a lot of richness back into our personal relationships, making them juicier, more vibrant and energised.

The 6 and the 3 together also suggest that we might become more creative in how we express our love. If you are in the sort of relationship where you bring home flowers or do something unexpected for your spouse, and their response is, "What did you do?!" as though the only time you'd do something nice or unexpected is if you felt guilty, then the 6 and 3 are definitely bringing you some guidance on this subject.

Sometimes in the midst of our daily demands and emotional tribulations, we can forget that relationships can be a rich resource and that we get back what we put into them. We can sometimes become focused on whether our own needs are being met, yet a relationship that is truly functional and healthy will flourish with an injection of love, and give us a huge amount in return. That which is unhealthy will not be able to return any energy you put into it in the same way. No matter how much you put into it, it might never seem to be able to give back to you. You might end up feeling drained and denied rather than supported.

When the 3 and the 6 come together, you are being asked to do a love test on your relationships. What happens when you offer more love into a connection? Does it blossom and become more mutually supportive and enhancing? Or does it suck it all out of you and leave you empty, exhausted and in need of some love yourself? The former response is love. The latter response is woundedness. When the 3 and 6 are coming up, the guidance is for you to notice how you are fed, or not, by the relationships in your life. Who responds to the nourishment of your love and nourishes you in return? What you choose to do with that knowledge is then up to you. Some relationships may then be given more of your attention, time and value, and others less. Or you may continue on for a while with things as they are and see what happens to your wellbeing as you do so. You are certainly being given a chance to grow in wisdom with this number combination. How you apply the knowledge that you gain is how you grow your wisdom.

3 with 7
(e.g. 7.33, 37, 3.37)

The 3 and the 7 is a combination that brings you guidance to trust your intuition, instincts and spiritual inclinations. These are important for you to develop and explore so that you can be more balanced and well in your life. If you have an issue or even a health problem that you can't seem to get a handle on, even if it seems to be a purely physical matter, the appearance of the 7 in combination with the 3 is guiding you to look deeper – the issue is actually a spiritual matter, and not solely an earthly or physical one.

An ex-boyfriend of mine, who was a deeply spiritual man, once went to the dentist. His teeth were hurting and he figured that he had better get it sorted out. Usually the kind of person who would instead look for the emotional causes of any illness or discomfort in his body, he stepped out of character and took himself off to the dentist! I didn't know whether to be impressed or shocked. The dentist looked in his mouth for about a minute and said that he had been grinding his teeth, that he must be stressed about something and that there was nothing physically wrong with him; he just had to learn how to let go and relax! My boyfriend at the time returned home and rather sheepishly reported the diagnosis. He became more emotionally aware of the stress he was under and took some steps to change it. His teeth grinding stopped soon after. We both found it rather ironic and amusing that he had essentially received his spiritual guidance from a dentist, while he was actually a spiritual healer himself, as was I!

If you have an issue going on in your life or your health or wellbeing and you are seeing this number combination, then there is guidance that the solution to the issue you are having is going to come through intuition and insight, rather than only a practical action. The 3 and 7 are telling you that a new way of looking of things, a higher perspective and even maybe a flash of intuition, are going to support you in attaining greater wellbeing and energy.

The 3 and 7 combination also speak of something very special – that of a spiritual gift that is coming your way. It could be falling pregnant with a child; that new spirit being a spiritual gift into your life. It might be a sign that you receive confirming that a hope in your heart is possible, or that a wish is going to manifest right before your eyes. It might also be a new idea that will end up being very important to your life's work.

An example of a spiritual gift coming to me was the *Kuan Yin Oracle*. I had wanted to write an oracle deck for years and years. Some time after I had met my publisher, who was interested in republishing the three meditation CDs that I had self-published several years earlier, he asked me if I would like to write an oracle deck dedicated to Kuan Yin. It was completely out of the blue. I had no idea he was even thinking about it and for some reason I had not even told him that I wanted to write a deck. He said that he didn't even know that I could write, until I had sent him a manuscript for an e-book called *Heart-Centred Living*, which I sell on my website. He had been going to approach a more well known author, but he kept thinking of me for the project instead.

When I received his email with the offer, it was at a time when I had been working very hard to help people and I knew it was the Universe's way of saying, "Hey, we see what you are doing and we want to help you out, to make your work reach people a bit easier – so here, we are offering you this." I agreed with much enthusiasm and many exclamation marks in my emailed response. The deck is now being translated into other languages and is helping people all around the world to connect to the loving ascended being, Kuan Yin, who has such an exquisite energy and supports those on their journey to find love and faith, and let go of fear. That was my spiritual gift, one of many, and I find with all true spiritual gifts that in receiving them, many others are helped in some way or other also. I wrote about Kuan Yin not only in the oracle deck dedicated to her, but also in the book *Crystal Masters 333*, published by Blue Angel, which also contains many stories about spiritual gifts and how they can come into our lives with synchronicity and humour.

If you aren't certain what your spiritual gift could be, that's just fine. Even if you are not certain you 'deserve' one, that's OK too. You just need to open up to receive it, trusting that if something is meant to come to you, it will. And at the right time too. Trusting in right timing is another important message of the 3 and 7.

A good way to open up to the energy of the 3 and the 7 is to ask for help. You can say, "Through unconditional love I accept any spiritual gift coming to me now and through unconditional love I open to higher perception in any issue of importance to my growth now. Thank you!" Then surrender any expectations about what that gift is supposed to look like, and just get on with living your life. What is meant for you will find you in the best way, and according to the best timing.

3 with 8
(e.g. 3.38. 38)

The 3 with an 8 is an opportunity to heal your relationship to authority and power. It is about finding a balance between power as justice and strength, and power as kindness, gentleness and surrender. It might seem strange to think of power as the latter, but just think of bamboo. It is so powerful because it is flexible. It is very hard to snap or break it. Power is not just about force. In fact as we grow, we learn to move beyond personal demonstrations of power and into an alignment with the greatest power, that of the flow of life and the love behind it, which we might call God, or Goddess or the Universe (or perhaps 'the Force' if we were 'raised' on *Star Wars* movies!).

Many of us have actually learned not to be powerful and taken on that learning at a deep and relatively unconscious level, so that we don't realise that we are trying not to be powerful! With a willingness to open up to a different experience however, even if only out of curiosity, we can begin to sense what it genuinely can feel like to be powerful. It is often not what we think at first. We might have had negative experiences with those in positions of authority and power and unconsciously decided not to be like those people, figuring it would be best not to take on their negative qualities. Unfortunately we might not have realised that just because they expressed power in that way, it doesn't mean that is the only way for power to be expressed. It can be expressed in a more healed way that has nothing to do with dominating or controlling another person, and is instead about empowering ourselves and others with freedom and appropriate responsibility. We might have rejected our power in a quest to be a different sort of person, but lost an important and useful part of ourselves in the process.

The 3 and the 8 ask us to heal our sense of power and authority. This combination asks us to remember that we have the responsibility for ourselves and our own happiness and wellbeing. If we give the power to another to decide that for us, we are still the ones that have done so. For some of us that were perhaps asked to do too much as children, to take on emotional responsibility that was not age-appropriate, we might associate taking responsibility with being tied down, burdened and overwhelmed. That is not necessarily true, however. Part of mature responsibility is knowing when to say no to someone else's issues just as much as when to step up to our own duty to deal with stuff going on in our lives rather than expecting someone else to fix it for us. Appropriate responsibility is actually very freeing. It helps us live a life that supports our wellbeing and sets boundaries for manipulative behaviours of others who are yet to discover their own healthier relationship to power.

The message of 3 and 8 is that we have power in a situation where we might not believe it at first. We might think the other person, or the set of circumstances, or the situation at hand, perhaps an illness for example, is where the power lies and we are victim to that. But the 3 and 8 in combination are asking us to shift our view, and to realise that we can make choices and through our willingness to make choices based on what feels in integrity with our body, heart and mind, then we will exercise our power.

We might be scared of this at first, scared of the consequences if we assert ourselves. For all its apparent freedom, Western culture is still very driven by fear, and history is littered with examples of those that were punished by the masses for being empowered, for daring to stand tall. In Australia we have a term for this: the Tall Poppy Syndrome, where if you "love yourself" too much or seem to be too successful, people will try and undermine you, to cut you down to size. I remember as a child growing up in Australia, being told, "You love yourself!" was considered to be the worst kind of put down! Perhaps Australian culture has matured a little beyond that now, celebrating individuality and originality more so than it used to, but there is still an element of fear of greatness in Aussie culture. Unless you are a great sporting hero – then that's generally considered worth worshipping!

The 3 and the 8 vibration are telling you that you are ready to step out of any fear of your empowerment, whether culturally or historically driven, that you are growing to the point where you can become more accepting of your power, and realising that the power that you truly have is not in controlling life, but in choosing how you respond to it, which in turn changes your experience of life. It is a liberating realisation, when you are ready for it. This number vibration is telling you that you are ready.

The 3 and the 8 also bring you guidance that you are healing from any negative experiences with authority figures – parents, employers and religious leaders, law enforcement officers or school teachers being some examples. Just because a person is in a position of authority doesn't mean that they have the consciousness to be able to hold that position with the same values that might have meaning to you – such as respect, compassion, justice, mercy, wisdom and a sense of service. They might have their own issues to heal that are as yet unresolved and seep through into how they exercise their position of authority.

That might have made for a toxic emotional experience for you, or even an abusive experience spiritually (with them demanding that you obey them and believe in what they tell you to believe), emotionally and psychologically (where you felt like your whole self was not accepted, but rather shamed, denied or otherwise rejected in some way) or even physically (where you were touched without permission, or manipulated into giving that 'permission,' where you were taken advantage of financially or sexually or in any other way).

These experiences don't make you a victim. In order to heal any upset or trauma from those experiences, you'll need to reclaim any power you have given to a person or organisation that treated you in such a way. It's important to acknowledge at the same time that it is their issue, their wound and it no longer has to be yours from the moment you decide to reclaim your power.

The healing process in Chapter Eight will help you with that process. And remember, you've done nothing wrong, you are just growing and learning. The 3 and the 8 bring you compassion and encouragement to take the next steps to learn and grow beyond those negative experiences with authority now.

3 and 9
(e.g. 3.39. 39)

The 3 and the 9 come together to indicate that a healing is happening through what I would refer to as spiritual grace. This is not a religious term for me personally, but a universal spiritual one, that is available to anyone who asks for help through unconditional love. No matter whether that person believes themselves to be good, bad, unworthy or the most pious and deserving person ever, spiritual grace offers itself in service to our evolution and spiritual maturation process. It helps us to heal – often in miraculous or unexpected, brilliant ways.

The 9 often relates to the energy of unconditional love also known as the Christ energy in some traditions. In others it is the energy of spirit, in others again, it is a Universal healing energy. The 9 brings notice of healing that is not only of the mind and body, and emotions, but of the spirit or soul in us too. The spirit or soul is the eternal part of us, the animating force that makes us human, rather than just an animal body (as amazing as that body is–in all its intelligence and creative design–there is so much more to us than that). If you have a strong religious or spiritual background, then this message will be easy for you to receive. If you feel uncertain about spirituality, about any sort of connection to the Universe at all, or even to life as a greater intelligent force, then this number pattern suggests that there will be some healing in this for you, some resolution that can come. It will come in the form that is best for you. That may or may not be anything to do with a more traditional religious or spiritual path. It will be based on what suits your temperament and helps you to grow, not on what anyone else says you should believe in, for example.

The 3 and 9 bring a rebalancing and refinement of our spiritual connection to all of life around us. That is a very real experience, irrespective of how comfortable we are with whatever spiritual or religious doctrines we have explored, or even if we have not explored any. A spiritual connection with all of life affects us physically and emotionally. We feel compassion for others, we feel that we are in a greater process together, we feel the sense of life that animates all of creation, ourselves included, as though we were all rising out of the one ocean of light, perhaps. It brings us a sense of peace and diminishes anxiety because it helps us feel that we are not separate and alone anymore. This sort of experience can sometimes mean that we need to withdraw for a short time to find ourselves, our own feelings, our own thoughts, but through that process, we can come to a place of feeling far more connected to life and the Universe in a personal way that feels real and genuine for us.

The 3 and 9 combination says to us also that it is unconditional love that will bring us into the deepest state of wellbeing, happiness and playfulness in life. It speaks of recognising that although we might be an adult in body, in our hearts, we are always the sacred or divine child, cherished and nurtured by life in growth and spiritual maturity, so that we can love according to the capacity of our hearts, which is often far greater than we realise. Some of the great masters and sages through various spiritual and religious traditions have been somewhat childlike when it comes to communing with whatever face of the Divine they believe in. Stories abound where they are happy to be led, to delight in life as an unfolding of Universal genius, just as a child delights in a new set of bubble blowers and some water and detergent, determined to experience the magic! It can be healing to surrender into trust of life, of the Universe, like a child into the loving and protective arms of a parent. Yes, we still have a life to live and adult decisions to make, and that is appropriate. Yet there will be moments when in our hearts we can feel safe and secure like the eternal child, secure in the love that the Universe has for us, urging us not to give up on life, not to give up on ourselves, and to keep doing our best to live and grow and love.

When the 3 and 9 come to you, the message is to let yourself feel loved like a sacred child. Let that feeling into your heart, even amongst your daily adult responsibilities.

The presence of the 9 also indicates an ending of some sort. For creative projects, business ventures and even raising children, there will be moments when they have to leave the nest. The artist finishes the painting and it can finally go out for public view. The child gains some independence and doesn't need his parents in the same way. The business grows and changes form dramatically, involving a need for more employees and a completely upgraded method of operation. So we have to let go! It can feel like a dramatic ending, even like a death of sorts. It is an ending so that the new cycle can begin. That is the 3 and the 9; an ending for a new cycle to start. The 9 has the quality of surrender, so when it appears you are really being asked to trust and let go, to allow for growth as it needs to happen through you and your life experiences. It is going to be OK. Just let it happen.

3 with 0
(e.g. 30. 3.03. 3.00)

The Divine wants to be born. It happens all the time, in every spring with new life, in every morning with the dawning of a new day. Every time we go through a challenge and rise up again afresh in a new direction, there is a trumpet that sounds somewhere in the depths of the Universe and new life is announced!

When you see 3 with 0, you are getting one of those divine announcements. New life is upon you, new birth – look out for it! If you can't feel it yet, it's coming soon! Congratulations are in order.

Healing Process

This healing process is to integrate the messages above, or if you are noticing 3 coming to you but aren't sure why, this healing process will integrate the guidance of the 3 at a deeper level, helping you even though you aren't consciously aware of what needs to happen. The mind is vaster than we realise and what we are consciously aware of is only the tip of the proverbial iceberg. So follow through the simple instructions below and don't worry about how it's going to work, just trust and go with the process, and the greater intelligence of your own mind will take care of the rest.

Look at the image below. Just relax and gaze at it. Allow your eyes to travel where they want to go and breathe in and out slowly for at least 30 seconds, if you have a timer, or even better, for up to 3 minutes. You may prefer to work with breaths – from 3 to 33 long, slow deep inhalations and exhalations as you gaze at the image.

Take your time; don't focus so hard that you give yourself a headache! Just relax, gaze, and if your mind wanders off into a stream of thought, just gently bring it back to the breath as you focus on the image.

When your time is up, you have completed your healing process.

CHAPTER FOUR

The appearance of the 4 suggests an inflow of gifts, both spiritual and material. When the 4 arises on its own or in combination with other numbers, it heralds the successful manifestation of our dreams in the physical world. At the same time it promises spiritual growth through the process of engaging with issues in the physical world, working through them according to our own integrity and heartfelt truths. The promise of the 4 is that we can attain spiritual growth, and therefore inner peace and happiness, even whilst manifesting our dreams and visions in the physical world. We do not have to 'choose' between the spiritual path and the world around us, we can ground our spirituality, our visions, our dreams, into the physical world to 'walk our talk,' or to put it another way, to live so that our insides and outsides are in harmony.

When these two aspects of ourselves—our physical world and our inner or spiritual growth process—combine, we have the blessing of genuine fulfilment. The message of the 4 isn't about empty attainment, which is what happens when the material things that we might desire nourish us for a fleeting and passing moment, before leaving us craving more. The attainment indicated by the 4 is more substantial, particularly if there is a 6, 7, 9 or 0 in combination with the 4. When we have our heart involved in a process of creation, the manifestation is more nourishing. The success is in our own growth personally, our own inner accomplishment, as well as the outward expression of the dream in the physical world. This is the beauty of the 4 – it brings together the inner and the outer, the spiritual and the material, integrating them as one. This can bring us so much serenity – even amongst the cut and thrust of engaging with the physical world. When we know that we are being supported by the Universe to live the life that is meant for us, that we don't have to live a different life to make someone else happy (but ourselves miserable!) then it is easier to have faith in ourselves, to have discipline to back ourselves through action and to fall in love with our own life.

With the 4 comes the message that our heartfelt dreams are on track and the Universe is helping us. The 4 lets us know that our work is not just going to remain in the realms of ideas or possibilities, but will actually translate into form. What we are working on at the time–our dreams, our visions–will actually become real, tangible, concrete.

The 4 relates to the four points of the square, the most solid and stable form. The energy of the 4 is not about rushing things; it is all about the foundation, the preparation and the discipline that lead us to success. The 4 brings messages of patience and application, of working towards the goal, and that our progress will be assured, even if it is labour intensive at times, because it is in harmony with the greater Universal plan, or flow of life, unfolding. This is especially true if the 4 combines with a 0 or a 9, or other 4s which you'll see in the section on combined numbers below.

When you see the 4, it is the Universe telling you to keep going because it's 'on your side' and it wants you to succeed. Sometimes visionary and creative personality types are so much more comfortable in the world of aspiration and ideas. The hard work and sometimes even drudgery of putting one's beloved dreams into the physical world can be a shock. For such types, ideas are easy to come by. Certainly I know that I have many more ideas on a daily basis than I have the physical time to act on and bring into being, even with my tendency to create reasonably quickly. I remember when I used to feel frustrated when I would see ideas that I had already had coming out in other people's books and so on. Now I am so busy writing and working on bringing my own ideas to life that I don't have the time to worry about such matters. I have been learning to really accept the 4 message which is to put in the physical work necessary for your success. There are times when I don't want to do it – even though there is so much that I love about my work. There are times when it is hard, for various reasons, to keep going. The 4 doesn't mean that it will always be easy, but it does indicate that there will be success if you put in the effort. If you are working on something where there is love present, be it a creative project, a job (even if you don't love the job *per se*, but you are doing it to earn an income to support a family that you love, for example) then it makes the application of hard work more fulfilling and energising.

The 4 is also letting you know that the Universe will match–or even double or triple or quadruple–your efforts. It's a bit like those government matching schemes, where if you invest a certain amount of money in your retirement fund, the government might match your investment, to encourage financial security in old age, for example. The 4 indicates that you are not to believe that you are doing all the work on your own. Life will support you. We are the gardeners, and life provides the raw materials. We do our part, and life does the rest. We are not in this process on our own. So the 4 brings a message that there is divine assistance for you, if you will only ask for it (keeping in mind how necessary that is, given we are living in a free will zone) and that help includes unconditional love and the helpful genius of the angelic kingdom, which is particularly associated with the 4.

It seems relevant to mention here that the angelic kingdom is of assistance to you no matter what your religious or spiritual background. We'll talk about this more in the section on combined 4s, which is when those beings appear most powerfully present, but it is important with the appearance of any 4 that you realise that spiritually, you are being assisted and that assistance will flow more powerfully in a very palpable, physical way, when you ask for help. You may believe in angels readily – perhaps you have had a lot of personal experience with them, as I have, in which case you will know that they are powerful beings, far from fluffy, lovey-dovey types, and that they respond to requests for help instantly and powerfully. I have lost count of the times that angelic energy has helped me in my life, and the many ways that any person can call upon and benefit from that help too. I wrote an entire book about it called Crystal Angels 444.

If you are new to angelic energy or not too sure about it, thinking maybe calling on angels might turn you into a new-age fruit-loop, then please don't worry! Angels are very practical. They don't care what you believe in. If you ask for their help, they'll help you. They'll not require that you undergo an entire wardrobe change into tie-dye organic hemp clothing, nor will they require that you stock your bookshelves full of spiritual self-help titles. If you want to do those things of course, great! But if you prefer designer threads and political thrillers as your bedtime stories, that's not going to cause an angel to back away from you! What angels are interested in is helping you to attain your best life.

That will include assisting you with anything that you ask for, provided it is in harmony with Universal law. So that means that if you are asking for assistance with something that is helpful for you, or another, they will respond. If you are asking for them to help you in hurting someone else, such as through revenge, they will actually help you heal the hurt in you that is prompting such a request in the first place. They are not at the beck and call of your ego. They serve your soul growth instead. They always come from unconditional love. This is why they are so safe to call upon for help. Even if you aren't exactly sure what you are asking for or what the best-case scenario in any situation might be, you can say, "I ask the angels of unconditional love to help with … now, thanks!" and be sure that you will receive genuine and most helpful assistance.

The 4 also sets things in order. When you are going through transitions of some kind, there can be chaos and also excitement. Transitional phases naturally happen throughout our lives as things end and new starts open up. In the 'between times' when the old phase is over and settling into a new phase is yet to occur, the presence of a 4 indicates that we are going to be able to successfully cross the bridge between old and new, to just 'hang on' and keep going. No matter how rough a patch we might be going through, if we are feeling tentative, insecure, uncertain, or even bold, confident and adventurous, the 4 gives us a message that the Divine is with us, guiding and helping us, and we are going to look back at this time and see that it was an important stepping stone for us in our greater life journey.

The 4 also brings us a message to pay attention to our foundations and preparation. That could be literal! If we are building a house and receiving 4 messages, we might want to check on zoning regulations, building permits, the qualifications of the architect or even that the concreter is attending to the task at the right time. Foundations can also be emotional. For example, if you are preparing for a new job, new relationship, new adventure of any description, then the message to tend to your foundation might relate to you reaffirming to yourself that you are deserving and capable. You may need to work on whatever self-belief is needed to go ahead and do your best in the situation at hand.

Whatever is going on for us when the 4 arises is significant, no matter whether it appears to be at the time or not. When we see a beautiful lush garden, mature and full of perfectly arranged plants, do we stop to think of the time when there was nothing but soil to be tilled in preparation for the planting? Perhaps not. Yet the 4 is a reminder of the importance of preparation for the planting, and the weeding once the garden starts to grow, and the reorganisation when something isn't working quite well enough. The 4 reminds us of the attention to the detail and getting things done on a practical level, which allows for the drama and beauty to flourish later on. The drama and beauty might be what gets all the attention later on, and what seems to be the success itself, yet the 4 holds the secret to how that success can be achieved – the preparation and steady application.

When the 4 comes to us, it is reminding us of all of this. If you are working hard–even without much reward at the time–the 4 is letting you know that in time your hard work will lead you into success and attainment. You must tend to your foundations however. Sometimes that will mean that you realise your self-worth and stop slogging away for a company or employer who doesn't have your interests at heart, and instead invest your precious time and energy, skill and effort in something that honours you. It doesn't mean immaturely stomping feet and throwing a tantrum because you are not an overnight success (well, perhaps just once or twice, in the privacy of your own home!). Rather this means that there is no point in trying to grow something in barren soil. If you are putting all your energy into something that doesn't offer you a hope of commitment, of support, of promotion, of growth encouraged and rewarded, then you might want to check your foundations of self-esteem and self-worth. The 4 promises us due reward. If we are not receiving it, we need to check in with ourselves. Is it a timing issue? Or is it a self-esteem issue? If you are not sure, ask the angels to help you see and act to resolve the situation, through unconditional love.

I once knew a man who was a naturally talented singer. He was also a gifted spiritual healer and intuitive counsellor. He took to meditation naturally and psychic readings flowed easily from him also. I suspect he would have also been gifted in many other areas, if he wished to explore them. The problem that this man had was that he struggled to bring these messages of the 4 into his world. He couldn't anchor his many talents, anchoring being a quality of the number 4, for a number of reasons. Growing up in a painful family environment that featured frequent violence and alcoholism, as a child he was often told he was useless. At some times, he was also treated as a special child, used as an emotional support by certain family members, and as a result, he had the painful combination of inflated self-importance, believing that he was and should be responsible for the emotional wellbeing of others, and at the same time crippling self-doubt. That programming from his childhood made it hard for him to commit to a path that would allow him to become acknowledged and successful. Perhaps he was unconsciously scared that becoming known would place yet more emotional responsibility upon his already weary shoulders, having to then care how his fans felt about him too. What if he let them down? And of course there was the belief that he wasn't quite enough anyway, and that he would be 'exposed' as being inadequate, eventually. Without healing those original wounds, he couldn't put the energy of the 4 into action, which was a shame because he wasn't a lazy person, nor was he lacking in talent. So success in these fields didn't happen for him, whilst it did for others who were far less talented than him. He needed the 4 to help him apply himself consistently enough, with enough 'positive' stubbornness that he could move further along his path and have the patience and determination to accept the opportunities that he naturally attracted to him through his talent.

I share this story with you because you need to know that the influence of the 4 will not make things happen against our own will or way of being. It supports us in doing our part to bring about success, which often requires a lot of hard work and determination, persistence and most of all, consistency in application, whilst the Universe does it's part, which is to provide the magic of how it all comes together. We don't need to make anything happen, but we do need to do everything within our power to be prepared and ready for the manifestation of our dreams. As in the case with the gifted man in the story above, and certainly in my own journey too, that often involves dealing with our own sometimes hidden fears about success that can keep us from fulfilling our potential.

I still remember the day, more than ten years ago now, that the most prominent new age bookstore in Sydney at the time agreed to sell my three self-published meditation CDs in their store and reviewed them in their monthly newsletter. I was so incredibly excited. After years of slogging away on my own, this felt like the first real hand of assistance that I had received to bring my work more into the public eye. I did a spontaneous victory dance in my apartment after I heard the news, squealing with delight and shocking my sleeping orange puffball of a cat straight out of his nap on the lounge. As he scurried for cover away from the strange and uncharacteristic antics of his owner/slave/door-opener, I did a few air punches and then, having got all that glee out of my system, went back to writing or whatever I was doing at the time.

A week or so later, I had to deliver the CDs to the store, which I chose to do in person. As I did so, one of the store employees, the same one who had reviewed my work came rushing out excitedly to meet me. She was so enthusiastic about my work. I felt overwhelmed with shyness, quickly dropped off the delivery, smiled and then ran out of the store! It was many years later, and after a great deal more personal work on myself, and having attracted a publisher for my work, that I was actually comfortable with people acknowledging me for the work that I did. I am able to receive people now, very comfortably and with great joy and love, in a way that I wasn't able to do back then. I just wasn't ready. Each day on this path, I feel that I am being asked to shed more of my resistance to allowing life and success to unfold according to a greater plan.

The point that I want to make with this is that back when the store first accepted my CDs I was delighted because I thought I was ready. It wasn't until I freaked out at the first bit of public acknowledgement that came to me in person that I realised I wasn't as ready for stepping forward as I thought I was. When the 4 comes to us, we are asked to prepare for success, which is just as important as the actual success itself. That success is defined by us. For me in that instance, it was being able to reach people with my work and be of benefit in their lives. For another it might be a loving relationship, or finding meaningful work in some way. For another it might be the manifestation of wealth and eventually perhaps finding that genuine wealth is much more than financial prosperity, but includes abundance in love and relationship. For yet another, success might be having a breakthrough in an anxiety pattern and being able to socialise without constricting terror for the first time in years. Success is not absolute. It is about what has meaning for us and what leads us to our fulfilment. That differs for each of us, and at different times in our lives.

The 4 promises a sense of fulfilment – regardless of whether we believe we know what will fulfil us. Sometimes it will be far simpler than we realise, sometimes it will involve so much growth for us to be able to receive all that is spiritually destined for us, that we also need the healing guidance of the 4 which is to have patience and not give up. If we have a lot of growth to do to become ready for the success destined for us, then it can take a while. I know from my own life there were quicker successes and then those that have taken more than a decade of preparation and still others that are yet to be, that I sense will come to fruition in some way, but they might take another ten years of preparation at least! The 4 reminds us to keep the faith, keep working and prepare, prepare, prepare (and prepare).

In the Tarot, the Emperor is associated with the 4. He is usually pictured as a successful and mature man in a position of authority, rulership and status, symbolised by the throne on which he sits, often holding tools of authority – a staff perhaps, a sceptre, an orb, for example. Usually his kingdom is pictured around him – having attained structure, stability and success through his own maturity, he has been able to rule a developed and abundant community also.

This is the long-term return that the 4 promises us. It is the positive father energy (regardless of our own gender) that helps us learn how to behave with honour, dignity, responsibility and fairness, and to feel good about ourselves in that process. If we have had a wounded relationship with our father, perhaps because of his emotional immaturity, addiction, or through his absence in illness, psychological or emotional dysfunction, death or divorce, then bringing the qualities of the Emperor into ourselves and our lives can be a steep learning curve indeed. We often have to do some work around letting go of the father wound and realising that although it was perhaps unfortunate, it doesn't have to define who we are as adults. The resulting maturity can allow for greater success in whatever way has meaning for us and our life journey (keeping in mind that success might look very different for different people). The 4 promises that heartfelt success, the fulfilment of that which carries the most meaning to us.

Whatever the number 4 is combined with will help us understand how to work with structuring our lives for that success to manifest most perfectly.

4 with 1
(e.g. 41, 4.14, 4.41, 1.44, 11.44)

The 4 with 1 is a cosmic 'yes'. It means that there is a new structure, approach or foundation that is being created to ensure your dreams become a reality, and that you must trust in those new starts presenting themselves.

Those new starts might necessitate a decision on your part, an action or a willingness to take a step in a certain direction. If you have been contemplating this, the 1 and the 4 together promise that the decision or step that you take is not only in accord with heaven, or the Universe, or the divine plan, or the flow of life, but also that it is a step that will lead you in the right direction for successful manifestation of your dreams in the most effective and fulfilling way. This doesn't mean that everything is going to unfold as it we imagined it would, however. It does mean that the twists and turns that happen along the way, following our decision to act, will be inspired and useful for the ultimate manifestation of our success.

If you have sudden intuition, sudden feelings to act in a particular way, or a new person who appears in your life, follow up on it. Sometimes we just need to add one simple element into the mix, and it's enough to get things moving. Sometimes we won't understand why we want to take a course of action but we just feel to do it anyway. I have had this sort of dilemma through most of my adult life. I have learned to trust it because over time I have realised something funny and strange about life and manifesting my own personal brand of success. It is often those things that seem the most odd, the most off-track compared with what I am already doing, or whatever would 'logically' be the next step, that bring the most benefit to me and to my career development. It takes courage to follow this, and certainly whilst I have my supporters I also have well-meaning comments from others at times questioning what on earth I am doing. And more often than not the only way I can get close to an explanation is to say, "I don't know! I just feel this is what I need or want to be doing now!"

I recently did a reading for a young woman who was making a similar choice for her own career development. I could see her very clearly at a deeper level. She had a blend of rational and intuitive, of practicality and inspiration, and she was learning to bring them together. So despite her background in finance, she suddenly felt the urge to enrol in psychology and philosophy studies, and also learn various healing modalities! I could see what her plan was – though she wasn't so certain herself of all the details, being rather surprised by what she was drawn to do but trusting in it enough to take the steps. The plan was that the financial background together with her new studies would support her in doing work in organisations where both credentials would be of benefit, recognised, and supportive of her being able to do great work, using her skills in developing programs of a humanitarian nature. From a more narrow view of things, what she was doing at this time didn't make much sense, but when we widened the lens of perception by a few years, we could see how it would come together and it was a very wise course to take. Now we don't always get the opportunity of such clear vision. So we have the choice to rely on our internal compass instead, and take the steps that we feel inspired to take, simply because we want to do so. That is enough to take our commitment towards our own personal success to the next level.

If you have been trying something new already, perhaps a new habit or approach to fitness or wellbeing for example, then this number patterning is encouraging you to stick with it until it becomes a new habit. Let the new way integrate into familiarity. It will be helpful for your long-term success if you do. The 4 with the 1 brings guidance to allow what is just starting, the new cycle, the new habit, the new way of feeling about yourself or thinking about a situation, a new sense of identity, for example, to really take root and ground itself in your being and your life. The Divine is saying yes to what you are beginning, and encouraging you to stick with it. You are being given a message that these new starts, new seeds of action, will become the garden of your tomorrow.

4 with 2
(e.g. 4.42. 2.44. 4.24. 42. 22.44)

The 4 and 2 bring a message of stability in relationship, connection, partnership. This bodes well for the resolution of any relationship issue through a compromise, which can bring with it a more workable arrangement. This could be about two lifestyles integrating as you move in with a loved one, or about parents finding a workable custody or child-care arrangement, and it could be about the foundation of a new relationship in business or in your personal life.

If you have started a new romantic or business relationship, particularly the latter, this is a sign that it's time to sort out the details, to get grounded and not caught up in the excitement of the possibilities or vision, but instead deal with the responsibilities, practicalities and details of the here and now. Who will manage which parts of the relationship? How will the finances be run? How will the daily chores be divided up or the relationships with others outside of the partnership be managed from within the partnership?

My grandmother had an expression, "From the first day of marriage you hand your husband the tea-towel – you start as you mean to go on." She was speaking of the importance of setting of expectations and intentions on a very practical, day-to-day level as soon as possible. This is the message of the 4 and 2. Bring some structure to relationship responsibilities. This might come easily to you or you might be terrified to assert yourself and express your genuine needs on a practical level. Perhaps you are more romantic at heart and the practical side of getting down to details is a bit intimidating to you. You already know that the 4 also brings angelic assistance. So, ask for help! Say, "Angels who love me unconditionally, please help bring structure and practical support to me through this relationship, thanks so much."

The 4 and the 2 are also an answer to a question that you might not have known you were really asking. If you have been struggling with a situation or issue in your life or have just wondered if your life could maybe be a bit easier, then the appearance of the 4 and 2 affirms that yes, it is possible for you to receive more help in a practical way and that will happen through allowing yourself to be supported by the relationships that you have, or that are going to come into your life soon.

I often share the story of a woman who sat in one of my spiritual classes and spoke of wanting to be open to abundance. She then spoke of a course on the topic of abundance that she wanted to do. Another woman, who was wealthy financially and emotionally (in that she would give without wanting anything in return other than the joy of the other person receiving from her) piped up and offered to pay for the first woman to attend her course. She would love to do this for her, she declared. As we sat there, wondering at the instant manifestation that was happening before our eyes, the first woman rejected the offer, saying that she couldn't possibly accept.

I understood where she was coming from but I felt sad for her too. She was being given the gift of the 4 and 2, but she couldn't accept it. Perhaps if she had have received it willingly, that course would have opened her up and she would have been able to 'pay it forward' to another, with a gift of some kind in future. Or even pay back the investment to her original benefactor.

It can be hard to accept generosity from another, or even help, especially if we have been raised to believe that is a sign of personal inadequacy or weakness, and that true strength lies in always doings things on our own. But those are just beliefs. Sometimes we gain strength and power through learning to work as a team with others. If we are going to grow and be all that we can be, we have to learn to let ourselves be helped sometimes, so that our strength (and our narrow definition of it) doesn't become a weakness that ends up undermining our success rather than supporting it – especially when the Universe is giving us such a nudge through the 4 and 2 message.

4 with 3
(e.g. 3.44, 4.34, 4.43, 43)

The 4 with a 3 brings a beautiful message of something being born out of the structure, discipline and commitment that we have been acting upon. That could be in health, where we are being told that our hard work–not only in training and exercise, but in learning to live more moderately and love ourselves– is going to pay off in improved wellbeing, the end of an illness or a fitter body. It could be in financial matters or creative work, where our attention to practical matters is going to bring about a whole new way of being for us. It could also be in setting up a new business or relate to a dream or project that we have been working hard on. The presence of the 4 with the 3 indicates that something new is coming from what we have been doing, and to stick with it through to the birth process. It is an indication of an imminent harvest.

It can also indicate that the way we have been approaching something is about to become more creative, or a new method of operation is going to be very helpful indeed and assist us in reaching our goals.

When you see the 4 and 3 together, you can be sure that your efforts are bearing fruit. Sometimes these signs will come when you need them – just before you see the truth of the new reality. There is a saying that it is always darkest before the dawn. This means that often we are at our most hopeless, most discouraged, most faithless, just before the breakthrough into a new reality is upon us.

That darkest hour can be when we most need a sign that our dream will manifest into reality; that success will come. That is the message of the 4 with 3. Our work is bringing results. Like water that drips slowly into a cup, we cannot see the evidence of it sometimes, until there is a tipping point and the cup overflows, and suddenly we realise how full that cup had actually become. We couldn't necessarily see evidence of it as we watched the water slowly dripping. Yet it was happening, it was only a matter of time. Imagine if we had have given up one drip too early? What a waste of all that time and effort!

When the 3 is appearing with the 4, you are being asked to have faith that your birth will happen in the sense that whatever you have been working on creating will actually come to fruition, and probably rather soon at that. You are probably just 'one drop' away from success. Hang in there!

4 with 4
(e.g. 4.44, 44, 444)

This is a powerful number stamp which brings the message that the angelic kingdoms are with you, helping you. Another way of saying this, without the angelic interpretation (if that is not in your belief system or you don't feel comfortable with angelic helpers) is that your life is unfolding according to the intelligence of life and the Universe and all is well, so there is no need to worry.

People respond instinctively to numbers, often without even knowing why or what they are supposed to 'mean'. This is one reason why I wanted to write this book; to help make the messages being given clearer and more accessible. However, the message in the number is received by us at a deep level regardless of whether or not we know what it is supposed to mean. The meaning helps us, of course, but it is not essential that we have a perfect understanding of a particular message in the numbers for it to have beneficial impact upon us and our lives. It can be helpful when we do–we can co-operate with it more intelligently and consciously–but healing can come to us even when we are lacking in clear understanding.

The repeating 4 is a powerful example of this. We might have no clue how anything that is happening in our lives at the time could be working according to a higher plan. It might seem like anything but that! There could be chaos, mess, confusion, uncertainty, or ordinariness and we are just trying to keep our head above water, so to speak.

The presence of the 4 in repeat is a powerful sign that no matter what appears to be, invisible help is at work, so do trust in it. Ask for help through unconditional love (are you sensing that is a repeating theme? Good!) but also trust in what is taking place. There is an expression that God works in mysterious ways. Whether a belief in God is part of your particular orientation to life or not, we can probably all agree that life is mysterious at times! Have you ever had something happen that you didn't think you wanted at the time, or something that you did really want to have happen at the time *not* happen, only to later realise that it happening (or not happening, in the latter example) was actually for the best?

I have had this realisation so many times! Sometimes not getting what you think you want at the time is actually taking you closer to what you really do want (and need). And sometimes what we get is what we need, even if we think we don't really want it right then at all!

This is the 4 in action – the divine plan unfolding in a benevolent Universe that wants us to succeed by leading a fulfilling life that really nourishes our heart. Sometimes, especially in the midst of those times when we are struggling with doubt, we need to know that something, someone 'up there' or in our own hearts, really cares for us, has our best interests at heart and is doing their all to make sure that we can flourish and be happy and free. The Universe is that being and the 44 or 444, or any repeating 4 pattern, is a reminder of this, at those times when we just need to know that we are loved.

I must tell you a little story of 444 in my own life. My publisher from Blue Angel told me that he was thinking I could write a book on angels. I didn't leap at the idea at first. There were so many angel books already around. I didn't want to just repeat what was already written. I wanted to make a different contribution. I began playing around with how to combine a book on angels with other topics.

My publisher and I spoke of a couple of ideas but nothing really clicked. That night, I mentally shrugged my shoulders and said to the angels, "Well, it's up to you – of course I will write something, but you'd better work it out because I don't know what to write!"

The next morning my publisher emailed me and told me that he had woken up suddenly and received this message, "Crystal Angels – Healing with the Power of Heaven and Earth." He looked at the clock and it was 4.44am. He asked me if I wanted to write such a book and I agreed with alacrity. I loved crystals, and I loved the angels. And I loved the title that he suggested – Crystal Angels 444. It was different and I knew it would be a way to reach people through an unusual title, to share so much of this incredible spiritual path that has helped and inspired me. It gave me a chance to share so many of the experiences that have happened to me and my students and clients, and to show how spirituality is very relevant to daily life. The feedback I have had from that book is that it is very helpful and actually just really interesting, which is very rewarding to hear. Through the angelic help that book is doing what it is supposed to do – help people.

Now that is the angels at work, making things clear and getting life moving in the right direction! Once I started writing that book, within a day actually, I had an entire series show itself to me. And the messages in the numbers, which already came up in my life from time to time, became crazy! It was near constant. I was seeing number patterns 'randomly' many times each and every day. I felt like the Universe was going berserk and was really giving me a message about working with numbers; that it was powerful, that it was real, that it would help people and that I needed to share this information with others. I started to include number guidance in my talks at Mind Body Spirit festivals when speaking about the Crystal Angels 444 book and the other books in that series (such as Crystal Masters 333 and Crystal Goddesses 888, Crystal Stars 11.11 and so on). People responded with a great need to understand. They loved it. The messages were simple and helpful and they could relate to them. They shared some of their own stories about numbers, including one about 9.11 which I shared earlier in this book, and it made me realise that the Universe really did want people to speak this number language as it was a way for wisdom and guidance to get through to us via the means of technology, which must be made to serve love and life, if we are going to really prosper and thrive as a species. Once I was a good way into the writing of the book, it calmed down. A little!

One day some weeks back I was uncertain about a financial decision that I needed to make. So I made a brave prayer. I said, "Archangel Michael, I am trying to make a decision that would result in me investing considerable time and money into something that I do want to do, but I am not sure if it is the right decision or even the right time. I have some doubts but I really want to go ahead with it, so it's making it hard for me to be clear intuitively about it. I give you full permission to show me if this decision is going to be the right one." I was feeling a bit nervous about how that rather bold request for help, and absolute permission for the angel to intervene would manifest, because I know that angels are powerful beings – although I wasn't scared that I would be hurt, I also knew that asking for a clear sign would deliver it. Because I was confused about the decision, I obviously had some resistance to knowing the best choice for me, so it was possible my clear sign wouldn't necessarily be easy to witness. However I really wanted an answer!

Later that day I went to shop for groceries, but stopped off first at a pop-up store for an Australian designer that made funky outfits. I had purchased one of their jumpsuits in Byron Bay with my best friend the year before and worn it for a performance. It was comfortable and looked good on stage and when I saw it at half price and in another colour, I thought it was heaven-sent. As I went to pay for my purchase, the card didn't work. I couldn't explain it! The girl at the shop counter apologised and said that there must be something wrong with their machine. I didn't have much cash on me so I just let it go, trusting that the jumpsuit would be mine if it was meant to be, and I moved on to the grocery store.

After getting my groceries I proceeded to the self-serve checkout where the same problem happened! I couldn't believe it. As I stood at the grocery store checkout, I checked via internet banking on my mobile phone and discovered that I did in fact have as much money as I thought I did available in my account. I couldn't understand why I couldn't access it.

I was very grumpy, having wasted that time in the grocery store, only to have to leave empty handed! I called my bank, and was transferred from one customer service assistant to another without any help. Then, during some particularly annoying 'hold' music, the proverbial penny dropped. I wondered if this was Archangel Michael answering my request for his intervention earlier that day. He was giving me a sign, letting me know that I was not to spend the money at that time. I knew he wasn't particularly subtle but I appreciated his directness.

Just as I came to that conclusion the next customer service person finally took my call and told me that there had been a temporary hold put on my account for security reasons and it was now released. I ended the call and as I did, the phone slipped out of my hand and I managed to catch it before it hit the ground, unintentionally pushing some random numbers as I grabbed a hold of it. The numbers that I had pressed were, of course, 444.

I went back and purchased my groceries–and yes, the half-price jumpsuit–without a problem. When I got home, I logged into internet banking. As I reviewed some transactions, particularly the one that had apparently (under the guise of Archangel Michael I think!) caused the block on my funds, I decided to check how much money was available in one of my accounts whilst I was still waiting for funds to clear in it. As I did my calculations, I realised that there was exactly $444 available at that moment. I laughed out loud! The angels were in my bank account and helping me manage my finances. I asked them if, whilst they were in there, they could arrange for some more funds to come in, and, lo and behold, several new orders for work came in that evening and the following morning.

4 with 5
(e.g. 4.45, 5.44)

The best way I can sum up the 4 with the 5 is to say that you aren't going to like this vibration or message if you are still trying to control the ocean and its waves, but if you are keen to learn how to surf, you'll love it!

The 4 is about stability and settling into structure and the 5 is about change, chaos and upheaval for creation. Together, however, they are not in conflict. You are being told that you have a strong enough foundation for change to happen and even dramatic growth, without losing your footing. In other words, don't waste your energy trying to control the waves, just learn to surf them! This number combination tells you that you can do it! Surfing the waves means responding to what is happening with a sense of being present and dealing with each matter as it arises, knowing when to let something go and when to really chase a great opportunity. Much of it is instinct and that comes from learning to trust yourself.

Now if you were getting a triple combination of 4, 5 and 7, the message would be to learn to trust your instincts to deal with changes or unexpected onslaughts as a way to open up to even greater success. Be flexible, believe in yourself and trust that even apparent obstacles to your success can be ways to make you stronger and more assured, more skilful and therefore more capable of sustaining the manifestation of your dream.

So in short, this 4 and 5 number combination urges us to respond to what is happening, not to read it as a sign to stop or give up. We might need to adapt, to become flexible, but not to the point that we give up on what we have laid down as our foundations. Allow for the original structure to support you even through the changes that are happening. Then you can be both strong and flexible in response to life, and to situations that are outside of your immediate control.

As a more personal message, this number combination asks you to support yourself with what works for you – relationships, healthy lifestyle, grounding and being in nature, for example, and in setting healthy boundaries in meeting your own needs, so that whatever changes or unexpected diversions are arising, you will still feel nurtured and supported within, even whilst you wait for whatever is happening within you or around you to settle into a new pattern and stabilise once more. It will do so eventually.

You are also being reminded not to worry about losing your footing with so many changes in your life. No matter what happens, you will always be you! So if you are worried about not being grounded or connected to your family anymore if you take on a new identity or training course, for example, you can relax and know that you can ask for support. If you are hesitant to explore new groups of friends or interests because you are worried you won't have as much in common with your loved ones anymore, don't fret. You have enough solid connection with those in your life that you can afford to grow a little and still remain in connection with your loved ones. It's OK to expand. You won't lose your foundations in life.

If you are experiencing the sort of change that is so deep and profound that it feels like it is shaking your foundations, then don't worry. The message in these numbers is that the change is not going to destroy your foundations, just broaden them. Perhaps you've been working on too small a stage or you've outgrown a way of life and you need to expand. The message in the numbers is to trust in the flow and grow.

4 with 6
(e.g. 4.46, 6.44)

This is a romantic and practical number combination. It is talking about some 'divine intervention' in your love life, amongst other things. It can also be divine intervention in your financial affairs and in anything to do with beauty, attractiveness, feeling like you need a make-over or a wardrobe revamp. It can be about grounding love in your life, instead of having perhaps a great fantasy lover, you can begin to experience the physical intimacy and sensuality that your heart desires through the messages in these numbers.

The 6 brings matters of love, beauty, wealth and attractiveness into view. You might think that these are rather unimportant, superficial matters, but whilst it is wise never to mistake the glitter for the gold, or the shininess for the substance, enjoyment of beauty and love can bring so much pleasure to our lives. We more than likely have enough struggle and stress in our lives already! It can be very healing to balance this with some pleasure and beauty in a healthy and conscious way that is about enjoyment (rather than not feeling good enough if we aren't wearing the latest fashion) and appreciation of beauty (rather using it to exacerbate old self-esteem wounds through comparison or competition).

The message of 4 and 6 is to take a healthy and healing approach to beauty and our enjoyment of it. That can involve discovering the beauty in ourselves or others, in appreciation of objects of beauty and also being able to see and experience the beauty in life in a more ethereal and less concrete, but perhaps even more moving, way.

In terms of relationship, if you have been asking for some help from the Universe, preferably in the form of a soul mate love connection with another, or in the form of a financial healing if you have struggled with your financial wellbeing, or in the form of learning to love yourself, or to really live with passion and love for life, then this number combination is letting you know that your requests for help have been heard and are being answered. If you have forgotten to ask for help, and these issues matter to you, then the numbers are telling you that the Universe knows what you are in need of, so ask for help and let it come to you.

The other message in this number pattern is the counterbalancing of all the hard work, discipline and application of effort that the 4 can ask of us – which is to learn when to let go, to rest, to step away and let life happen. The 6 is about living well. That means appreciating what we have, and enjoying it, without fear or guilt getting in the way. It might sound easy, but if we have been raised with a disciplined work ethic or to abhor laziness in any form, it can sometimes be very hard to let go and enjoy life. We might have to learn how to do so without sabotaging ourselves with guilt!

I remember once living in a beautiful apartment that had a pool and spa in the building complex. I think even though I lived there for around a year or so, and the pool was heated and great for use all year round, I only allowed myself to go there two or three times in total. Now to give this little story some meaning, you should know that I love being in water. I find it to be so relaxing that it's therapeutic for me. A part of me would have liked to have been in that pool daily. But it was at a time in my life when I was very fearful. I had left my job and was working as a spiritual healer full-time for the first time in my life. I had no idea if I would survive financially and was very stressed out about it. It took me years to learn how to surrender and trust and realise that I would be OK, even when I didn't feel in control. I recognised the bitter irony at the time – here I was for the first time in my adult life in a beautiful place with a pool that I could use anytime I wanted, even during the day when most people were at their 9-to-5 jobs, and I just couldn't let myself indulge. I felt too guilty about it. I felt that if I were suffering in anxiety and stress enough, the Universe would somehow see fit to bestow success upon me. What happened of course is that I made myself miserable and exhausted. Eventually I did learn to let go, but not before I had moved out of that apartment and away from its very nice pool and spa! Fortunately at the time of writing I am living in a quirky little home surrounded by beaches on a peninsula at the very outskirts of Sydney. The Universe did eventually give me another shot at living a life where therapeutic opportunities are relatively easy to access and it's something I can allow myself to do more readily these days.

However it took genuine inner work for me to learn how to live my life well and not feel guilty about it. It was hard to face the demons of self-doubt, fear, distrust and lack of self-worth at the basis of that difficulty. What helped me was to realise that living well made me better at my job; more productive and ultimately of more benefit to the people I wanted to help. That awareness supported me in cultivating enough self-esteem to eventually realise that if I wanted to lead a happy, healthy life that suited my temperament and abilities, I didn't have to prove or justify myself to anyone, I just needed to do it. It took me more than ten years to get to that place. When I did, I was secure enough within myself to deal with the jealousy or criticism or misunderstanding that others might have about the way I choose to live. I understood it because I knew that sometimes when we see that another enjoys something that we would like to have, rather than being inspired by it, we sometimes become resentful and angry about it. It is always our choice if we stay that way or take the action needed to earn that for ourselves of course. With the 4 and 6, we are given permission, indeed encouragement, to do so.

I also learned during that time, that I was often extremely productive in my rest. I would gain ideas, become inspired and solve issues during those restful times lying in the sun during my lunch break, or on my afternoon walk or jog that would help me create better work. Sometimes there wouldn't seem to be much happening at all during those times though, but I knew I needed them anyway!

I realised that you can prepare all the ingredients, set the cook-top aflame and get that meal happening – but you still have to wait for it to cook. That meal can then be eaten, but you still have to wait for the digestion to take place so that it can nourish your body. In any creative process there is a time during which we are best to wait and allow it to happen.

Life is just like that. The 4 and 6 speak of this. It is like the law of attraction, the invisible magnetism that draws things together in accordance with their frequency. It is the magic of inspiration and solution that comes when we stop thinking so hard about something. It is the sudden burst of energy that comes after we have a rest. It is the enthusiasm that returns when we walk away from a project for a time. It is missing our lover during a time apart and delighting in the reunion. We need to give life and our desires room to breathe and grow. The 4 and the 6 in combination let us know that it is safe to do this, to have faith in our own ability to attract whatever we need through the love that emanates from our heart and our willingness to allow that love to help us live a fulfilling life. When we feel safe enough in that, we also feel safe enough to allow for some breathing room, and to let go.

4 with 7
(e.g. 4.47, 7.44)

With the 7, you are receiving a message that there is a new way of understanding or looking at something–perhaps in a deep and profound new philosophy of your life–that is going to create a far more successful foundation for your life journey. A short way of saying this is that the Universe is trying to get you to view something through a different filter. Sometimes this is so simple. It is just to stop looking at how something apparently isn't working for you (by it not turning out the way you wanted it to or the way you thought it should) and instead ask the question, "How is this trying to help me?" You can turn an apparent negative into a positive by looking for how you can 'win' in that situation. It doesn't mean you have to control the circumstances in any way. It is about mastering the situation internally to find a way that you can choose to grow. Through your own inner wisdom you can find a way to master any situation, whether it is pleasant or not at first. This is a tremendous spiritual power to develop. It leads to a sense of freedom and trust in yourself and the recognition that life loves you and is always going to be helping you to grow into all that you can be. If you recognise this, you'll work with it more consciously and grow accordingly, becoming more empowered and stable in your emotions and mind, and able to help others heal too.

The 7 is a healing and particularly spiritual number. If you are thinking about studying or teaching or healing–either as a vocation or through further training in a practical sense–the 4 and 7 together affirm that yes, this is a good and appropriate path for you at this time. If you are thinking that you might benefit from spiritual exploration or healing on your life path, to help you put some of the pieces of your inner puzzle together, then yes, the message in these numbers is that the Universe agrees with you.

If you have been having intuitions or insights and you want to know if they are 'in accord' with the Universe, if they are accurate or genuine, then this number combination affirms that you are seeing through the eye of wisdom, according to the greater plan of life. It means that what you are thinking and feeling is in flow with what should be.

If you are considering a change in religious beliefs, adopting another spiritual tradition, or disbanding from any formal association with any religion in order to deepen your own personal spiritual path, for example, then 4 with 7 encourages you to honour your choice and act on it. Or if you were considering taking a deeper step into a religious or spiritual organisation, in some form of service or support, and that feels truthful, authentic and loving to you, then you are encouraged to follow your intuition on that. If at any moment it feels as though that is becoming exploitative, trust your intuition and your sense of inner value, and support yourself and your own intuition enough to let it go and move on.

The 4 and 7 brings another message to us. We might have been thinking about healing a certain issue for some time, perhaps dreaming about a different life or waiting for a sign that we are ready to deal with a matter that we have been struggling with for a time. This number combination lets us know that the time is ripe for healing. Sometimes if we are impatient, we can take the leap even before we are quite ready. We might find that we jump from the proverbial frying pan into the fire and the situation is not better but rather worse than what it was, or we just aren't quite ready to sustain the new level of life that we are reaching for. We might be rather close, but just not quite there yet in terms of development or readiness. It will undoubtedly only be a matter of time, and perhaps not much time at that, yet if the greater timing isn't right, if we aren't truly ripe and the circumstances to support our leap aren't in place, our attempt at healing through taking certain action might fall flat. Just for now, because the timing isn't quite right.

I have tried to leap numerous times only to find that my rather impatient nature had me foolishly leaping where angels feared to tread. I just wasn't ready; I hoped that I was and leapt, and perhaps I needed that to learn and grow. That's fine, but the changes really happened for me when other people were there to catch me when I leapt dramatically into the unknown!

So instead of blindly just leaping (OK, I still do that at times, I admit) I learned that there are times when that is wise and times when I just have to wait.

If we trust in this and look to guidance for direction–the numbers being one such guide–we'll sense when there is more structure and support for us to take the leap, not only a vision. The structure and support will usually be in the form of circumstances and relationships that support us. It might be financially. It might be creatively. It might be emotional or physical support in other ways. Whatever it is, the appearance of 4 and 7 lets us know that the timing is right, the moment for healing is upon us and it can 'take root' in the physical world successfully. Another way to explain this 4 and 7 vibration is to say it brings good luck. So leap and enjoy being perfectly caught on the other side (instead of landing flat on your face – which I have done many times, before dusting myself off and leaping yet again!).

4 with 8
(e.g. 4.48. 8.44. 48. 4/08)

This is a powerful combination of numbers that speaks of new power and authority. If you have been promoted and are questioning yourself, don't! You will be fine! You are stepping into more responsibility and the Universe is letting you know that it is well earned and you will be able to handle whatever comes your way. If you are thinking of applying for a promotion or more training, taking on more responsibility at work (particularly if that involves management or leadership in some way) then this number combination encourages that wish in you.

If you feel that you are more informally leading those around you for a time, perhaps family or friends, with your heart-inspired decisions and way of being in the world, and they are leaning on you, then this number combination is an acknowledgement that yes, indeed this is happening and you are handling it.

The message in these numbers is also to call on assistance through unconditional love for all matters of authority or leadership in your life. Now this might mean in your role as a leader or authority figure, formally in work situations or more informally (but just as legitimately) in your personal life or even in unofficially mentoring others in a work setting. It might also mean that the Universe is helping with your involvement with authority in some other setting that relates to this theme. It might relate to a custody dispute or other court related matter you are involved in, or some connection with the law that is causing you distress or that could certainly benefit from a little angelic help. We have to remember that asking for divine intervention is not about us asking for things to go the way that we personally think that they should. Divine justice is very real, but it is not always easily understood from our human perspective. Karma is unfailingly accurate but it unfolds in its own wisdom and timing. We may or may not always–or even often–see it in action, for better or worse. We can either trust or distrust; that choice is always ours, but when the 4 and 8 arise together, we can be sure that the Universe is up to something and if we ask for help in whatever matter is important to us, we'll receive assistance to understand more fully what is happening and why. It is also a sign not to worry about people 'getting away' with something. It isn't possible according to higher karmic law. The 8 and 4 arise when karma is kicking in. This isn't about punishment, it is about learning. If you have come out of a situation where perhaps you were treated unfairly and the perpetrator seems to be getting away with it, the message in these numbers is to leave it to the Universe to deal with in its own timing. It is not always for us to bring about justice. If we feel an obligation or duty to act, then of course, we must assess if that is wise and act accordingly. However the karmic rise and fall of fate is determined by life, not by mere mortals.

On another note, if you have a specific interest in publishing or being published as a writer or artist in some form, in being managed and having an agent, this number pattern can indicate that this can happen for you, if you (you guessed it!) ask for such help. It is wise when asking for something specific to happen–such as more money, or an agent, manager or publisher to come to you–that you end all such requests with this statement: "With harm to none and for the greatest good."

Here's an example of what happens when you don't do this!

A woman once shared a story with me. She wanted ten thousand dollars. She wanted it to purchase a car that she desired. Instead of asking for help in manifesting the car, she said, "I want ten thousand dollars." What happened was that her apartment got flooded and she received an insurance cheque – for exactly ten thousand dollars. Which was used to repair the damage to her house. She got exactly what she asked for and rather quickly at that, being an expert manifestor, setting clear intention and holding absolute belief that her intention would be answered by the Universe, which, of course, it was!

It would have been wiser and more useful to ask for help with what she really wanted – in this case, to manifest a new car (with harm to none and for the greatest good) or to ask for ten thousand dollars if she really had to be specific (adding in with harm to none, and for the greatest good, of course).

The 4 and the 8 vibration tell us that we are master manifestors in the making. With clear intention and some wisdom (which is adding in the phrase, "May it harm none and be for the greatest good"), this vibration is letting us know that what we put out at this time in particular is either on its way to us or already being demonstrated.

If you already know this about yourself – that's great! You are then also probably receiving this message in the numbers – use your manifestation for the greatest good; see what loving contribution you can add to the world through your manifestation ability. You will be richly rewarded even as others benefit.

4 with 9
(e.g. 4.49, 49, 9.44)

This is a number pattern that says, "Surrender your material concerns to the Universe and let them be taken care of according to a higher plan." Of course to do this, we might have to face our issues of fear and distrust, that if we let go and stop trying to force or take things, we will still have more than enough. It also asks us to surrender that toxic disease of the modern Western world – a sense of entitlement! People sometimes confuse this with healthy self-esteem, believing that entitlement is not a bad thing at all. Entitlement in this sense of the word however means believing that you should be able to take whatever you want simply because you want it, usually when you want it, irrespective of whether or not that causes harm to another or disrespect to our planet, and irrespective of whether or not you have actually earned what it is that you are seeking. Entitlement is about taking for oneself from a childish and selfish place. Surrender is about trusting and receiving. They are completely different. If you recognise a sense of entitlement in yourself, that is wonderful! It is often very unconscious.

I have met people with that sense of entitlement that were also deeply spiritual and wanted to help others, yet when it came to me, they believed that I was there to serve their ego, not their soul. To their soul, I would hold nothing back, but to indulge the whims of their ego that demanded that I instantly make them 'feel better' if they were upset, rather than teaching them that their pain wouldn't kill them and they could sit through it and grow – well, that was just not on! Eventually I had to cut ties with them. Their disrespect of me, their attempt to use me to prop up their own sense of importance felt very sick to me. I didn't want to encourage that in any way. To get them to see where I was coming from proved to be impossible, despite numerous efforts.

A sense of entitlement is a very difficult thing to bear witness to because it usually covers up an almost unbearable emptiness within. Healing a sense of entitlement allows us to stop acting as a parasite upon the resources of the world and others, and instead genuinely learn how to receive. This is empowering both to the giver and the receiver, rather than leaving the 'giver' drained and exhausted, depleted and perhaps feeling used and abused. It takes a lot of effort to transform a sense of entitlement into a more humble and trusting sense of receiving our due. It requires that we acknowledge and feel the pain that has been fuelling the sense of entitlement to begin with – usually an enormous rage. Most of us avoid going into our inner pain more than anything else in our lives! It becomes a survival instinct when we are young and vulnerable, and when that pain is so excruciating as inner rage, well, there is usually no way that we will open up to feel it as adults if we can try to avoid it instead. The only time we tend to get into such painful emotions is when we are apparently forced into expressing and feeling them through life disappointments or circumstances beyond our control. The hidden gift in this is that it shatters defences that might have kept pain out for a while, but are keeping out life too, and preventing us from really receiving all that we could possibly receive.

I knew that the frustration that I caused by thwarting the demands of those ex-students of mine could either push them to look within to the source of their painful responses or to try and avoid doing so by instead blaming me for not being a good enough mother figure for them, even though I had never signed up for such a role. The choice would be theirs but I would be offering them the possibility of healing in a way that I couldn't if I remained in their lives and allowed them to continue 'feeding' off me. I went through a 9 and 4 experience myself – allowing my surrender to create physical world actions that were serving unconditional love.

Sometimes we might imagine that the material world and the spiritual world are quite distinct, and even that the material world and all its energy might distract us from the serenity promised by spirituality. However the spiritual part of us can also grow strong through engaging with the material world. When we are receiving the message of 4 and 9 in combination, we are getting guidance that we will grow spiritually by engaging with what is happening in the physical world, whether that be through tending to our health, emotional, physical or mental, or just dealing with a particular situation or circumstance which might call for us to develop the qualities of persistence, or trust, or compassion, which leads in turn to our spiritual growth. Don't turn away from what is – engage with it, ask for help, surrender, and you'll earn the next phase of your spiritual development. Even if you don't relate to taking a spiritual path, you can be assured that this approach of surrender will lead you towards your fulfilment and success, however you define that according to your own values.

The 4 and the 9 together also bring a message that a physical situation that has been causing us some limitation is on its way out of our lives. The Universe has got it handled and it will be soon over. We just need to hang in there! And–yes–ask for help. The message of the 4 and 9 is to do as much as you can do and then let the rest go. Don't try to wrestle with something that you cannot change–whether that is an external circumstance or situation, or the behaviour of another person. Instead deal with what you can deal with– your own body, mind, emotions and spirit – and allow the Universe to take care of the rest of the situation and sort things out for you according to the best possible plan.

4 with 0
(e.g. 40, 00.44, 00.04, 4.00, 4.40)

The 4 with a 0 is a dramatic proclamation saying, "Don't worry, this situation is being handled!" It's a sign to do our part, but then to 'let go and let god,' as the saying goes. When I see 4.00 or some other version of 0 and 4, I know that the Universe is reminding me that there is a plan and I am right in the midst of its unfolding, that I don't have to be fearful or concerned and that I need to remember to trust absolutely in how my life is turning out, especially if it's going in a rather different direction than what I had anticipated.

Considering my journey has taken me from acting to law to singing and dancing, to DJ'ing and shamanic healing, just to name a few choice moments, it is good to remember this! Somehow all those things tied in together and are useful for the work that I currently do. I have no doubt that strange but effective trend will continue. That just seems to be how my particular life path unfolds. I get reminders of that–often when I am embarking upon even stranger new territories or adventures–when the 4 and 0 appear. Just because it doesn't always work the way I thought it would doesn't mean it isn't working out! In fact, 4 and 0 let us know that things are working out perfectly, so loosen up, let go and go with the flow because things are coming together according to a greater plan than our own.

Healing Process

This healing process is for any time you need grounding, connection with the angelic kingdom or the guidance of the 4 in any combination or on its own.

Sit on a chair in such a way that you can place both feet firmly on the floor in front of you. If you cannot do this you may wish to stand. Feel both feet connect with the floor and see if you can sense all 'corners' of your feet – front near the toes, the sides where the arches lift, the back near the heels and the outer side of the feet. You might want to move your feet on the ground a little to get a feeling for each of the corners of your feet.

Then sit comfortably and feel both hands resting on your lap, palms down and lightly pressing onto your legs. Feel the fingertips, the backs of the palms near the wrists, the outside edges of your hands and the inside edges near your thumbs. Move your hands slightly to become aware of all four 'corners' of your hands.

When you are ready, say the following aloud, "I call on unconditional love to help me manifest my best life and for assistance for my greatest good, so be it."

Gaze at the image below for as long as feels right for you, but at least for four long, slow inhalations and exhalations. Without straining, see if you can 'trace' the outline of the circle, stopping briefly at each of the four points – at the sides, top and bottom of the circle. Do this four times (moving around the circle in any direction, starting at any point that feels best) with your non-dominant hand (usually the left hand) and/or your eyes.

Don't worry if you feel weird or strange because you don't understand exactly what you are doing or why you are doing it! The healing process will still work for you!

CHAPTER FIVE

The 5 vibration was something that I had to learn to love. Earlier on in my life I was rather more controlling than I am now. And that's an understatement. As I processed and released the profound levels of anxiety that I carried with me for most of my childhood and young adulthood, I found that I didn't need to attempt to control life quite so much, and instead I could learn to surrender and trust more, even if there were great changes taking place and I was being led by life into unfamiliar circumstances and surrounds. In fact, especially then, because those were the times when life really had something wonderful in mind for me that I couldn't appreciate until I had the benefit of hindsight.

I mentioned in the previous chapter that the guidance of the 5 is going to be something that you'll find challenging if you are trying to control the waves (by that I mean the movements of life far beyond our personal control) but that you can learn to love if you are willing to learn to surf. I mean that as a metaphor for learning to sense the direction that life is heading, and jumping on board (no pun intended!), moving with, rather than fighting against, that direction.

This can sound simple, and it often is, but that doesn't make it easy. Sometimes we feel that change is happening fast, or in a way that we can't anticipate. If we are trusting in change and open to it, the 5 lets us know that life is going to take some interesting and likely unpredictable turns. If we are nervous about change and perhaps the unfamiliar, the 5 might evoke some apprehension in us which is actually a chance to heal distrust (that we possibly learned subconsciously through the fears of our parents or society early on in childhood) and begin to feel more secure within ourselves so that no matter what happens, we know we'll be OK.

I remember in my early thirties meeting a friend at a boot camp fitness training program. I was going because I wanted to challenge myself and conquer some fears about what I thought my body was capable of doing. As it turned out the program was nowhere near as terrifying as I anticipated. Actually it was fine. I just got very fit but also very tired because I felt strung out from the early mornings and inadequate rest. Nonetheless I turned up to every session, completed the program and felt proud of myself and my accomplishments. I just decided not to keep doing it because although the short-term results were good, I could sense how much it was going to tip me back into the over-training that I mentioned earlier on in this book and that would, in the longer term, ultimately compromise my health.

For my friend however, it was a different story. She was there because she thought it would be interesting. I tended to initially meet any challenge with fear and a resolve to get through it, which I always did eventually. For her however, there was no fear. She just had a different personality and approach to life. She was interested, curious and thought it would be exciting. Because I had often doubted myself, and learned to be rather insecure in many ways despite my general competence in life, every challenge brought me face to face with a fear that I wasn't good enough and would fail. My friend thought rather more highly of herself and assumed that she'd just cruise through and have an interesting experience in the process, before she got bored and moved on to something else. So even when facing the same challenge, with similar fitness levels and abilities, she would see something as fun and I would see it as something I just had to get through. I often remarked how different it must be to live like her, with her attitude to life, which was so much lighter than mine.

Now of course one is not superior to the other, though obviously one is less stressful! We gain our childhood experiences to help us grow and fulfil our spiritual learning this lifetime. So whatever happened for us, happened for a reason. When the 5 appears however, we can be sure that whatever happened for us to make us either controlling or trusting will arise to be dealt with. I am happy to say that when I see a 5 pattern now, I am very happy about it. I have learned to appreciate that change brings me more happiness and joy, even if at first there is some difficulty in getting through it. I welcome these messages now where once I wanted nothing to do with them! If I can have that approach to the 5, then you certainly can too. It is not a number to be nervous about, but excited about, when we trust that life is actually helping us to grow.

So when the 5 appears, you are being given a notice that something significant is about to change. Any uncertainty, lack of clarity, or confusion present in your life at this time is there because there is an undercurrent of change and you are sensing it brewing. Perhaps you just haven't quite got through to the other side yet. If it seems like your life is getting a bit out of control, and we are typically taught that this is not a good thing, the message of the 5 is this: "Things are changing and you'll be disoriented for a while, but it's for the best and you'll be guided through it – and all is still well and exactly as it is meant to be."

5 with 1

(e.g. 1.55, 5.15, 5.51, 51, 11.55)

The 5 combined with a 1 is rather exciting because it indicates that change is going to be happening soon or has already begun. The 5 and 1 are strong indicators that energy is moving, shifting and soon you'll experience the result of that in the physical world through a change in life circumstances. These are not small changes that are just little bumps in the road of life. These are changes that are rather more significant – the starting of a new life chapter or phase.

It might be that you are starting study, starting to travel (the 5 is also associated with travel in particular, especially the sort of travel that changes your perspective) and you end up deciding to live in another country that you visit along the way. It might be a change in attitude (attitude being another quality of the 5) that is so profound that it starts you on an entirely different course in life, attracting different sorts of people and situations into your life and making you almost unrecognisable as your former self.

With the 5 and 1, the message is that such change won't be contrived or artificial, it really will be in response to life internally and externally. That means that we will be asked to grow as well. Sometimes that can be confronting as we meet and release old limiting beliefs or choose to feel and surrender previously unprocessed emotional pain. What this promises however is the sort of change that feels substantial, supportive and real. It is not like the temporary willpower associated with trying to force something to happen, only to slump back down under the weight of inertia some hours, days, weeks or months later, back to where you started. This is the real grit of change that is transformation; that is irreversible; that is about leaving the past behind and embracing life in the present moment with a view towards experiencing a different future. It is not predictable or conformist, but it is real and nourishing to the part of us that craves authenticity and fulfilment.

When in combination with the 5, the 1 lets us know that we have a lot of power in the situation. We can have an effect on what is taking place. We cannot force life to be other than what it is, but we can have a powerful input into what is taking place, if we so choose. In the Tarot, the number 1 relates to the Magician and he is usually pictured with one hand pointing up to heaven and one down to earth. This is a visual representation of the teaching 'as above, so below' which refers to the movements of the heavens affecting the earth and all within her field, which includes human beings of course. It also refers to the macrocosm in the microcosm, the sense that the entire substance of the Universe could exist within a grain of sand, which is rather a beautiful thought and is based on the notion of holographic consciousness (essentially that within each part there lies a blueprint of the greater whole). It means that within us is a creative power to affect life; not to control it, but certainly to choose to constructively contribute to it if we wish.

When the 5 and 1 appear together, it is not just about going with the flow of change. The magician and the 1 that it symbolises are also about evoking change, using intention to bring it to be. We don't have to move the heavens to do this; according to the teaching of the macrocosm in the microcosm, we only have to make a change within us, and through that, there will be ripples of change that spread out into our life so that eventually our life will mirror back to us the change we have made within.

That might be a change in self-respect which eventually translates into being treated very differently in relationship with others. It might be a change in the smallest way within, but in time, that change will have an impact in the world around us and change our life. This is the wisdom teaching of the 5 and 1 together. It lets us know that we have a lot more power than we might think and that we are not only learning to flow with the greater movement of life which we cannot control (such as the orbit of the planets, or the rising and setting of the sun, creating day and night) but that we can contribute much to life through how we consciously choose to be and act. That is the power of the magician, and the 5 and the 1, within.

In this message then, the 5 and 1 are letting us know that it's OK to use our intention to declare what it is that we want, or confirming that we already have been setting something in motion within, through our actions, and now the outward demonstration of that is gathering momentum and will soon make itself seen in the physical world.

If you have been doing inner work on healing yourself or a particular issue, then the appearance of this vibrational pattern is a good sign that the effects of your inner work are soon to become visible. When the 5 and the 1 combine, there is a message about your intention bringing about change. It might be that it is already happening, or in other words, you are getting what you asked for, so let it happen!

5 with 2
(e.g. 5.52, 2.55, 52, 552)

The 5 and 2 indicates change and fluctuation in relationship, partnership or any issue of balancing – such as parenthood and career, for example.

This instability is not necessarily a bad thing however. It could result in something ending but it could just as easily result in a deepening of commitment, or finding that through the failure of one approach, a far superior solution arises. Change requires the instability of the old form to break down so that a new form can emerge.

In terms of relationship, that can mean that you have a sense that you are outgrowing a pattern in the relationship and the result is a moment (perhaps a long moment spanning weeks or months or years!) whereby you realise that how you have held on to each other no longer appeals. The opportunity in that is that you can learn to relate to each other differently. If one party, or ideally (but not essentially) both parties, to the relationship are able to change, then the dynamic can change in the relationship. It only takes one to make a change but it takes two to accept it. This is why the 5 and 2 can indicate both a crisis leading to commitment or a crisis leading to an ending (which is really just a doorway to new beginning). When you resonate with this message of 5 and 2, you are really being guided to experiment with new ways of responding to your partner rather than getting stuck in old patterns or habits. This is certainly easier said than done at times, but it is not impossible – especially if we ask for help through unconditional love.

The 5 with a 2 is also a nudge from the Universe to allow for partnership to support you during great change. The 5 with the 1 vibration has a very independent quality, more about what we are doing within ourselves and for ourselves to evoke or respond to change. The 5 and 2 is much more connected to others and about letting close personal relationship support us. It can also mean that a close partnership–professional, personal, or both–will be the tool through which great change is going to take place in our lives. The quality of the 2 is also responsive rather than dynamic, so the appearance of this number pattern is also going to emphasise allowing the change to occur, rather than feeling that you ought to be initiating it.

No matter how the 5 and 2 are manifesting for you, know that trust will help you accept the changes that are happening because deep down, you can know for sure that the movement of life is about helping you become all of what and who you are. So just go with the flow.

5 with 3
(e.g. 3.55, 5.53, 53, 535, 553)

The 5 and 3 together speak of something creative; a new birth arising out of change that is taking place. Sometimes life can be lacking in subtlety! We might be experiencing dramatic and even painful changes in our lives – losing relationships or a lifestyle that we have once loved, perhaps we have to move house, or have lost a beloved through death, divorce, illness or maybe financial shifts have occurred and we are without our usual resources.

No matter how dramatic, or how subtle, the changes sweeping through our life may be, the message of the 5 and 3 is that the way is being prepared for new birth. Think for a moment about a woman in the midst of giving birth to a child, if you will. She will be wild, messy and free, totally engaged in her process. It is rather less likely that she will politely be arranging the ornaments on her mantle, so that they all sit in perfect alignment. The energy of the situation will be rather more raw and uncontainable. That is the energy of birth. It is the quality of the 5 with the 3. It isn't polite creativity. It is messy at times, a bit unwieldy perhaps, a bit chaotic and you might not be able to make heads nor tails of what is going on, but it is effectively leading you to rebirth nonetheless.

So this number pattern comes with a message that no matter how messed up our life may seem, or how much our plans for perfection and order might be falling into disarray, there is nothing wrong! It is just birth that is happening now. Trust it, ask for help using this simple phrase, "Through unconditional love I ask for grace in managing the changes in my life that are leading to new birth! Thank you."

This number pattern is also confirmation that if you have been thinking about making changes in your life or lifestyle, now is a good time to do so because they will bring about constructive effects for you and help you start a new cycle in your life.

There is also a special message with these numbers about children. If you have a child in your life that you are concerned about, perhaps because they are going through changes like emotional disruption in a family situation, the guidance is that they are protected and they will come through it. Later on in life they will even benefit from the struggle they are in right now. For now, you are being asked to request help on their behalf – simply by saying "Through unconditional love, I ask for help for ... Thank you." Do this every morning or evening for the next 3–5 days or weeks, whatever intuitively feels appropriate for you.

5 with 4
(e.g. 5.45, 5.54, 4.55, 54, 545)

The 5 with a 4 brings more balance to the changes that are taking place, a grounded quality that assures us that it is no longer in the wild phases of birth, but that the change is leading us towards a more stable and secure foundation. At least eventually! At first, the 5 and 4 might seem to manifest as a profound change in our foundation – the things upon which we rely for certainty or security might be slipping from our grasp. Yet sometimes we are holding onto a penny when the Universe wants to give us a pound. Sometimes we have to trust and let go even if we are worried that what we are releasing is just too great a loss to risk.

I often say that the Universe offers us a dangling carrot or a smack with a stick; we get to choose how we move ahead. The 5 and 4 suggest that we become open to receiving security from life – even from changes in life that might not promise us any sort of certainty. This number combination is about trusting in change to support us rather than trying to hold on to how we felt secure in the past. It is about learning to trust in life's changing flow, knowing that it will lead to new form and structure again eventually, before changing again.

To try to avoid having to trust life would be like trying to resist too great a wave; we'll just end up being dumped, with a lot of sand in places we'd rather it not be! Sometimes we have to let go to receive, and although the exchange isn't simple and might take us on a journey through some changes, it can still lead us into greater security.

This is the wisdom of the 5 and 4 together. Greater stability and foundation for future success sometimes requires that the current system and organisation be dissembled – just like a garden that is completely stripped back and tilled with readiness for future planting and abundance.

I once had a dream that I was trying to plant a garden just outside my home. A wise gardener leaned upon his shovel as we worked together and he said simply, "Alana, it's not going to grow there." As I looked out beyond my home, symbolising what I knew and felt comfortable with, and down at the gravel-ridden patch of dirt that would not make a fertile garden bed, I realised that the wise gardener was correct. I would have to bear the rigours of change if I wanted to build a foundation for planting my garden so that it would flourish.

Upon waking from that dream, I realised that the garden was the work that I wanted to share with the world. I couldn't remain in my small known world if I wanted it to succeed. I would have to seek out unknown territory to find my fertile ground. In the years following that dream, many changes took place, including adventures into communities and groups that were truly outside of my comfort zone! There was also a development of my work in directions that were surprising and at times challenging for me. Through these and many other personal changes, a new foundation through which to reach and help people was created. I would hope that if I met that gardener again now, he would nod approvingly at the more fertile soil into which I am planting my garden of life, so that it may flourish. As I glance up at my clock on my computer and see 10.55 I am hoping that it is a sign that the Universe is behind my new beginning as a result of much inner personal work and the changes are indeed set in motion now.

5 with 5
(e.g. 55, 5.55)

I love multiple 5 messages! They are so exciting! They herald change of the most dramatic sort, the kind of 'wild card' where you know that you have no hope of controlling any of it, so you may as well let go and see where it takes you. It is the energy that I get from travelling when I have got past my culture-shock and am just going with what I experience, really soaking up a new culture and often learning something about myself and people more generally, in the process. It can feel very liberating, stimulating and exciting. Of course also challenging and frightening sometimes too – but at the very least, I feel very alive when travelling.

The sort of change heralded by multiple 5 patterns is so much more than that which we could evoke on our own. It is more like the hand of destiny stepping in, which is why I find it such an exciting message to receive. It means that the Universe has taken something out of your hands, usually in response to a prayer or request for help that you have made. Sometimes it could even be a divine act of grace and help on your behalf that you are not conscious of having asked for, but that has been granted nonetheless. You could call it a miracle, or a changing in the tides of fortune, or in the Tarot, it would be a shift in the wheel of fortune, where even that which seemed to be absolutely stuck and beyond shifting, suddenly just moves, and a whole new vista opens up before us.

Think of multiple 5s as the hand of the great universal creator reaching down and rearranging the various pieces of our life on earth as though she/he was moving around chess pieces on a board and suddenly, the whole game changes. That is the multiple 5 effect. Everything changes and anything is possible.

If you have been worrying about an issue from your past, or feeling downtrodden or exhausted because life has just been so hard for you, the 5 in multiple pattern is letting you know that just because something has always been a certain way, it doesn't mean that it has to continue in that way! In fact, the 5 in multiple is letting you know that even the most apparently implacable, impossible change IS possible and will happen. Ask for help ("Through unconditional love, I ask for help in changing ... *[describe the situation]* according to the highest good, thanks so much!") and let it happen.

5 with 6
(e.g. 5.56, 6.55, 5/06)

The 5 partnered with a 6 brings a softer edge to the wild 5. It speaks of change in fortune, fame, beauty and love. It speaks of instability in those things that can lead to greater abundance if we trust in it.

With the change of the 5 and the love of the 6, we are being asked to release belief systems that don't resonate with love so that we can open up to a brand new experience of love (and wealth and beauty – all qualities of the 6) in a more healed and helpful way.
Sometimes we have to let go of our fear of having wealth, for example, if we have never experienced it for ourselves or only experienced it through others in a negative way, such as them behaving as though having money made them better than others or gave them permission to behave in ways that were arrogant and disrespectful.

Many years ago, early on in my personal healing journey, I decided to do some work around my beliefs about money. It was an interesting exercise. I simply wrote a list of what I believed about people who were wealthy and what I believed about people who were not. It was very revealing! I didn't consciously realise until I read my list exactly how much negativity I had been holding onto with regard to those that had wealth and how much I had hero-worshipped those that had little as survivors and more deserving people and so on. Now those were nothing more than stereotypes. I could certainly find examples to support those beliefs, but when I looked a little deeper, I realised I could also find examples that challenged them. I realised that they were just beliefs, but it took a lot of effort to change my attitude about being wealthy, and to not consider that I would become the sort of person that I detested if I opened up to greater wealth.

Fortunately the 6 brings a quality of compassion and patience to the 5, so we have all the time that we need to open up to changing our views around money, wealth and love, of course. When we ask for help through unconditional love, even apparently stubborn beliefs can soften and all becomes more possible.

For you, the message of the 5 and 6 in combination may be encouraging you to choose to shift the issue away from money in order to become more relaxed about it – whether you have as much of it as you may wish, or would be open to receiving more. The 5 and 6 in combination offer you grand prospects for change, but you must ask, of course, for that help. You can do so by saying, "Through unconditional love, I would like help in opening to receive more abundance, prosperity and wealth in my life. With gratitude for all that I already have, I thank you for this." I write about this in much more depth in *Crystal Goddesses 888* in the chapter on Lakshmi, the ancient Indian goddess of wealth and spiritual enlightenment, because when we ask for healing about money issues, sometimes issues of self-worth come up that we didn't even realise that we had. Keep asking for help using the simple request above and the healing process at the end of this chapter if this is happening for you. The 5 and 6 in action together will trigger healing and change within you to allow for more abundance to become a part of your world. That may mean facing up to some self-worth issues or dealing with some outmoded beliefs about money.

The 5 and 6 together can also bring us in touch with our sense of our beauty, inner and outer. It doesn't promise to turn us into super-models, but then that is no guarantee of genuine attractiveness either. I recently heard a comment about someone being good-looking but not attractive because there seemed to be no love really present in him. That is the nub of the 5 and 6 together, with healing guidance around beauty. We can have all the right framework—the appearance and the good genetics—but what makes someone truly beautiful is the substance, the content of their heart. That is what gives people an energy of being alive, of being someone that you want to be closer to and connect with. There is much more to a beautiful person than having an appealing body shape.

When the 5 and 6 are coming to you, you can be sure that you are going to have some shifts in how you think about yourself, your own self-valuing, your sense of your own beauty and how you feel within yourself. If you open to this process, you come out of the other side of it feeling more attractive, worthwhile and deserving of love than ever before. This is very conducive to attracting loving, supportive relationships in your life. You can expect with the 5 however that you'll go through some changes and even challenges in your belief systems to get to that place. You might be confronted with all the ways you talk down to yourself, believe that you are ugly or unattractive or simply not enough. It can be quite a confronting process. However if you realise that you are simply being given a nudge by the Universe to witness and then choose to no longer believe in these assessments of yourself, you'll be able to let them go and become loving and self-accepting of yourself in a way that may astound you.

5 with 7
(e.g. 5.57, 7.55)

The 5 and 7 together bring the message that the Universe is supporting you in taking risks based on your intuition, to trust your instincts and allow yourself to be guided through changes that just feel right to you, irrespective of whether others understand them or not.

This number combination also suggests that there is a new philosophy, belief system, spiritual tradition or teaching that will be very supportive of you living your potential and growing spiritually through your life experiences. This may be an effortless awakening, but it may also involve some pain in questioning what you have believed up until this moment, perhaps even some anguish around whether or not you will be punished or mistaken for questioning.

If you are going through a crisis of faith in any way, questioning the religious or spiritual tenets that you were raised with, then know that this number message is urging you to give yourself a break and know that this doesn't mean you are turning away from your inner journey, or even away from the creator, it just means that you are likely outgrowing the religious or spiritual container you were originally given this lifetime. This can happen as we grow; we might outgrow a religious tradition psychologically or emotionally, and if we try to keep forcing ourselves to honour something that doesn't feel right for us anymore, it's a bit like trying to force ourselves to wear shoes that we wore as a child but that don't fit our adult-sized feet! Uncomfortable and rather impractical! Better to be open to a new pair of roomier shoes.

So the guidance here is to explore spiritual ideas, be open to different religious practices. My very Catholic grandmother used to say to me, "Alana, there are many roads to Rome." By that she was referring to the Vatican, the headquarters of the Catholic religion, but what she meant was that there are many ways to get to the holy place in our heart, which is about love more than anything else. This tolerance made it easier for her to accept my various religious and spiritual explorations, which really began when we studied comparative religions in the sixth grade. I was about 11 or 12 years old and I was fascinated by the different colours, architecture, symbols, cultural associations and places on the earth that were attributed to the various world religions that we briefly studied at the time. I knew then that there were many paths to divine fulfilment and each person needed to choose their own way. It was rather an unconventional belief system to have, especially for one raised in a Christian household and at such a young age, however, the 5 and the 7 (which I personally relate to quite strongly) is a rather unconventional pattern!

So the guidance here is to be bold. Open your mind and question what you have been taught. This can be scary. I still remember having to confront my own beliefs in a literal hell and the devil when I was exploring the pagan religions in my early university years. I never once stopped believing in Jesus or Mother Mary, whom I loved and still do, nor did I stop believing in God or the Holy Spirit, whom I talked with as a child, and still do as an adult. I just added to my spiritual repertoire, bringing the Divine Feminine in the form of the many faces of the goddess into it, and eventually the faces of the Divine as Allah and the Black Madonna, and eventually the Hindu and Buddhist deities were thrown into the mix and found a place in my heart too. It was all the one divine energy I was loving and adoring, just with many different faces. I am a complicated being with many facets and it was easy for me to love a divine being that also had unlimited faces. I could recognise it was all one behind the variety.

I have been blessed with that easy grace in acceptance of the Divine and I feel very lucky in that. Not everyone is the same though. I have encountered a lot of fear in people as I talk about such matters which are very natural and acceptable to me but can rouse fear of damnation, as though the Divine can only love through one religion and would cast aside a beloved child who is trying to get to know him/her better through different spiritual and religious exploration.

This is not to say that such a varied path is for everyone. Of course not! We must find what suits us – that is the 5 and 7. We must find our own truths and follow that path. For many that will be a simple path of one religious tradition or perhaps one spiritual tradition that is not particularly religious in orientation but just about love and kindness as an approach to life, taking some of the most beautiful healing aspects from all of the key religions at this time. However when the 5 and 7 are appearing, even if your path is simple, there is wiggle room to explore. There is a spiritual and philosophical shift taking place within you, encouraging you to go deeper. Don't be scared of it. Embrace it. It is the Divine reaching closer to you and you are responding, even if it seems like you are turning away from what you have known. Even a crisis of faith can be a vehicle through which we eventually slip deeper into our wisdom and inner knowledge. The 5 and 7 together speak of faith through crisis and change.

Even if that change has not much to do with religious or spiritual matters, the 5 and 7 together are promising that you shall come through any change or chaos through trusting yourself, trusting in your faith (whatever that may be – in a higher being, in love, in yourself, in truth eventually coming to light) and knowing that it will see you through this change into the next stage of your life.

5 with 8
(e.g. 5.58, 8.55)

This number pattern indicates a noticeable change in the status quo! This vibration brings to mind the expression: "Every dog has its day." Whoever runs the world today, can be under the thumb the next day, and vice versa. You could take the example of someone who was forced out of a leadership role in a company through circumstances beyond his control, perhaps stripped of authority and status that he once considered to be a part of his identity.

The vivid image of a powerful man who now is in a weaker position in society describes the 5 and 8 in its dethroning aspect. This can apply literally to people and situations – so if you have the boss from hell you might soon be breathing a sigh of relief that they are about to move on. It can also apply to parts of our own psyche. If we have been dominated by an inner critic, perfectionist or some pattern of self-hate or other that has been holding us under its power, this number pattern is alerting us to the fact that such a pattern will not continue, and is instead on the way out.

Now of course there is a flip side to this, which is that if something is no longer in power, something or someone else will be. We can work consciously to ensure that whatever is coming into power within us, at least, is based in love. Although we cannot control how others behave, we can choose how we are within ourselves and what is acceptable or unacceptable to us. Being dominated by the pain in ourselves or another is–according to the 5 and 8 together–being subjected to a shift that will change it for good. It is time for a new king to be placed upon the throne and we get to choose how we wish to move through that change. If you are noticing patterns of 5 and 8 with a 4 as well, then the change will be quickly stabilised and grounded. If you are noticing the 5 and 8 with a 1, then it's going to happen quickly and soon. If you notice the 5 and 8 with a 2, then the change in power dynamic is going to happen within a personal relationship or be supported by a personal relationship or partnership in which you are involved.

In short, the message is that you will have your time in the sun, your time to shine. It's coming and events are conspiring to bring this into being. If you feel that this is already happening for you, then the message of the 5 and 8 is to journey deeper into what power is for you. Consider how you might handle it with a lighter touch, to allow it to constantly reform itself through you, to not become attached to how it is currently expressing itself, and to allow for the authority and power you currently have to shift and flow without fear, for what goes up must come down, but also when we are down, the only way is up!

5 with 9
(e.g. 5.59, 9.55, 59)

If you have been struggling to accept a situation, then this is a sign to let it go. In your active choice to surrender and 'hand it over' to the Universe, you'll find that things will shift very quickly.

This is an indirect acknowledgement that you've been growing because it is in the choice to embrace change and open up to life, that life can flow more easily through us. We actually invite change into our lives when something isn't working for us through surrender. We let go and in doing so, things can shift.

The 5 and the 9 together are a beautiful message of absolute surrender into change. It is a sign that a karmic ending is happening. By that I do not mean a punishment! Sometimes even people who work as healers with a deeply spiritual commitment to love still believe that the Universe has something of a mean streak or at least, they believe in 'an eye for an eye'. Karma is not about retribution or revenge; it is about learning, spiritual growth and love. That doesn't mean we get away with behaving poorly. Everyone learns about responsibility for the consequences of their actions over time. That is karma and that is about growing up, not being judged and condemned.

Sometimes love, especially unconditional love that is at the heart of our Universe, wants us to become fulfilled human beings, and that can ask a lot of us. Sometimes it asks us to let something go that we would really rather hold on to with all of our might! That could be a job, a relationship, an identity, a status symbol of some description or even a particular lifestyle. We could equally be asked to release something that we really don't want to hold on to anymore–at least consciously–but are struggling to release out of a hidden fear or shame within us. Either way, the appearance of the 5 and 9 together says to us that it's time to let go and if we are finding it hard, we ask for help! We can say, "Through unconditional love, I ask for help in letting go of ... [*whatever the circumstances are*] so that I can grow in love, thank you."

Sometimes an ending, a change, is a sacrifice on the altar of life; an acceptance of how life needs to have endings and beginnings to actually be, to exist. The 5 and the 9 together are letting us know that whatever change is happening now—whether it be welcomed or mourned—is in service to our growth and in some way, will be a form of spiritual healing for us, and the way to bring an end to a cycle in our lives so that a new cycle may soon begin.

5 with 0
(e.g. 5.00)

We know that the 0 adds impact and intensity to a number. With the 5 and 0 together there is no doubt about it, change and movement is upon us! And it is likely to be big!

This is exciting. It might involve travel, movement to another home, country, relationship, vocation or career, or even a complete change in how you see yourself and your place in the world. Because it has the 0 with it, it is a change that is absolutely brought to you by the Universe. So it comes to you through love, because that is the fundamental nature of our Universe.

You are being told to embrace the change that is heading your way, to accept it as being a gift from the Universe and to know that this change is being brought to you according to higher wisdom and as a part of your own life path. Exciting times lie ahead. Surf's up! Get ready to go with it!

Healing Process

This healing process is to help you adjust to change and accept it more graciously, opening up to the benefits and gifts that may be hidden at first.

Sit or stand comfortably, in a private space where you will not be interrupted if possible.

Lightly touch your feet and say aloud, "These feet are blessed through unconditional love to help me find my way."

Lightly touch your knees and say aloud, "These knees are blessed through unconditional love to help me kneel before that which is truly sacred and worthy of respect and devotion."

Lightly touch your lower belly and say, "This sacrum is blessed through unconditional love with the power to give and receive life."

Lightly touch your heart or the centre of your chest and say, "This heart is blessed through unconditional love to always know love and truth."

Lightly touch your lips and then say, "My words are blessed through unconditional love."

When you are ready, sit comfortably and gaze at the following image for at least five long, slow inhalations and exhalations.

CHAPTER SIX

I mentioned in the introduction the notion that there are not good or bad numbers but if we are going to rise above the challenges inherent in claiming freedom of mind, then we are going to have to face some fears. In any predominantly Christian society, even if we weren't raised Christian, we are likely to feel some negative association with the number 6, especially 666, because of the reputation that number pattern has acquired as being the number of the devil or anti-Christ.

I still remember when I was a little girl dreaming of a big red devil-creature. I suspect that was right after seeing the movie *Fantasia* which featured a devil-like creature in it that terrified me! I remember at the time also thinking, "Well this isn't very appropriate for children," which was rather an adult response for a child to have, but the fear co-existed with that adult response and I remember covering my eyes in the darkened theatre, trying to manage my level of fear by blocking some of the stimulus out. In my dream, I could sense a similar devilish being outside my bedroom window, lurking about, and I was terrified. He couldn't come into the room for some reason, although I had the sense that he was very aware of who I was and would have liked to have entered my room! Eventually he moved on and didn't return, but the vividness of that dream, or vision, remained with me. So did that fear, for many years following, until I actively confronted it as an adult during the course of my personal healing and conscious spiritual growth work.

I was in my early twenties when I finally decided that for me at least, I could still love the Divine, and Jesus, without having to be a formal Christian. It was a pretty radical thought at the time, and I remember having a moment of extreme fear as I wondered if I would go to hell because of it! I was shocked by that fear, because at an intellectual level I didn't believe in hell as a literal place that one could go to, but rather as a state of consciousness. I realised that my fear at that subconscious level–that I only became conscious of when I was choosing to step away from it–was part of what I had 'picked up' in cultural conditioning from going to mass every Sunday when I was a child. The fear of going to hell passed pretty quickly once I noticed it because I genuinely believed with all my heart in a God of love, not a God of fear or punishment. I was shocked at how powerful the fear was as it was leaving me though. It really made me hesitate for a moment and wonder if I was making the right decision! I had enough awareness by that stage to understand what was happening; that the fear was simply something that was leaving me, and indicated beliefs that I had picked up, and was not God trying to frighten me into remaining in a religious tradition that I felt was actually not needed for me to access the Divine and have a meaningful spiritual life. It might be necessary for some, but clearly, through my personal experience, not for all.

Having been able to move through that surprising moment by trusting the love in my heart rather than the fear in my mind, I decided that I wanted to expand my religious and spiritual education and explore other religions too, like Wicca and Buddhism. I wasn't looking for one path to belong to, I already felt love and conscious connection with the Divine. I was looking for wholeness in my spiritual and religious education; I was searching for the other paths, the other pieces of the puzzle. I didn't know what I would find, but I was keen to follow my curiosity! Wicca came first because I loved nature and I knew nature-based religions would love nature too. I wanted to learn about those ways and explore how people who practiced such religions experienced the Divine through their rituals and ceremonies, which were in some ways very different to those in the Catholic church in which I grew up, yet in other ways, so very, very similar that I began to believe that all religions are telling the same story, just with slightly different words or actors playing the key roles. All that focus on the divine energy in nature, helped to ground me at a time when I was getting caught up in my head at university, studying law (which I deplored!) and trying to figure out what to do with my life.

Eventually I was drawn to explore Buddhism, particularly Buddhist Tantra, which really helped me deal with my passionate and powerful emotions, and learn how to be present, to accept what was happening and not try to analyse the life out of it! I learnt instead to honour my emotional energy as part of my reaction to life, as part of what made me alive, rather than something to have to fear or suppress. Later, as I became more comfortable with my emotions and learned to channel them back into music and dance – which is what I had done as a child, but stopped doing during my studious teens when my head was constantly in textbooks instead. I became very drawn to Sufism, the mystical tradition of Islam that features dance, music and poetry so heavily, and I began to see the divine relationship as a great love affair. When I was searching for a way to understand what happened to me when I did healings for people, all the energy that poured through me when I was teaching and writing, I eventually found Hinduism–or it found me, I should say–and from that I learned about shakti or life force, and how it operated. I found a very expansive notion of spirituality and the Universe in Hinduism that I absolutely related to and found very freeing. I also loved, and still use, their ancient Sanskrit prayers, for sound healing because they are extremely effective and helpful. When I was exploring the feminine energy in great depth, and learning about the power of letting go of the action-oriented way of life in favour of allowing for non-action and becoming a surrendered vessel to life, I was very drawn to Taoism and the ancient Chinese wisdom teachings therein.

I found that I was naturally drawn to whatever religious or spiritual teaching I needed to help balance me and help me move forward on my spiritual path to be as close to the Divine as possible. For me that meant learning how to systematically free myself from fear or intolerance born of ignorance, as I opened up more to love and trust in myself and in life.

I still draw aspects of all of these religious traditions into my life, and the way that I naturally relate to the Universe every day. To me they are all pieces of the puzzle, all expressions of the beauty of human intelligence devoted to love. I should explain here, to be clear, I never converted to any religion formally. I explored their teachings and found within myself whatever the truth of the religion was to me. I believe that every spiritual truth exists within our own hearts; we just have to be open to feel it. I mention this because although I make comment on various religious or spiritual matters throughout this book, I am offering it to you irrespective of your religious or spiritual affiliation, or even if you don't have a particularly spiritual streak and aren't really interested in anything other than what number patterns might mean. The Universe loves us all the same – religious or spiritual or apparently not so much of either.

I will also mention that I never lost my connection with Jesus and Mother Mary through all of that exploration. If anything, that connection became increasingly personal and strong over the years and they are now two of my most powerful spiritual teachers on a personal level, even though I don't consider myself to belong to any particular religious tradition at all. I just seek to love the Divine in all its forms, and I accept that all genuine religious and spiritual traditions have value in their own way. What feeds one may not quite feed another and we all have to discover what helps us find the spiritual nourishment that we need in life. Some of us need a lot of that, others seem to need it less. It is just a matter of working out what serves us this lifetime.

Now I mention all this because in dealing with the 6 vibration, which is a part of life whether we wish it to be so or not, we are going to meet with some fear. Although what I described above was just my journey, and it won't necessarily be the same for everyone, the lesson that to experience love we will have to meet and move through our fears and intolerances, applies to us all. We just might have that learning through different life experiences or situations. We might have a gay child and need to learn to love that child regardless of our intolerance or fear of their sexuality or difference, as just one example. The 6 brings us a message of love. Love can be so much more, so much more healing, so much more powerful, than we dare dream, but we have to be able to receive it and only we can choose how much we are willing to receive by our attitude and choices. To receive the endless love in many forms offered to us by the 6, we are most likely going to need to face some fears and grow at various times in our life.

Due to the association of the 6 in Christian culture with the devil, a lot of that fear is going to centre around religious matters, and the material world which is often taught to be the devil's way of seducing us away from divinity and purity. In many spiritual traditions the world is seen as little more than a distraction or at worst, a manifestation of the devil's work, and is to be treated with suspicion and fear lest we end up cast into hell. Now even if we intellectually challenge that idea, I realised through my own experience, that releasing the emotional charge of such indoctrination is another matter. If you do still believe at an intellectual level that such a teaching has merit, and these are often the deeply spiritual people who love purity and fear being tainted by the ways of the world, then learning to accept all of creation as part of the divine plan, part of the divine work is going to be hard. Even for me, though I truly believe that, there are still things that happen in the world and around me that are just too easy to judge as 'wrong' sometimes. There will be moments when it is really hard work to learn to trust and accept and love all of life!

If the notion of the material world as separate to spirit is not part of your belief system, then you'll probably find working with the power of the 6 much easier. If that indoctrination is part of your belief system, however, and you don't feel ready or wiling to challenge that, I absolutely respect your right to choose your beliefs and what has meaning for you. We have to take our own path, according to the timing that is right for us. I have no interest in converting anyone to anything, only to offer a voice of love to assist those that would like to live with less fear. That's it. What I would offer to any reader that is uncertain about whether the material world can be just as spiritual as the spirit worlds, is that there is healing in the 6 vibration that is not about the devil or hell, but about the Universe wanting to assist you in the physical world so that you can live your spiritual truths in the world. More like the teaching of "be in the world, but not of the world" That might be more accessible for you. You'll see what I mean below.

The interesting thing with the 6 vibration is that it holds a lot of power. One of the idiosyncrasies of human beings is that we tend to fear that which holds power – until we confront the fear and integrate that power, learning to use it responsibly and with compassion.

We can fear our body, the material world, sexuality and femininity, particularly in Western or Christianised culture. Yet these are all parts of us that hold a lot of power and can actually help us to grow spiritually and be a more empowered presence of love in the world, when we learn how to love and accept rather than fear them. Until we get to that place however, we might judge those parts of us as less than spiritual or as being unclean. We don't have to feel ashamed of this–it is mostly just what we have learned through social, cultural and religious conditioning since we were children– but we do need to decide if we want to continue with that fear or face it and become more mature, challenging those beliefs and choosing new ones.

If not, trouble can brew. One example is that we can remain stuck in unconscious fear of women which leads us to want to judge them, objectify them and treat them as servants to our needs, or as competition for attention, not as independent divine beings in their own right. In that we would miss out on feminine connection, nurturing, genuine love and healing tenderness, not to mention receptivity to life and the ability to feel and flow with creativity, intuition and sensuality – all wonderful, life-affirming qualities that flow from the feminine sensibility. If we didn't challenge our fears we would continue to unconsciously distrust the body and therefore want to dominate it, control it, make it behave according to our ideas of what it should be, and therefore miss out on all the pleasure, intuition, wisdom and instinct it can bring to us. Without doing this work of challenging our belief systems we can end up not realising exactly how much we disrespect and even hate our body, our mother, other women, sexuality and so on. Those attitudes all come from unconscious fear and if we are held in those fears, the power of the 6 vibration will never be within our grasp.

I briefly dated a man who was deeply fearful of what the 6 vibration represents. He was good looking, charismatic and successful. He ran his own building business and also entered bodybuilding competitions in his spare time. He was very disciplined, determined and able to bounce back after some truly heartbreaking challenges in his life, where he lost everything he had built, and he had to start all over again, rebuilding his finances, his work and his economic security from scratch, which he did successfully, on two separate occasions. There was much about him to admire and appreciate.

Dating him however was truly a disappointing experience. He was blessed with a lot of masculine energy, which I enjoyed, but he was unable to connect with his own feminine side which meant that he couldn't connect emotionally, he couldn't connect to his heart or genuine feelings, or with the idea of spirituality as being loving rather than punishing. He didn't understand my work as a spiritual healer at all, which he responded to with either fear or mockery. He wanted to control me (and being a free-spirited woman, I didn't respond well to that) and any kind of romantic interaction with him lacked tenderness and a feeling of loving connection.

Suffice to say that we did not date for very long and I felt very good about my decision to not see him anymore. I did have compassion in my heart for why he was that way, though. He came through a very difficult and punishing childhood that featured some shocking abandonment by his mother. He had a lot of fear in him of all things feminine as a result. At first he responded to that fear by building up his masculine strength, drive and determination. I could relate. I had similarly responded to my own fear of the feminine, learned through cultural conditioning, in that same way, becoming very driven, learning to shut off from my feelings, my instincts, my body, and learning to live from my head rather than my heart. It was painful, and resulted in problems with eating and weight, depression and anxiety. It was only in having to heal those issues that I realised I had a problem in accessing my own feminine nature, and only in accessing that feminine nature, that I could heal those problems. It took years of inner work and self-healing to change.

However he had not taken that next step. He was yet to believe enough in his own strength to learn how to become vulnerable. He simply couldn't do it. He was unconsciously unresolved about his mother's abandonment of him and resisted any kind of vulnerability that would lead not only to deep connection with another, but the possibility of that person being able to cause him great pain by leaving him again. I guess you could say he learned a lot of distrust from his childhood and he didn't know about how powerful his body was, not only through the masculine approach of weight-lifting, but the feminine side of being able to bear pain consciously and release it if allowed to do so.

Given the circumstances, that was understandable. However it was up to him as an adult to choose to deal with that. He had to confront the fear that his past had created within him and it seemed that at least when I knew him, he was not ready to do that as yet, so all the unconscious fear in him kept him a slave to the world that he knew and prevented him from reaching out in tender and loving connection with another. I was sad about that, not only for myself, but for him, because it was tender and loving connection that he needed so deeply for his heart to be able to heal from its painful past.

Working with the 6 vibration requires that we begin to challenge what we fear, making it more conscious, so that we can overcome it. We can't heal what we don't acknowledge. Now you might think, well that all sounds easy but how do I do it? It is simpler than you think to heal this fear. We start by reconditioning our mind to accept the 6 when it comes to us. When I started to work with the 6 vibration, I was a bit anxious at first. It wasn't completely conscious, but when 6s would pop up on my mobile, I'd try to ignore them!

Then I realised what I was doing and began to tell myself, "Hey, a 6 means the Divine Feminine–love, the body, money, sensuality and beauty–don't be scared, embrace it!" and I began to recondition myself to have positive responses to the number patterns with a 6. Now I don't feel fear when I see it, I feel curious about what lovely energy it is telling me is going to come my way.

The healing process can start with that shift in mind-set. Give yourself time to adjust to it. It might happen really quickly or it might take a while. You don't have to tell others what you are doing – get used to it yourself first and then share it if you want to do so. Fear can be contagious. Sometimes it's better to clear our fears out first–sort of like putting our own oxygen mask on first so that we are strong enough to help others–and then we can share what we feel later, and others can choose for themselves how they want to deal with those issues for themselves.

I acknowledge the fear that this number can generate in us. I want to lay it to rest. There is no need to fear the 6 or 666. In fact it is extremely likely– especially if you are interested in this chapter particularly–that you are one of those souls who are strong enough to help the world overcome the fear of the feminine, of the body, of the material world, of the Goddess, and so reconditioning yourself to love the 6, and be open to its gifts, is part of your special spiritual journey this lifetime, and you can become an inspiration to others in that process.

I recently spoke with a friend of mine. He is straight, but his brother is gay. He is one of the most open-minded people that I know. He went to the Sydney Gay and Lesbian Mardi Gras a few nights ago to support his brother. I was teaching interstate at a spiritual festival over the weekend and on the Monday after the big weekend, he called me for a catch-up of our respective weekends. He told me something that I found very interesting. He said that the lesbian community seemed different to him. They weren't carrying the energy of anger in the ways that he had noticed in years gone by. Instead they seemed to be absolutely radiant with feminine power and strength. I had chills pass through me when he said that, because I realised that with his typical insight he had picked up on something true – the feminine was healing, and this was one way to see that for real.

It is not that only lesbians who can access the Goddess energy of course. She is living in each one of us, men and women, plants and animals, crystals and all of creation – that is her. She is the manifest aspect of the Divine, she IS creation. It was just that in that moment, in that particular community, the feminine energy revealed that she was healing herself through human evolution. My friend and I were very moved by this realisation.

What healing of feminine energy means in psychological terms for humanity is the release of fear and stepping into love, getting out of our heads and into our hearts, not retreating from our feelings, but engaging with them intelligently in order to live a truthful and authentic life which honours who we are (and how we were created) rather than who we think perhaps we should be! If this is something that has meaning for you personally and spiritually, then it's part of your life journey to help with this process. You can do that by 'making friends' with the 6 vibration and working with it consciously.

Even if you don't relate to this discussion as much as others in the book, if you are receiving 6 number patterns, the Divine Feminine wants to gift you with more love, attractiveness, wealth and wellbeing, which are some truly lovely gifts to receive. You can receive those more easily in learning to condition your mind to accept the loving messages that come with the 6 number patterns.

6 with 1
(e.g. 6.16. 16.16. 166. 6/01)

6 with 1 brings messages of new beginnings in romantic love, in our relationship to our body and our sexuality, and in our finances.

It brings us guidance to take loving action in our lives, to get clear about what we want and to realise that setting a loving intention is a very powerful way to attract what we want into our lives. My grandmother used to say that we get more flies with honey than vinegar. This is the difference between love and fear. If we are warm and inviting to what we want to draw into our lives, rather than fearful of never having it, then it can more easily come to us. It sounds simple, and it is, but it does involve us going through the lesson that I mentioned in the discussion above on the 6 – learning to access the gifts of the 6 often requires us confronting and overcoming our fears. Sometimes that means facing fears that we aren't worthy or deserving of what we want or desire. I believe that if a desire is in your heart, it's part of your life journey to experience it. We have to learn to give ourselves permission to accept our desires and to open up to receive them. With the 6 and 1, you are going to need to accept your own intention to create what you love; then you will be inspired to act in a way that tends to attract what you want towards you. You'll be acting in harmony with love.

This number combination also has special resonance for our attitudes towards women, the body and the feminine. When we are able to feel empowered but also respectful towards women and femininity, we will not feel threatened by life. It is only the discord or disconnection to our own feminine energy within us that makes us fear the feminine in others or in the world, or the happenings in life itself. By the feminine energy within, I mean that energy which exists in both men and women, and is about loving relationship, receiving, vulnerability (which can be a sign of great strength rather than of weakness) and sensuality. If we are having trouble with touch, with receiving affection or gifts, with being received and really held by another in word or deed, in feeling supported or loved, in accessing our natural sensuality and sexuality (which will very naturally differ in degree, intensity and orientation for each person) then we are having difficulty in accessing our feminine energy, whether we are male or female. That is OK. It just means it is part of our learning this lifetime. If we know this, we can do something about it, which is the call of the 6 and 1. Take action in service to love!

The 6 with the 1 asks for us to take action around new ways to relate to the feminine. It might be to stick some notes with loving words where we can see them – on the computer, on the bathroom mirror, or in our diary. Try it! Write: "You are beautiful" and "I love you" on some notes and stick them to a mirror. I bet you will smile when you see them! What we think and hear becomes part of how we are mentally conditioned. Changing our mind is the first step to changing our life. If you want to heal your relationship to your body, to food and eating, to relationships and love, to receiving, to abundance and wealth, then this is how you start. If you want real, genuine change in those areas, not just exercises in will power, then you need to change from your mind first. This is the message of the 6 and 1: change is coming, or more change can come, because of how you are working with your intentions and decisions, and that is good, that is healing, so keep going with it.

If you have been asking for help in these areas–love, wellbeing, romance, health, sexuality, finances, self-worth–then this number pattern lets you know that a fresh start is imminent. Ask for help (say, "Through unconditional love I ask for help with ..." and say this morning and night for six days, or even better, every day!) and take action that feels positive and constructive in these areas of your life. The best way to do that is to get out of your mind and what you think you should be doing, and start to be kinder to your body, listen to your intuition and get to know what steps are right for you based on what your heart tells you. With the 6 and 1 you are being guided to listen to your heart and get to know how it speaks to you. Like all things, it can become much easier with patience and practice.

6 with 2

(e.g. 6.26)

The 6 with 2 brings messages to do with loving partnership. This is most likely marriage or some other sort of romantic love relationship that is mutually enhancing, loving and tender, that has a sexual or physical aspect to it. It can however also refer to a heart-centred business partnership or a partnership that will bring more love or money into your life without having the romantic association to it. It can mean a relationship that contains all of those aspects too of course.

The 6 and 2 also brings a message that loving partnership will help you to open your heart and become more receptive and surrendered to life, and through that process, you can receive healing – financially, emotionally, physically (in your relationship to your body and issues to do with that relationship such as food and eating, exercise and overcoming bad body thoughts or criticisms, learning to feel more beautiful and accepting of your body).

If you are in a relationship, this number pattern speaks of a deepening love connection between you, which is very beautiful. Even if you are not in a relationship, the appearance of this number pattern suggests that you keep your heart open, and ask for unconditional love to assist you in all matters with relationship.

6 with 3
(e.g. 6.36)

If you want to get pregnant, this is a good sign! If you want to become more creative and express the love in your heart in some new project or business, this is also a good sign, especially if combined with a 4 or 8.

The 6 with 3 indicates creations of love. Obviously a child is one such example, but it can also indicate smaller groups forming in love and service. Meditation or support groups that are based on love and helping each other are one such example. Groups of friends that come together to heal the heart are another example. The 3 doesn't mean such groups can only have 3 participants. The 3 represents gatherings, anything from 3 to 3 billion!

I had an experience of this recently when I was dealing with the ending of a relationship. I truly loved the man in question and we had been together for five years and discussed marriage and yet there were basic incompatibilities in the match that made day-to-day happiness together a great challenge, despite the passion and love we felt for each other.

Leaving him was one of the more painful things I've had to do in my life and my heartbreak was acute. At the time I decided the best way to heal would be to get away from daily reminders of him and start a new life afresh elsewhere, so I moved rather far north where I wouldn't be running into him or his family and friends and tried to process my grief and move on with my life. In that new environment I very easily ended up meeting people who were going through similar issues. We just naturally gravitated towards each other, perhaps unconsciously seeking out moral support! For some months, whilst I needed that external validation and support, I was blessed with it – usually in groups of two others plus me. It was the 6 and the 3! Small groups and heart healing.

With the 6 and 3, we are asked to allow ourselves to be supported by loving group energy. For some, they will be lucky enough to have this in family. For others, with more dysfunctional and fear-based or generally 'toxic' families, they will need to seek support and loving group community or connection outside of their biological families. That might be found in a meditation, yoga or conscious dance class, in spiritual support groups or art therapy groups, as well as reading groups or art classes, for example.

If you are in need of this–and most of us can benefit from more love in our life–then ask, "Through unconditional love, please may I be assisted to connect with loving, supportive groups of people for the highest good, so be it!" There have been times in my life when I have really struggled to find my soul tribe – those people who really just get me; the ones I don't have to try and tailor my remarks for, or explain myself to so that I can be understood. At one stage earlier on in my life, I felt deprived of such people for a number of years. I just couldn't find a group of people where I felt I could be myself and belong. I was socialising, but I can pretty much talk to anyone about anything and although on the outside it seemed like I had a lot of social activity happening, on the inside I didn't feel received or heard. I didn't feel like the people with whom I was interacting were actually that interested in who I was. Actually I felt as though it scared some of them, and in such cases polite small talk was all that they seemed capable of engaging in with me. That led me to feel a sort of social disconnection and dissatisfaction which was frustrating. Even though I am more introverted than probably any other person I know and I actually enjoy a lot of solitude, I do also have a highly social side and like to 'play' with others when the mood strikes.

Eventually a series of circumstances led to me being invited to sing at a drumming circle. I was so nervous on the day of the gathering. I had no idea what was really involved in the drumming circle. Not knowing who would be there, and really for no particular reason that I could see, I just felt as though

I was about to take a great leap into the unknown. All day I hoped it would be cancelled! Then on that evening, when of course, it was not, I somehow summoned up enough chutzpah to force myself to go to the evening and not give into my mysterious fears and hide under the duvet at home instead. I had a marvellous time! I met a whole new group of people unlike any I had met before. They were free spirits, like me. I had thought I was the only one! I relaxed, and I laughed, I met new friends, two of whom are now two of my most loved male friends, the three of us playing music with a spiritual twist together upon occasion. That evening marked a new beginning in my life that helped me open up to be more of myself than ever before. No wonder I was nervous! That growth was not always easy. However it was worthwhile and my life has never been as lonely as what it was before that time. That is the promise of the 6 and 3, the ending of loneliness. But we have to take the risk to open to love too, of course.

6 with 4
(e.g. 6.46)

This number combination gives stability and constancy to love. It can suggest that there be planning for love or physical space created for it. This might sound odd, but clearing out some stuff from your life–even just old physical stuff–can be enough to create the space needed to attract something new into your life.

I will give you a little story to explain this.

I often go through wardrobe clean outs. I find that as my sense of self changes, and as I grow, my sense of fashion and style changes too. I love to express myself through clothing. I find it fun, creative and freeing to do so. That means I also keep topping up the local clothing charity bins from time to time, and also, that I sell some of the higher end pieces on eBay sometimes too. I had recently moved to a new area and had a donation that I wanted to make to a local clothing collection bin. The clothes were sitting in the boot of my car however because I didn't yet now where the local charity bin for my new area actually was!

At the time, I also had a beautiful dress for sale online that curiously– despite being a great bargain at the price I had listed it for–was not selling easily. I even had one buyer who purchased it and then didn't want to pay because of a list of excuses, including that her twelve-year-old daughter had bid on it and she hadn't known, followed up by her husband having been in a car accident and so she could no longer afford it, and then saying that actually maybe she did want it! And on it went. I got fed up with her constant changes of mind and just cancelled the transaction. I didn't feel it was right to force her to honour her commitment to purchase, so even though I had to relist the garment again, I just went with that. Eventually my guidance said to me to release the garments that I was donating to charity as well, which I easily did that day by searching for a local charity clothing bin online and then driving up the road and putting my donation in it.

As soon as I had released that changing-her-mind buyer and released the other clothes to the donation bin, I was contacted by another buyer through eBay–this one genuine and committed–who purchased the dress, and enquired if I had any others to sell her, which I did. The transaction was easy and effective and through releasing the clutter of my donations and the clutter of the uncommitted buyer (giving up on trying to hold on to what was not easily coming to me, which would have been what I was doing, had I tried to force her to honour her commitment and pay), I opened up to another solution. The new buyer loved her new dresses, and I cleaned out more space in my wardrobe, through donations and sales, and we were all happy. That is the operation of the 6 and 4, letting love work out the practical details!

With these numbers, we are promised more wealth (the 6 and 4 are great energies for growing financial wealth) but also more security in love that is constant, stable and long-term. Love needs room to breathe. If you want more of anything that is represented by the 6 vibration–wealth, beauty, connection, love–then you need to make some space for it to reach you, as I mentioned above, and also room for it to breathe and not be suffocated. The first way to shut down abundance is to try and grab on to what you have through fear. Likewise if we try to force initial affection or interest into long-term declarations before such things happen naturally, then we can end up killing off connection rather than strengthening it. Life needs breath, and we all need room to breathe. That space can be physical but it can also be mental space, just taking some time out to relax and float on the ocean of life for a while, rather than surfing or paddling madly against the rip tide! When we take this approach, we are actually allowing love to build in our lives. We take the physical steps, yes, we make the commitments and attend to our disciplines (the 4) but we also trust in the magnetism and worth of our hearts and that the Universe will respond to our efforts naturally (the 6) and in the best way, so that we don't have to try and force things to happen. We put in the effort, yes, and then we trust in what comes.

The 4 is a foundational number and with the 6 it can bring a message of building a foundation in love. My grandmother used to give me various relationship tips when I was growing up. She talked of foundations of mutual respect, trust and both partners putting in the hard work needed to build a secure future together. This is the 6 and 4, the practical work of love, and commitment, and the rewards that it brings to us on so many levels including a palpable sense of physical, emotional and mental wellbeing. She had a loving marriage and I took her advice seriously. Though I did ignore one of her tips when I fell in love with the man that I mentioned above. She always said, "You have to be compatible!" and she was right. That was a lesson that I had to learn the hard way though.

If you are getting a 6 and 4 together, then trust that you are being told that your efforts in attracting stability into your life–in relationship, in wealth, in love more generally–are not in vain. You are building foundations. If in doubt, ask for help through unconditional love, with whatever is troubling you. Help will be on its way even before you finish asking for it! No matter what appears to be in the physical world, the 6 and 4 let us know that love will always find a way to heal it.

6 with 5

(e.g. 6.56)

This is an exciting though not necessarily comfortable number pattern, at least initially. The 5 brings upheaval and change. Now that can mean new spice in your love life! It can also mean a temporary rocky road in finances or love. Most people don't enjoy such a thing, however the benefit of the 6 in that pattern is that there is some sort of healing energy behind that change. Sometimes when a plane is shifting altitudes to reach a higher cruising level, there is a lot of turbulence. Once the plane settles at the new altitude, the discomfort settles down and the journey continues even more briskly–and more calmly–than before.

It is the same with our changes in altitude in life. A change in altitude means that we are operating at a different frequency. We go through such a change every time we shift our belief systems out of fear (I am not good enough, I can't do this, I am not as good as so-and-so, I'll just stay with what I know because I am scared to fail) into a more loving consciousness (I deserve happiness, I'll give this a go because no matter what happens,

I'll learn something new and that's helpful, I love myself, every failure is a chance to learn how to better succeed). We do this as we conquer our fears and believe in ourselves more in life. It might be subtle such as through dealing with a challenge at work and getting through it successfully or getting to the yoga class that we wanted to attend and praising ourselves for making the effort to care for our body and love ourselves. A shift in frequency might come through a big leap of confronting an illness head on and healing it through changing our behaviours and braving treatment. It might happen through internal work where we change the way we relate to ourselves over time, choosing more loving words or beliefs about ourselves, giving ourselves the benefit of the doubt instead of rampant inner criticism with no alternative loving inner voice speaking up on our behalf against negativity directed towards us – by ourselves or another.

When the 6 and 5 combine, the guidance is that there is a change in frequency headed your way. It will likely have physical effects in your world, and internal effects in you and your relationships with others. No matter how it is manifesting, in the 6 lies the clue in how to best deal with the change – be in your heart! Trust. Come from love. No matter what is happening, you can always call on unconditional love to help you by saying, "Unconditional love, help me with …" Then stay in your heart and trust that help will come to you in the best and most helpful form to assist you in navigating the changes and enjoying where they are taking you.

The 6 and 5 remind us that improvement typically requires change, and any change can be tricky to accept, but if we stay in our hearts and have enough self-worth to believe that if change is happening it is in order that we receive an improved set of circumstances in our lives, then we'll be able to accept that change as an expression of love and keep our hearts open to life, no matter what. The result of that will be greater happiness and more fun surfing the changing currents of our lives.

6 with 6
(e.g. 66, 6.06, 666)

This is probably the most challenging number message for us to receive as a positive message if we have been raised within religious traditions where it was considered negative, and yet if we can learn to see it differently, we will realise that we are being asked to release fear and find a more healed and loving relationship to the physical world. Greed and materialism are not about the physical world per se, though that is obviously where they tend to be acted out. Those feelings come from a place of lack within. That sense of lack or emptiness where love could be, is expressed in a sense of emptiness needing to be filled with things – toys, gadgets or other possessions and sometimes even endless activities in our lifestyle.

The messages that are associated with multiple 6s are often trying to help us be liberated from this emptiness. Unfortunately the way we often receive that message is with a sense of shame, or the suggestion that we are being distracted by materialism and need to focus on our spiritual path. Yet I have found the Universe to be loving, not shaming. The message of multiple 6s is not about a smack on the wrist or worse. It is about a gift of love that is coming to us, so we are asked to be open from the heart to receive it. Are you feeling open to love or fearful? It is OK if you feel some fear. Sometimes love is confronting! It might sound strange or illogical but genuine love can cause us to realise where our limitations in receiving lie – as if we are being offered an ocean but our heart is only capable of receiving a few droplets. If we suddenly feel unworthy, that is our heart letting us know that we need to open up more, believe that we are worth more in order to receive more. It isn't about being better than someone else; it is about being good enough within yourself.

When you are receiving messages in the numbers with multiple 6s you are being asked to be brave and open in your heart, and to realise that you are one of the those special souls who are learning to overcome fear and accept love in its place, and helping others to do the same this lifetime. You can also be sure that you have come a long way in that journey already. The Universe is benevolent. It will often start our journey with the 6 vibration through gentler paths–combining the 6 with a 1 or other numbers–helping us adjust to the message of the 6 until we are really ready for multiple 6 in our guidance and messages. Once we are ready for multiple 6s, it's really a sign that we are working with the feminine energy in quite an empowered way, and we are ready for the bigger challenges in overcoming not only our own fear, but global fear of the feminine that still contaminates so much of our modern social conditioning. So consider your multiple 6 message to be recognition of your own spiritual success as well as more opportunity for you to live your inner light radiantly in the physical world, bringing greater love into being.

6 with 7
(e.g. 67, 76, 6.07)

This is a powerful number pattern asking us to pay attention to our intuition and acknowledging the power of our intuitive feelings and insights in the heart.

Let me tell you a story that sums it up.

I owned a beautiful long silk kimono that I had not worn and thought to sell on eBay, as I mentioned earlier on in this chapter.

I listed the item for sale and received an email offering me more than my requested price. The email said that the offer was greater because they wanted immediate express international shipping. The email sounded fine, the buyer had positive feedback on his account (which is a way to check for references on eBay before going ahead with a transaction) and it seemed above board. My instinct however was that this was a deception and not to trust it.

The amount that was offered was $670. A nice little synchronicity! I did listen to my intuition and did not post the item, although many apparently legitimate emails were sent to me saying that the funds would be released into my account once the item was shipped and tracking number advised. Fortunately I listened to my intuition that said from the beginning that it was a scam and just let it go without much inconvenience to me except some time lost in emailing. Later that day I was emailed again, this time officially by eBay, and notified that the account this person had used had been closed, and that was the end of that.

I share this story with you because it ties in so perfectly with this number combination. The 7 asks us to trust our insight, our instincts and our intuition. The intuition in particular, and insight, lie within our heart. It is amazing what we can see from the heart.

I had another incident on eBay a year or two earlier (see, the material world does help us put our spiritual skills to use and grow on our spiritual journey!) when I was interested in purchasing a dress that was listed as being made of silk. I had a strong inner knowing that it wasn't silk at all, but actually viscose. I would not pay the same for a dress made of artificial fibres as I would for a silk dress of natural fibres and I wanted to know if my intuition was correct about the fabric of this dress, despite the seller describing it as silk.

I showed the photographs of the item to a seamstress with a lot of experience with textiles. She couldn't be sure what it was, she said it was possible that it was silk but she couldn't tell from the photographs. Somehow I just knew that it wasn't silk though. I asked the seller to provide a picture of the tag with the 100% silk label on it, which she did. Yet I still knew that it wasn't silk! The thought of it being mis-tagged or someone purposefully sewing on a tag that indicated a more expensive material to gain a higher price seemed ridiculous to me, but nonetheless I listened to my intuition and told the seller that I didn't believe it to be silk, even though she probably thought I was crazy because she had just shown me the tag indicating that it was! Far from thinking I was crazy, a day or two later the seller emailed me back and said that she had taken the dress to someone to identify the fabric in person and it was actually viscose, an artificial fibre, and far less valuable than natural silk after all. I was grateful for her confirmation of my intuition, as it was kind of her to take the time to let me know, but I didn't need it. I knew what I knew.

The 6 and the 7 together tell us to trust what we feel when it comes from the heart. We just know. We might think that others will judge us, or think we are crazy, but we don't doubt what we know.

This combination in particular tells us to trust our instincts in love. We might have all our ideas and fantasies about how we want someone to be, but deep within our heart we often know with striking clarity if someone is right for us or not. I have suffered a lot in love, because I hear that voice so clearly and immediately, but rather than listen to it and act accordingly, many times I have sought to prove it wrong! Of course I failed in all those attempts because wanting someone to be right because you love them doesn't make it so. I don't begrudge my experiences. I learned a lot from them. But I also know that the heart speaks clearly and the 6 and 7 are telling us to listen to that and trust it and I have learned to love myself enough that I don't wish to keep trying to prove my own intuition to be wrong anymore, I would rather love it and allow it to guide me on the path of love, creating more happiness and peace in the long term.

6 with 8
(e.g. 68, 686)

This combination speaks to us of leadership from the heart, of being able to be powerful and empowered in love and perhaps even a career that beckons as a relationship coach, or as a leader or authority figure or mentor in some heart-related field, from cardiology to heart-math to counselling or heart-healthy foods, fitness or beauty consultancy for example. This number combination speaks of success in any field that relates to the 6 – property and real estate, emotional healing, heart healing, love and romance, beauty and appearance, counselling and psychology with an emphasis on the emotional journey, or any project or field that really means something to us, that is our heart's passion. It is an indication that success will come through really loving something enough to go for it.

This number combination also reminds us to remain in possession of our own empowerment in all heart-related matters, including personal romantic relationships. To remain empowered in love, in connection with our own inner sense of authority and not handing that unconsciously over to our partner can be tricky, especially when we want our partner's approval or devotion and we believe that is going to be conditional upon us behaving a certain way. This is particularly so for women with men who might believe in traditional values of the man making the decisions for the woman rather than the woman making decisions for herself. This can also happen where any partner decides to play the role of the weaker party–whether they are actually or not–and hands over their power to their partner in order to make the relationship seem more secure and stable. The 8 with the 6 lets us know that love doesn't have to make us feel or play at being weak. We can be in our strength and be in love too! Sometimes the only way we can challenge such (often unconscious) power games in love relationships is to tackle them head-on by choosing to hold on to our personal power, choosing to remain responsible for ourselves as individuals, and cultivating enough self-respect that we can naturally attract more respect in our relationships too.

This combination actually suggests that we might be able to find more of our personal power and authority through love or any path of heart, that we might need to bring more love and heart-centredness to our experiences of responsibility, authority and power to be able to fulfil our life journey. If you have been recently promoted or are thinking of stepping into a leadership role that contains more responsibilities, for example, but have concerns that you will turn into a heartless management person and lose your connections with your colleagues, this number combination tells you not to worry! You'll be able to combine your friendship, regard and like for those around you with a leadership role. When leadership is carried out with love, it can inspire respect and devotion from those being led. It doesn't have to be an either/or situation. Love and authority can co-exist, indeed it's the best possible outcome that they do.

The 6 and 8 also indicate loving yourself is going to lead to you being able to step into a more powerful expression of yourself and your life. This is your guidance to step forward, believe in the love within your heart as being enough to empower you to guide others, if that is your calling in life.

If you are in a leadership position and struggling with a decision that needs to be made, or how to cope with those around you in positions of authority, this number pattern guides you to call love into the equation, to come from your heart. Simply do this by asking for help by saying something along the lines of, "Through unconditional love, I ask for help with this situation ..." and the rest is up to the Universe.

6 with 9
(e.g. 69, 6.09)

Flipped sideways, 96 or 69 become the sign for Cancer in astrology, which is the energy of the Divine Mother and of creation. The 6 and the 9 together bring about a connection with divine love. When things don't seem to be going our way, it can be hard to remember that the Universe loves us unconditionally. We can feel that we are being challenged or victimised, treated unfairly or having to suffer something that we just don't understand. In those cases divine love can seem like a 'nice idea' but not of much relevance to our daily lives.

Yet the appearance of the 6 and the 9 lets us know that no matter what appears to be, there is truly great love around us and within us, wishing for us to know it and let it heal our lives. The trick with the 6 and the 9 is that for it to be able to work its magic, we have to give up our ideas of control. That might sound easy but surrender is an art that we have to learn. We only know when we have truly surrendered something because we cease to worry, or usually even think much if at all, about it. Even if it used to dominate our thoughts obsessively night and day prior to the surrendering!

No matter what happens, we can accept it, even if we don't understand it or it seems unfair. That's when we know we have surrendered.

Through surrender, great things are possible but we have to give up the idea that things will turn out the way we think that they should. Sometimes in the game of checks and balances called life, we have to lose somewhere, so that we can win somewhere else, somewhere more important for our life journey.

My grandmother (who had a lot of sayings, as you are probably working out by now) used to say to me that sometimes we had to lose the battle to win the war. The bigger war in life is that between fear and love. It can be so hard to let go of fear at times! We might not know that a small loss here and now will help pave the way for a bigger win later on. We just have to surrender if we are going to find peace amongst all the ups and downs of life. I am the first to admit that is often easier said than done. However when we do, the greater plan of our life can flow and even though there will undoubtedly be times when we don't like some of the journey because it is painful for us, there will be many times when we are so grateful that we were able to get through the pain because we realise it has led us to somewhere profoundly more fulfilling and we are all the happier for it.

When you are given a 6 and 9 number pattern, you are being reminded of divine love and some sort of blessing or spiritual gift is coming to you as you ask for help in letting go and surrender into the mysterious workings of that love. I can tell you from experience that this is always worthwhile, no matter how hard it seems at the time. Sometimes of course we just need to know that surrender is 'allowed' and we feel relief at letting go of the struggle, which is a far easier way to respond to the guidance of the 6 and 9.

This number pattern also speaks of an ending in love. It might be the ending of a karmic pattern of attracting the 'wrong' sort of partner for you, or a harmful pattern in relationships that is being healed within you now through your own spiritual growth and unconditional love coming to your aid. It might also be the ending of a phase in relationship so that a new phase in that same relationship can open up. It might be a death–another sort of ending–and a reminder that love is in all aspects of life, even death, and that you are not to fearfully hold on to anything in your life, because there is no need! You will find that there is always more love awaiting you after a loss of any kind. Processing the loss can take time, but there will be a healing purpose behind any sort of loss we are asked to bear in life, and in going through that experience, we can open to receive a deeper expression of love in our lives. The 6 and 9 speak of a deepening experience of love, which is increasingly unconditional, and you are being brought notice of that gift. If you are doubting yourself in your choice around another – in letting them go, in surrendering your relationship, for example, then don't doubt any longer. This number pattern brings you a message that you have been loving without condition or attachment and you are to trust in your own loving nature, no matter what else may appear to be on the surface of things.

Finally this number pattern asks us to remember the healing power of love. It can conquer anything. We just have to remember to ask for unconditional love to heal our hearts and minds, and bodies. Ask for help. Allow the Universe to assist you. Invite it in, with all its compassion and genius, to help show you the way through any matter of concern now.

6 with 0
(e.g. 6.00)

When the 6 combines with 0 you can expect the unexpected in your life, particularly in matters to do with love, money, beauty and the feminine (perhaps in the form of your own body if you are a woman, or for men, with the women in your life). The presence of the 0 brings the message that there is divine assistance for you in these matters. It could also indicate that something from the past in these areas of your life is going to 'come full circle' and appear again in future, or that there is a pattern (perhaps a physical habit or psychological tendency) that relates to the areas of money, women or the feminine, beauty and how you are in the physical world, that is going to be subject to 'divine intervention,' where life itself seems to step in and offer a chance for fresh starts. That could be through a windfall, an unexpected change in circumstances, or even an experience that triggers an inner healing for you, allowing for your experience of all matters relating to the 6 energy to improve considerably.

Healing Process

This healing process will assist you in integrating the messages and guidance of the 6 more easily. Even if you don't understand the process intellectually, it will still work!

Place both hands on your heart and gaze at the image below. Say aloud, "Through unconditional love, I ask for kind assistance to release fear and open to love in all ways, for my own highest good, so be it."

Breathe in and out for six breaths, and with each inhalation imagine 'sucking in' the image below and on each out-breath, imagine that it is gently released into your heart.

When you have completed your breaths, rub your hands over your eyes and ground yourself again and you have completed your healing process.

CHAPTER SEVEN

The number 7 is the number of universal wisdom. It reminds us that everything in life is unfolding according to a higher guiding principle, no matter whether we can make sense of that at the time or not. Even if you believe that life and all its events are completely random, the 7 reminds us that there is, beyond that randomness, a guiding principle of life, some may say a divine plan, others might call it a higher consciousness, but no matter what we call it, the effect of it remains the same. That means that no matter what is happening in our lives, we can trust that there is love behind it. That love might be hidden in a lesson that feels painful but has the purpose of freeing us from something that is holding us back from living our best life and ultimately causing us even more pain in the long term. The 7 on its own or with other numbers brings us a reminder that no matter what appears to be, life has a goodness to it and it is guiding us.

To be able to accept this requires trust. That is the major message with a 7. Trust. Trust in what you have asked of life, what your heart is telling you, where your life is leading you, in the people that come into your life to help you, and the gut feelings and instincts you have to let others leave your life or not really become a part of it at all.

The beauty of the 7 is that it brings us healing. It is the number that appears to many healers (whether you typically think of yourself in that way or not) because the universal wisdom that it represents is essentially love and love is the ultimate healing energy. When we can connect with love, life has a habit of happening more beautifully, more fully, more freely and more wildly. That in itself creates greater trust and allows us to be caught up in the momentum of our own lives, so that we can consciously choose to participate, with intelligence and responsiveness, in what is presented to us each day.

Whenever the number 7 appears, I feel reminded in that moment to trust in the goodness of life, no matter what appears to be, for all is leading us into that universal wisdom of love that is at the beginning of all creation and at its end. It is all that continues to exist when our fears have passed away and our dreams have been fulfilled; it is that love that prevails. This is not some fluffy philosophy. When we really 'get' this message from the 7, we feel more peace in life. We can go after what we want, but we do it from a place of trust, not from a place of fear, anxiety, lack or emptiness. We trust that if it works out the way we imagined, that's great, but if it twists and turns and ends up going in another direction, that is fine too. I would sum it up with a funny post that I saw on Facebook recently. It went like this: "When something goes wrong in your life, just yell "PLOT TWIST!" and move on."

I would describe the 7 vibration by saying that it essentially reminds us that life is the therapist. We can do all sorts of healing work on ourselves if we choose, and that is wonderful, but the purpose of all healing work is to eventually become able to engage with life from a place of presence and a willingness to *learn* how to grow and respond. When we can do this, rather than attempt to resist life or try to make it other than it is, we are allowing ourselves to work with the 'great therapist' and from that place, we can grow naturally, engaging in life as a journey for the soul, maturing us not only in body, but hopefully also in heart and mind.

If we have been wounded in ways that were too difficult to process and resolve at the time, perhaps when we were young, we may unconsciously formulate a belief that life is too painful to be open to, that it is better to defend ourselves against it in order to avoid future hurts. Unfortunately this defensiveness also keeps us closed off from the pleasures in life, as well as the satisfaction that comes with feeling alive and growing. In such cases– which are fairly common–we need to learn how to respond to life and grow, how to trust again, even if that trust is basically that we are likely going to feel hurt at times, but we will be able to get through it and perhaps even derive some wisdom and compassion, rather than further defensiveness, through processing that pain.

This is a key to the 7's message about learning. When we feel like life is wanting to teach us something, or if we keep repeating the same mistakes or patterns and wonder if we are supposed to be 'getting something' which would allow us to create a positive change, then we are in the territory of the 7. In these cases the 7 brings a message to us that we are being offered a new understanding, if only we accept the opportunity before us, and learn to grow through it rather than fight against it or ignore it in the hope it will go away. Just so you know, I have tried both of those latter approaches and as it turns out, it is only by growing through life that it actually changes. You might, like me, need to be sure and check all this out for yourself of course. Someone can warn me something is hot and I'll burn myself if I go too close, but my goodness, how often I like to just make sure by doing the very thing and seeing if it's true! That's OK though. Painful at times, but OK. Life is for learning and growing – that is the message of the 7. It's nice guidance to receive if you are feeling like you are making plenty of mistakes and messing things up. The 7 is letting you know that you are just living and it's good, keep on with it, but remember to listen to your instincts too. Once you've been burnt, your instincts will guide you away from repeating past mistakes (or what I prefer to call learning experiences!).

Life will present us with answers to all of our problems or questions if we allow it to do so. It is a very responsive intelligence. When we ask a question, even if it involves standing in our back yard and sending a question or desire out to the Universe, we can trust that it will be answered through the events that then begin to weave the resolution of our issue or query into being. The man that I loved and was in a relationship with for over five years did this. He stood in his garden and said to the Universe, "I'd like a relationship now, with someone cool, like Alana." Although we had only dated briefly, for six months, many years previously and had not been in contact with each other all those years, within two weeks of him saying that, I had also been asking and felt guided to reach out to him. In a funny series of circumstances we reconnected and reignited our relationship and that continued for five years on. We had our karmic 'stuff' to work through with each other and it was painful, undoubtedly, but there was some deep love there too. I grew a lot through that relationship, and there were signs that I could see in my then-partner that showed some growth had happened for him too. We both took a journey through that life experience together and what we did with it marked it as success rather than failure in my eyes, even though the relationship came to an end eventually. But then I never judge the success of a relationship based on whether it is long term or not. Some relationships are just not meant to be thus, yet they can fulfil their potential to be all that they can possibly be nonetheless. I assess relationship success based on whether or not I grew and learned enough to become wiser and more healed within myself, and whether it had run its course and had become all it could be, before I had outgrown it. That is the approach encouraged by the 7.

For most of us, learning to trust is a big part of engaging in this process of living as a path to wisdom. If we developed issues about believing we needed to control people, places or things in order to avoid traumatic emotional suffering, then learning to trust can seem frightening or even completely beyond us. I have had private readings with very intelligent, educated people on their own spiritual path, and when I suggested that they needed to trust more, they would earnestly say, "Yes, but how do I do that?" Intellectually they understood, but emotionally they couldn't connect with it.

Until we can get to an emotional reality of trust, letting go is going to seem like a suicide mission. I am not exaggerating! People who have believed life isn't safe (perhaps because they were sensitive and raised in emotionally unsafe environments where their fundamental needs for care, security and unconditional love were not met) will feel tremendous pain as they begin to trust. They might even feel like if they trust in something or someone, without their usual defences in operation, they will literally die. If we have unresolved pain from experiences of rejection, abandonment and betrayal in our hearts (and that will be the vast majority of the population) then to be blunt, trust can really seem like a dumb idea. However without it, we will remain a prisoner to what we have already experienced, repeating that same reality over and over again, because we are not willing to open up to other possibilities that could come to us if we would just be willing to run the risk of putting ourselves 'out there' into unknown territory and letting down enough of our defensive barriers so that life can reach us in new ways. That might not ever be really easy for us to do, but we can learn to feel more able to bear the discomfort of it, or even to find it exciting, as we learn to resolve our issues about trusting.

We can learn to trust step by step, by choosing to take small risks on a daily basis that push us beyond our comfort zone but don't overwhelm us with fear and anxiety to the point that we shut down and zone out completely. For each one of us, at different times in our lives, what we can tolerate whilst still remaining present, will vary. We might be able to bear the stress of the unknown in some ways, but not others. We might be able to have a question that relates to our spiritual life remain unanswered for quite some time, but an issue about our material security might be very hard to let go of for more than a moment or two. That is fine. The Universe doesn't demand perfection from us, it simply asks for a willingness on our part to grow according to our own capacities and at our own pace.

We will know when we are growing and opening up to life, because our 'stuff' will come up. These are the feelings that we haven't quite resolved as yet, and that will be seeking resolution as the loving wisdom messages in the 7 seek to bring us more deeply into love. I can explain it like this. If you have been hurt emotionally, and you build up a shield to keep others away from you so that the hurt doesn't happen again, that will keep you happier for a little while perhaps. After some time though, you will realise that not only are you keeping out the possibility of another hurting you, you are also keeping out the possibility of another really being able to touch you, to love you. You might 'get' this intellectually, but then you are going to have to 'get' it emotionally if things are going to change.

The intellectual understanding brings you to the realisation that you are going to have to drop some of your walls with people, learn to share yourself more, be open to let people get closer to you. The emotional understanding comes with the practice. You don't run away from people the moment you become uncomfortable. You don't let your judgement of others prevent you from getting to know what they are about. You don't let your fear of being hurt prevent you from sharing yourself with others, of putting yourself out there in the world in ways that mean something to you.

This could include anything from showing your artwork, to accepting a promotion at work, to accepting a gift from another, to expanding your social network by saying yes to new invitations that would open you up to new communities of people. The 7 is a big "yes" to life. The more we can respond to life with a yes, the more we will grow and evolve into our fulfilment. I can say without exception that you are capable of so much more than you realise. The 7 brings us the invitation to say yes so that life can open you up to all that you are. The more that you trust, the more that you will naturally begin to say yes. The more you say yes, the more you realise that even when it is buffing off your sharp edges, life is love, and there is nothing to fear.

When you work with trust, accepting the guiding message of the 7, you'll notice that life brings you much synchronicity; those little (or big) sign posts along the way that help you know that you are on the right path. These are not limited to number patterns, though that is one way that the Universe can check in with you. I had an experience recently where I needed to move house. I mentioned it earlier in this book, in reference to other number patterns, but the final number that came through was the 7. When I finally found a place that I loved, there were quite a few signs to support me in my decision to move there, despite my concerns about some practical issues (although I couldn't have known this at the time, all of those issues later turned out to be not much of an issue at all – but I had to trust in what my gut instinct was telling me and wait to see how those practical matters would unfold).

The house that I moved into was number 34, the 3 and 4 adding together to give a 7. As I spoke to my manager about the move, and he asked for the new address he paused after I responded, and said, "You're kidding?" When I replied that I was quite serious, he told me that another author he managed had just moved out of a house in the same Northern Beaches suburb, on the same street and just up the road from the one I had moved into – from number 16, the 1 and 6 giving also giving a 7. We both recognised a synchronicity.

I felt something click in me. We work out our "life path" number by adding up all the numbers of our birthday as though it was a sum. My birth date is 15 July 1974. So the numbers $1 + 5 + 7 + 1 + 9 + 7 + 4 = 34$. Then you add those numbers until you get a single digit. So $3 + 4 = 7$. The fact that this house number was the same as my life path number felt like the Universe was confirming my intuitive sense that this move, on from the relationship, on from what I had known, was in alignment with my life path. It was necessary to allow my personal growth to happen on many levels, and that would translate into me being more effective in my spiritual work with people as well. I had the sense that the move would somehow support a forward step in my career as well as my personal life. Essentially, it was a step forward on my path and it was confirmed by the numbers, as well as by the life experiences that later happened through that move.

I have made a note in the introduction about life path numbers if you want to work out your own life path number too.

Back to the story, the other author who had moved a couple of beaches further up north was further along in her career than I was, at least in terms of being publicly visible, with me really just starting to build a public profile through my career as a published author, despite the 14 years of solid work in my field behind me.

I felt that the Universe was letting me know two things – firstly that the expansion of my career was going to be supported by this move, just as this other author's work had taken her into the public eye which allowed her to reach more people. I also felt that Mother Earth was telling me that she had specifically prepared a place for me with this particular property. I knew that when Mother Earth wanted you to be somewhere, nothing would get in the way of that and I would be safe and protected there, that it was meant to be. As the other author (being a healer too) had moved out of that area just weeks before I moved in, it felt to me like a type of spiritual posting had opened up for another healing energy to be anchored in that particular part of the world. It was like that other author and I had exchanged our batons in the healing race and she moved on, whilst I took over the role of bringing some spiritual energy, my particular frequency, to the area. I quipped to my manager that it was one witch out and the next witch in! I felt comforted by this knowledge. It was a move that was in alignment with my path and with what the Earth wanted from me and for me. I felt reassured, even whilst being open to the possibility that in time I might move elsewhere and some other (perhaps witchy) woman would be attracted to move into the property.

The decision proved to be a good one and I have spent much time in gratitude for all the powers that conspired to bring me to the home that I currently reside in. That was a 7 decision. Concerns about distance, starting somewhere afresh, being so far from my old life, living in a completely different place which held a very different 'energy' to other areas that I had lived in, and practical issues such as not having a long-term lease offered to me at the outset, all fell away. In trusting my intuition and trusting life, issues which were a problem for every other place I applied for – such as having a cat and not having any recent rental references (because I had not rented a house under a typical rental agreement for years), amounted to nothing. Instead I trusted my heart that said 'yes' and all the perceived obstacles melted away with ease. It was quite extraordinary.

I benefited from that decision, with practical matters sorting themselves out somewhat magically and I just realised when we are meant to be somewhere or doing something, doors open to us that would otherwise remain closed. That's the wisdom of the 7. If a door is opening to you, go through it. If it weren't meant for you, it wouldn't open for you.

Will this mean that you won't have any bumps or bruises along the way? Life will undoubtedly present us with odd bumps and scrapes as we grow, no matter how aligned we are, but it will do so in a way that you can find those knocks to be ultimately helpful and that the bumpy parts of the journey, along with the smooth sailing, will help you grow and live into your destiny – which is to be all of who and what you are in trust.

7 with 1
(e.g. 7.17, 7/01)

The 7 with a 1 asks us to trust in the changes that are happening, particularly in those new insights, experiences or intentions that we are setting in motion. Whatever is beginning anew at this time in our lives is trustworthy. Go with it! Say yes to life. Don't hesitate out of fear or uncertainty – just say yes.

If you have been through a cycle of negative or challenging times and are feeling at your wits' end because of it, worried that your future will hold nothing but the same, then this number combination brings you the hope and trust that you need to believe that a new start is possible! I am often guided to share with my students this piece of 7 and 1 wisdom – just because something has been a certain way doesn't mean that it will continue to be so!

The 7 and 1 guidance will often come at a time when you need to take new steps on your path. The message is to trust in those new steps, and in the instincts within that are telling you to take them (even whilst your fears might be causing you to question your sanity). In trusting, you'll open up a way for the Universe to lead you into the more loving reality and life that is waiting for you.

There is so much wisdom within us. Yet that wisdom exists outside of our intellectual and conscious mind much of the time. So when we are following it, through trusting our instincts and bodies, we actually won't consciously know what we are doing or why! That is because we are operating from a wisdom place beyond our mind. We have to trust ourselves in order to do this. That is the only difference between someone who is living from wisdom and someone who is not—the same divine essence dwells within—it is just that some are learning to trust in it and act even when their mind might be filled with fear or concerns or questions because deeper within, they feel the intuitive 'yes' to take a step. That is the message with the 7 and 1. You are safe to trust in whatever step you feel to take, whatever decision you might be wrestling with, whatever new beginning is arising for you now. Trust it. Act. Be bold. Have faith. Do it.

7 with 2
(e.g. 7.27)

The 7 and 2 speak of new levels of trust and understanding in one-on-one relationships. This means that if there have been issues of trust that have prevented you from really surrendering into intimacy, it's time to question that, to nudge yourself towards taking steps in trust to deepen your connection with others.

This pattern also suggests that you can learn and grow from your one-on-one partnerships whether they be romantic or in business. So that might be your clients if you are a therapist, or your students, if you are a teacher, and so on. I probably learn most on my path from my relationships. I then go inward to do my personal healing work, but it is through relationships that I often get stimulated to heal something in me that is causing pain. Following that process has been remarkable over the years. I look back at my life even just ten years ago, everything seems to have changed so dramatically in that time, that I can't believe that it is the same lifetime! Going back even further, it is even more remarkable. Now you might think that is just a result of the passing of time, but it is not. I know of people who have hardly changed at all during that time, with their lives remaining much the same over the passing of ten or fifteen years, perhaps with some superficial changes externally, but not much internally. This is not bad of course, not everyone will want or even need a highly transformational life experience this lifetime in order to grow spiritually. Some might need to have a more slow-paced existence for their benefit. However if you are working with conscious growth this lifetime and you feel the impulse, the inner nudge, to accept great change as a part of that, then you'll need to trust that to live your best life.

You'll know that this is you when you feel that change and growth is at the heart of how you approach your life experiences. You'll want to learn and grow, you'll feel that it is essential. For me this is certainly the case. Whilst my life heads off into new and ever expanding circles of connection and experience, it is because of the grace of life combined with my own willingness to grow. The passing of time doesn't necessarily indicate the expansion of life force into new fields and development. If anything, it often indicates the opposite, where people contract into ageing and an unwillingness to try new things. When the 7 comes to us however, we are asked to open up. With the 2, it is opening up to connection with others through which we can grow, experience more love and receive the wisdom of life. To whatever degree you feel you need and can accept growth in your life, the 7 and 2 are encouraging you to find that through your relationships.

This pattern also asks us to trust in our intuition in our relationships. What we see, sense or feel is accurate and helpful. We might be asked to express more of our inner knowing, intuition, instinct and insights in our connections with others as a way to bring more love into our unions.

It can also indicate that there is a relationship in your life, or that will be entering your life, that is going to give rise to learning about trust for you. That might be trust in yourself, trust in the other, trust in love or connection in some way. That relationship–whether it tends towards being easily flowing or more challenging–is going to help you grow in wisdom and intuitive confidence, so allow yourself to take that journey.

7 with 3
(e.g. 7.37)

The 7 with 3 brings us a message to trust in new birth and creations. We might have an instinct that something is being born or that we need to go in a particular creative direction in our life and we are asked to trust in that.

We might not see anything concrete yet, but the 7 and the 3 together promise us that our instincts and creative energies will come together in a manifestation. But we will have to trust!

Sometimes if we are an old soul, we will be asked to hold rather a lot of trust during a lifetime, because we are going to give birth to something far more profound and impacting perhaps, than a more transitory offering. That might mean that rather than a quick manifestation, or at least along with other quicker manifestations, we might be holding a vision for something that takes many years or even a lifetime to build. I have had to learn to hold patience over decades for creation to manifest. Now I am not in my fundamental personality a patient person. I write books in a month, and want music CDs to be completed in a similar amount of time. Sometimes that works out but sometimes it is impractical and not in alignment with my own process and life, which wants and needs more time to really marinate and absorb all the experiences and wisdoms that would come together to create something special. I recently gave a spiritual talk at a festival and Guidance asked me to give a specific message which I forgot about until one of the audience members asked a question which reminded me of the guidance I had been asked to give (yes, Guidance will get through to us when we need it, no matter what obstacles–such as human forgetfulness–might get in the way). That guidance was to have patience and to not, under any circumstances, give up! It was to give in to life, but not give up on our dreams, on our healing, on our desired manifestations, because even if we cannot see the results coming, they may only be just around the corner! And even if they are two or three corners away, we need to have faith and live our truths anyway, and that means not giving up!

If you are only going to accept quick turn-around successes, then you're going to struggle if part of your life journey is to build something for the longer term benefit of humanity that is going to take years to be born through you as you grow.

Sometimes we have to cultivate patience – and trust can help us not 'lose the faith' as we wait, and do our work, so that what we want to create can come to life through us. Sometimes when we are working on a longer-term vision for how we want our lives to be or what we would like to become within ourselves, we need to know that the Universe is 'on our side' and wants what we want too.

With the 7 and 3, there is a message that what you are wanting is what the Universe wants for you too, that you are in harmony with love and wisdom and you just need to stick with the process until it comes to fruition.

If you don't relate to the idea of a big vision of creativity that is fine. The 7 and 3 still have other messages for you. Sometimes the creation is the gift of a child coming into your life through destiny. Sometimes it is about a creative experience of some description that is going to open up your intuition. Sometimes the message is about exploring your creativity as a way to open up your insight and intuition. If you are interested in art, art therapy, creative healing dance or working with sound and music for healing, these are all in alignment with the message of the 7 and 3 and you are encouraged to follow up on those intuitive hunches with practical action.

As always, ask and trust in what you feel to find your answers.

7 with 4
(e.g. 747)

I can't help but think of a Boeing 747 aeroplane when I consider this number pattern. The 7 and the 4 together bring a message of building something that lifts you, that inspires, that brings love and wisdom into the world. You are grounded and will remain practically so, but you are also taking off and about to branch out into other worlds! That's very exciting!

It is also an indication that you are shifting to a more trusting way of being in the world and that this is allowing for the Universe to help you build a life that is more loving and supportive of your spirituality, inner wisdom, unique perspectives or perceptive way of looking at things. If you are a healer by trade and want your work to grow and earn an income whilst becoming more inspired and a source of wisdom for those on the path who need help from time to time, then this number pattern brings very good news for you!

The 7 and 4 also indicate that you are to trust your own wisdom and instincts in any matters to do with your emotional and particularly your physical health. You will likely benefit from some form of energetic or spiritual healing or counselling. Physical symptoms typically have spiritual or mental causes that, when dealt with, can at least improve the physical condition somewhat, sometimes heal it altogether, or at other times might not have a huge impact on the physical illness but will at least help you deal with it more peacefully.

Of course you are encouraged to consult with your health care practitioner according to your own choices, but you are also guided with this number pattern to ask for divine help in matters to do with health and wellbeing, and to add some form of spiritual or intuitive healing to support your wellbeing.

It can indicate that it is time to heal an old fear or block around spirituality, around trust, around listening to your own intuition and instincts, which can drain our energy and eventually show up in all sorts of health problems and behaviours that sabotage our best intentions for wellbeing.

Some examples of this are issues with food, eating and exercise (such as doing too little or too much), tension in the jaw or regular headaches that can indicate, amongst other things, that we are unconsciously restraining ourselves from allowing our energy to freely flow or placing too much burden upon ourselves mentally and we have to instead learn to get body and mind in greater and more loving harmony with each other, healing their connection with some practical compassion. Adding some counselling and/or spiritual healing into your approach to wellbeing will help you undo any unhealthy tendencies, which will in turn support you in being more easily able to live well – without quite so much inner struggle and effort.

This number combination also guides you to use your intuition and insight to solve practical matters, and to pray or ask for help through unconditional love and higher wisdom for assistance in practical matters. There is nothing too small or mundane for divine assistance as the Divine is in all things. I have parking angels and bargain angels and we work together well! I also have angels that help me reach people all around the world with my work which is rather more serious and important, but it is those parking angels and bargain angels that help me on a daily basis that really support my peace of mind and keep my energy flowing where it is needed – into how I live and my work, rather than getting regularly squandered in stress about finding a parking spot! This contributes to my sense that my faith and trust are best placed in service to all practical matters, not just the really big ones!

7 with 5
(e.g. 757)

The 757 continues the aircraft metaphor but takes it to a different level. It is about change and an opening up to new worlds that is so strong that it will not allow you to continue on the same foundation you have had (unless you are getting number patterns that combine with the 4 as well, which would suggest that your foundation is strong enough to be expanded perhaps, subjected to change, but will fundamentally hold or settle itself into a new pattern of stability).

The 757 energy tells us to let go, trust and allow our instincts and intuition to guide us, even if that means that great change is evoked in our lives and we don't feel in control or certain about where it is all heading.

If you are already in that sort of massive chaos of change, and wondering which way is up or if you are nose-diving into a big mistake, the appearance of 757 brings you comfort. There is a saying that 'only God can really mess up your life', which basically means that no matter how successful we are in making a big mess of things, only the Divine can really tip your life upside down. It's a completely different experience. It often comes as a result of us botching something and needing a helping hand to get us back on track, but sometimes that sort of change happens without any rhyme or reason (that we can see from our human perspective at least) and that might be through an illness, death, crisis financially or emotionally, for example.

Whatever it is–whether it is obviously an external trigger that is throwing us into great confusion or change, or whether it is an internal and somewhat inexplicable feeling of chaos within us that we perhaps cannot logically explain–the appearance of the 7 and 5 reassure us that no matter what the mess, it is unfolding according to divine love and wisdom and there's a healing in it for us somewhere along the line. We just need to hold on to our faith through the change until we 'get' that learning and can move through the process into calmer waters, which will happen in time.

The 7 and 5 also encourage us to rely upon our intuition and our trusting faith during big changes – it will be those qualities that help us move most gracefully through the change, guiding us into the healing gift that is the purpose of the change.

7 with 6
(e.g. 76, 677, 7.06, 07/06)

The 7 and 6 combined bring an important message about trusting in one's own intuitive insights and need for solitude and personal space when in love. It is healthy to balance time in your own company, in spiritual or personal reflection, with time in connection with another. With the 7 and 6, the message is to trust yourself to be able discern your own needs and thereby find the balance between time and energy directed into the relationship and time and energy directed into life outside of it.

This number pattern also brings a message that you are to trust that even if you are a unique or different person in some way, quirky or not looking for a 'typical' relationship, that love can and will still find you.

Everyone deserves connection, intimacy and closeness. It is part of the beauty of the human experience. You are being asked to have faith in love, to trust that it can be in your life and you don't have to choose between yourself and a relationship – you can have a good relationship with you and with others at the same time.

If you are experiencing challenges in love at the moment – whether with one relationship or with any matter of the heart more generally (such as feeling despair or depression, not really feeling passionate about life or purposeful, for example) then remember to ask for help (by saying, "I call on unconditional love, please help me with healing my heart and opening to love, thank you!"). The 7 and 6 are saying that healing of the heart is coming to you – just open up to it.

If you have been through a heartbreak or any kind of disappointment or pain in love that has caused you to shut down, this number pattern is telling you that it is time for your healing, or confirmation that healing is happening or has happened and your heart is opening. It also suggests that if you know you are in need of healing in some way, the above request for help will be beneficial for you because love is the great healer.

No matter what sort of problem you may be having, you can ask, "Unconditional love, show me the way through this situation with ..." and then wait for the response to show itself to you in your intuitions and instincts.

Remember that sometimes love will urge us to walk away from that which would close us down rather than open us up, and sometimes it will urge us to go deeper and not be fearful. You must trust in it to help you outgrow your difficulties and open up to new experiences that will help you trust more deeply in life and therefore shed anxiety and connect with peace.

7 with 7
(e.g. 77)

The repeated 7 brings us simple messages. Have faith. Believe in life and wisdom. Let Life help you get to where you need to be. Don't give up; help is on its way. And perhaps most hard to believe sometimes, you are doing a good job, so just keep going, no matter what others say!

The repeated 7 is also about spiritual rebels. Some people have negative associations with the world rebel, but I use it to describe a person who can think for themselves and chooses to live and act in authentic regard for their feelings, irrespective of what the popular press, religious authorities or anyone else has to say about the matter.

It takes a lot of courage to live from your heart and run the risk of being branded a fool, a troublemaker or something far more hateful. Sometimes those that live with love can be threatening for those who place their faith in fear. They might try and cut others down who threaten them, to make themselves feel better temporarily. Yet living from the heart might make us more visible to those that are ready to be inspired to live a less fear-based existence. Part of the message of the multiple 7 is to trust that if a higher profile is given to us for any reason, then it's part of our spiritual destiny and we can accept it and trust in it. Even if that means we are higher profile in a rebellious or non-traditional way.

The point of rebellion is not to be cool, although people who choose to live honestly from their heart in rebellion against the societal conditioning to play by rules that make no sense are certainly very cool people! The point of it however is not to win friends, but to live truthfully and to be loving enough of who you are that you are willing to respect yourself. This builds strength and love in the world. It often attracts devotion and genuine respect and appreciation from many, but it will undoubtedly ruffle a few feathers amongst those that prefer to keep you under their control, for whatever reason. To have compassion for that without getting locked into battling with those that aren't interested in win-win scenarios, is the highest expression of the rebellious 7 spirit. It is a 'live and let live' attitude that is drenched in compassion, love and care for the self and the human race. These sorts of rebels live lives that are inspired from the heart. They carry the flame of hope and the belief that anything is possible. The human race benefits greatly from such people, drawing strength, hope and courage.

Many people who have achieved such status are the saints and sages that have blessed the earth with their presence. They were often branded troublemakers and certainly they shook the foundations of what was considered possible or allowed, when their hearts couldn't bear an injustice that others seemed to believe just had to be accepted. I love these beings so much I have dedicated an entire book to their stories – funny, inspiring, moving and downright naughty in *Crystal Saints & Sages 777*, which is part of my Crystal Spirituality series published by Blue Angel Publishing.

7 with 8
(e.g. 778, 78)

There are stories in a number of religious traditions about King Solomon who was known as being very wise. People came to him for solutions to all sorts of problems and he ruled from his heart with wisdom, which is the guidance of the 7 and 8 together.

One story which always remained with me for its combination of astuteness, justice and compassion, was the story of two women who lived in one house together. Both had young sons. One of the babies died and the women both claimed that the living son was theirs, and that the dead child belonged to the other!

Solomon's response, as the rather emotional and shocking case was brought before him, was that the child should be cut in half, divided equally amongst the women who both laid claim to him. One of the women instantly cried out that the child must be spared, and the other woman should be allowed to have the baby, that she would give him up then and there, so that he would not be harmed.

Solomon made judgement that this was the child's true mother.

Whilst it is rather a dramatic tale, it does sum up the vibration of the 7 and 8 together which is wise authority. Solomon didn't make a decision on his opinions or judgements about which woman he liked more, for example. He created a situation through which the truth could be revealed, thereby making the decision far simpler and clearer.

When the 7 and 8 appear to us, there is a calling to us to step into wise leadership and authority in our own lives, and if we are in a position of leadership with others – whether that be with our friends and family or in the workplace or as a leader in the spiritual, political, educational, health or legal fields, we are being asked to exercise our power with due wisdom, care and consideration. Allow your wisdom, conscience and insight to be what guides your decision-making and exercise of authority. Anything else will land you in more trouble than it's worth, even if acting with integrity and wisdom seems to be harder at first.

Even if you are not in such a position, this number pattern has meaning for you. You are being asked to take personal responsibility for your feelings, your life and its circumstances. You are being urged to ask the Universe for help through unconditional love with anything that is bothering you, of course. And you are being asked to responsibly accept the help that comes to you by engaging with your life circumstances and following up on your instincts, hunches and intuitions without needing approval or permission from anyone else to do so.

If you are running into difficulty with people in positions of power in your life right now – be that an employer or a legal authority or council, then you are being encouraged to have faith and to ask for help from the Universe through unconditional love to get through it. The immoveable force of bureaucracy can be enough to make anyone feel frustrated, angry or victimised! It is important, if you have those feelings, that you come back to your heart and don't let any systems like that eat away at your sense of self or trust in life. When the Universe wants something to happen, it will, no matter what apparently immobile obstacles lie in your way. I have seen and personally experienced this many times. It is real and true. You don't always have to push through obstacles in life. Sometimes you can just move around them or step right over them. But you do this most wisely through calling for divine assistance through unconditional love. The 7 brings this wisdom, faith and love into all our dealings with power and authority, whether it be through us being in that position ourselves or in dealing with others holding such positions.

7 with 9
(e.g. 7/9, 7.09)

The 7 and 9 is a truly beautiful number pattern that guides us into deepest trust. The message of these numbers is to let go and let God, as the expression goes, and to absolutely surrender and have faith. In a modern society where asserting control and 'making things happen' is considered the way to be effective, it can be truly challenging to accept the guidance of the 7 and 9. However the message of these numbers is empowering in a different way. When we are willing to let go, life can happen.

You will notice, if you look with a broader and more detached perspective, that life moves in cycles, and is very adept at clearing out that which doesn't work anymore in favour of that which does. Just leaving the positive and negative effects of human intervention through free will out of matters for a moment, we can see that Mother Nature moves through evolution of seasons, through extinction of species and creation of new ones, through adaptation to circumstances outside of her control (such as solar flares or crashing asteroids affecting her), and manages to constantly bring herself and her vast creations back into balance.

The 7 and 9 remind us of these cycles. The 9 brings not only a message of surrender and faith that complements the guidance of love and trust in the 7, but also brings an additional message that something is at its end.

We might be at the end of a struggle, or also at a time when it is hard to let something go – a relationship, a job, a way of being because we have to move on for whatever reason. It might be something significant in our physical world that we are releasing or something subtle from within us – a belief system or old wound, for example. Either way it will be meaningful and have enough of an impact on our future that the Universe wants to bring us a message about it.

If we turn to nature we see that to everything there is a season and a reason. We have to trust in the greater cycles sometimes. This is one of those times. Remember that an ending is really only ever a doorway into a new cycle. Such are the wisdom teachings of nature and of the 7 and 9 in combination.

This particularly beautiful vibration also means that a prayer or request for help from the Universe has been answered and will be coming to you shortly, so open your heart and allow that answer–in all its wisdom, whether that is immediately obvious to you or not–to manifest as it will.

7 with 0
(e.g. 007, 707, 7.07)

The 0 adds a divine wildness to the 7 vibration. This is a call for radical trust – nothing less than absolute faith will do here. It is a sign that healing will take place. It is a sign that love and wisdom will prevail, no matter how much it may seem that negativity or darker energies have got a hold over someone or something. It is a call back to love and to faith and a reminder that everything is divine, no matter what appearances may indicate, and so of course to trust in that is the only sensible recourse. Have faith. Let the Divine handle everything because it is doing so now and the resolution, the healing and the answer to the confusion or mystery are on their way now or very soon will be. Trust. All will be sorted out.

Healing Process

This healing process will help you access the healing guidance of the 7 in all its combinations.

Repeat the following at least seven times:

"I trust. I have faith in the healing power of love. My intuition and instinct is trustworthy.

Then look at the image below for at least seven breaths in and out.

Relax for a moment. You have completed your healing process.

CHAPTER EIGHT

The message of the 8 has multiple aspects. Power and authority are one of the messages—to step into our power and to claim our personal authority—but more than this, it is also a number of abundance. To be empowered requires a sense of self-worth. To embrace the message of the 8 we need to believe that we are deserving of love and that we are capable of taking responsibility for ourselves and for our lives, and to feel good about that.

The 8's message is not only relevant to those who seem to glide through life with only successes. I remember once attending an interview at a prestigious law firm where the interviewer asked me if I would be able to deal with failure and set-backs, given that I was obviously so successful in everything that I did. I nearly choked on my laughter! I did my best not to blurt out, "What a ridiculous question!" because the interviewer actually seemed very serious. Perhaps I had written a convincing resume for the position. I wasn't about to list all my less-than-shining moments on my CV. I had experienced plenty of knock-backs and apparent failures in my life. I was just stubborn enough to keep plodding away at what I wanted anyway. I say apparent failures, by the way, because it has come to be a belief of mine that if we are feeling that we are failing at something, then there just hasn't been enough time passed yet for success or the success is just going to come to us in a different form than what we had anticipated!

Sometimes we just have to unlearn what we have been taught in order for success to come to us. The trick with that is part of what the 8 is telling us. It is about claiming our power. We can think that power is about dominating or controlling others, but that is not true power, that is fear-driven dominance pretending to be power. Genuine power is about what happens for us on the inside. There can be reflections of that in our outer lives, whether others acknowledge and recognise the power that we hold within and perhaps turn to us for support or guidance, or sometimes it will not be recognised at all, but genuine power is an inside job.

I have met many people who seem to have all the trappings of power on the outside – money, and plenty of it, flashy cars, nice houses and all the up-to-date gadgets. Yet that appearance of having it all is often just that – an appearance. Underneath, they had issues and doubts and fears just like anyone else. They worried about what others thought about them. They struggled not to take on the shame, criticism, guilt and judgement that they felt from other people and within themselves. They were learning how to be empowered too.

I have also met people with access to genuine power which I would define as the ability to master your responses to life from the inside, learning to find peace and love in your heart, whilst living with all your passion and purpose in the world. That means when others try to knock you down due to their own fear or insecurities, you deal with it from a place of mastering your responses to them as best you can and getting on with your life. You might be able to eventually hold compassion for such people because they will be acting out pain, but beyond that, you don't get drawn into their issues.

One of my friends is a great example of this. She runs a dynamic and growing spiritual organisation that reaches people all around the world with a beautiful healing practice. She is very ambitious in her work and helps a lot of people tap into the beauty and depth of their own experience. She has absolutely no interest in controlling the experiences that another has, she just wants to facilitate their awakening into their own journey. She is also one of the freest people that I have ever met. Her response to me from the first moment that I met her some years ago, that continues now with her as my dearest friend, is that she is open, curious and interested. I could, and do, tell her anything. We have been through some dark terrain in our respective lives and we bring it to each other with fearlessness. We just know that the other will show up for whatever is being shared. We bring out the best in each other and encourage each other to claim more of our innate talent, power and ability to make a positive contribution in the world. She is someone I would describe as having an abundance of 8 energy about her. She is abundant, beautiful, hard-working, dedicated to love and extremely kind. Generally the world is a better place for her being in it.

Sometimes the people I meet who are genuinely empowered, like my friend, also have an external appearance of being powerful as well. Other times they appear to be quite ordinary and average, at least upon first glance. I know a Chi Gung master who is extraordinarily powerful. He demonstrates his incredible physical and energetic mastery from time to time, but most of the time he is silly, playful and loving. He is like a big kid! He could be zapping so much chi into someone that he is healing cancer in one moment, or pushing enough energy into a $50 note to turn it into something as hard as rock, then using it to swipe through a chopstick, as if it were a blade, snapping the chopstick in two, and then at the next moment calling me "Alana Banana!" and running off giggling like a child in the school yard. His power is real and tangible and yet he has the most unassuming persona. You'd hardly know the power was there at all if you hadn't seen him doing his work, and yet if you are sensitive you would notice that you feel really good about yourself when you are around him because he is an evolved being and without saying or doing anything, he brings more love into the world.

People who have access to inner power are very permitting of those around them. They don't try to control them, they want them to be free, just like they are, to be who they are, to make their own choices and to believe in themselves. It is very healing to be around people like that. In modern culture where we are so often told what to do, how to be acceptable, what not to do, how we should look, behave and be almost constantly, to be with someone who places no such demands upon you, because they have no need to try and control you, is most liberating.

The 8 brings us the promise of stepping into our power, in this internal way, to let go of what others have told us about ourselves or the world, and to make some choices for ourselves. The power of choice can never be taken from us because it is not an external power, it is an internal one. No matter how restraining our circumstances, we can choose to be at peace by choosing how we perceive things. No matter how vast or free our situation, we could just as easily choose to be unhappy by what we choose to focus on! The choice is up to us and claiming that with awareness is the beginning of our empowerment.

The 8 also offers us a nudge to take steps, if this feels relevant to you, towards becoming an expert in our field of interest or an authority figure in some way. This isn't a selfish action when approached from a position of acknowledging our gifts or knowledge and wanting to use them as an offering to assist others on their way. The appearance of the 8 is a reminder that we have an effect, an impact, on those around us even if we don't realise it all the time. Choosing to believe in ourselves and recognise our talents and abilities and the ways that they can help others, is a way to step into the loving empowerment of the 8.

If you are contemplating whether you are to move ahead or take on more responsibility in your life–emotionally in your relationships or professionally in your career, or both–then the appearance of this number lets you know that you are ready for it and it will be beneficial for you to do so.

The 8 also relates to the Divine Feminine or Goddess energy which in the ancient spiritual traditions of India, is known as shakti. That tradition considers shakti to be power, life force, what brings the latent spiritual light of the Divine Masculine into thriving, pulsating, powerful life! The Divine Masculine energy is where things start, but the Divine Feminine energy is what turns ideas into realities, what makes fire burn, what makes water wet, what makes our lungs breathe and the planets spin. If we have been taught that the feminine is only receptive, surrendered, then the idea of the feminine also having a dynamic side might be surprising (although if you think about childbirth–birth being a hallmark of the feminine energy–that's a rather strong example of being dynamic!).

The feminine aspect of the 8 energy infuses power with qualities of love-in-action, of abundance (creating and receiving wealth in all its forms) and with the energy of the Earth herself which is about feeling supported, grounded, present in the material world with love in our hearts, and a willingness to be open to life in order to manifest creatively (which is exactly what the Earth does – look how much she creates on a daily basis, how much life she supports through her being).

The 8 is not only a call for us to step into our power, or an acknowledgement that such a step has been taken and is timely, it is also a reminder that we are loved by the Earth, that she will provide us with so many resources so that we can live and thrive and fulfil our potential. If that means we can create something that gives back to her in some way, with kindness to her creations, for example, or through wanting to leave the world a more loving and healed place than when we first entered it, then all the better.

When the 8 appears you can be sure that you are being guided into more empowerment, more life and more manifestation of your spiritual life in the physical world.

8 with 1
(e.g. 8.18)

The 8 and 1 speak of a new start in matters to do with authority, empowerment, money and wealth, abundance in all its forms and even in your mother issues. Mother issues are any unresolved issues that you have with your mother that are having a limiting effect on your current relationships. Mothering is an art and whilst human beings do the best that they can, that best is not always enough for the child in question. From our mothers we might learn that we are special, precious and loved. We might learn that we are not enough and need to earn love, if that mother has her own unresolved emotional pain which she unconsciously passes on to her child. We might learn that we cannot trust that our needs will be understood or met. We can learn lots of things! As adults we then need to choose how much of that learning needs to be 'unlearned' so that we can create more constructive relationships and not continue to act out old unresolved pain, bringing our issues of distrust from the past into the present moment.

The 8 and 1 bring you a message to get as clear as you can with your intention. What would you like to create? What would you like to be able to choose for yourself? What are you willing to claim for yourself as a new beginning? What do you want to initiate? What do you want to bring to life?

There are no limits here. The 8 is the infinity sign turned upright. Possibilities are endless, we just need to make a decision and set an intention.

The 8 and 1 are a good omen for new business projects or plans, suggesting that they have substance and will bring in money, love and success, provided that we are willing to do the work needed to see the idea through into completion.

The number pattern also suggests that new ideas will attract the loving support of Mother Earth, which means that the right people, circumstances and opportunities will present themselves so that you can be successful. To aid this process, begin to imagine yourself as a successful being, and visualise or intend that this is what will manifest for you. Also hold gratitude for all that you have in your life. Gratitude is magnetic and tends to attract more of what we are grateful for into our lives. Try it as an experiment if you wish. The 8 is a number that teaches us about magnetism and charisma, and those are both qualities that can most healthily flow from the heart. Yes, there are wounded people who use those qualities to seduce others for selfish purpose, but with a compassionate heart those attractive qualities can draw people to you for healing purpose too. The 8 and 1 message asks us to become clear and set an intention about how we will use our power. The 8 has a karmic energy too in the sense that it brings learning and often swiftly at that. Whatever we put out comes back to us multiplied. If we put out strong energy with intention to encourage and support others, that is what we generate in our energy field – and in doing so, what we receive too. Give as you wish to receive, is also the message of the 8 and the 1 in combination – start a positive flow of action through your intention and consequent action, and life will respond accordingly.

8 with 2
(e.g. 8.28)

The 8 with a 2 speaks of stepping into your power in the context of partnerships and relationships. You are being asked to own your personal empowerment even whilst in connection with another. You can imagine that you can both be empowered individuals, respectful and appreciative and/or loving of each other at the same time. This might be easy to imagine, or rather difficult.

If we have had a wounded relationship to power through childhood and social conditioning during schooling, for example, being told that thinking for ourselves was disrespectful to our elders or a sign of ingratitude or rudeness, then we may have come to believe that to be loving and respectful to another, we have to dispense with any conflicting opinion or personal successes, subsuming our needs for personal authority into an apparently greater need for harmony in a relationship.

This is more often, but not solely, the case for women, even relatively independent women who might feel more permitted to focus on their career development when they are single and more guilty about doing so when they are in a relationship. The 8 and 2 in combination offer a message of permission to balance both personal power and relationship. It is a question of balance, not exclusion of one over the other.

The guidance of these numbers is also that relationships will be supporting you in becoming more empowered if you open up to that reality. The 8 is about personal choice and we can always choose to respond to a challenge–at work or in a relationship–from a position of either feeling defeated and as though we must 'lose' something of ourselves in order to please another, or from a position of growth, where we can choose to work towards a win-win solution that goes beyond only one of us being happy rather than both.

I have a client who naturally understands this aspect of the 8 energy. She is quite remarkable. She worked in a corporate field for many years, is vivacious, bubbly, intelligent and very highly skilled in her field of work. This attracts many admirers to her – professional and personal. Some of that attention had a less than pleasant flavour to it. In one corporate role she ended up being the target of vicious jealousy and some of her colleagues, who were threatened by her abilities and magnetism became determined to undermine her brilliant career trajectory. Her response to this was not to feel victimised but to find a way to benefit everyone through her skill at her job. She was always looking for a way for everyone to win, and she got great results through that approach. This was not a tactical calculation on her part, even though strategically it worked well to earn her great business results and team building rapport, it was just part of her generous nature.

Eventually however the viciousness of the corporate world became something that she tired of, and she took her immense energy and talent to other, less fear-based arenas, including not-for-profit organisations where she was duly loved and appreciated for what she did without others feeling quite so threatened by her. Instead they felt grateful for her skill and supported her as she supported them.

One thing she has always claimed for herself, no matter what field she worked in, is that she has the power to choose her own course of action, to respond to whatever life delivers to her door. That gives her an ability to remain loving and open, and genuinely one of the most friendly-without-agenda women that I have ever met. She doesn't become bitter, even through some tough times that were exceptionally painful to endure where people behaved very poorly towards her indeed. Her work situation in the corporate field became something like a witch-hunt at one point. It was an appalling reminder not to underestimate the amount of unresolved pain and anger that people can take from their personal lives and try to off-load into the work arena, often with devastating effect on those who work for them or with them. Nonetheless no matter what comes her way, she is always looking for a win-win situation. That is the 8 and 2 guidance in a nutshell. Remember, if this sounds good, or relevant, to you, but you are not sure how to create it, ask for help! "Through unconditional love, I ask for help in creating as many win-win situations in my life as possible! Thank you!" That's it. That's your prayer of help.

The 8 and 2 also bring the specific message that you will attain greater success and take steps forward in your work through beneficial partnerships such as through business partners, managers, agents or publishers, investors or benefactors. Don't worry if you are not sure how that can happen. It might be that an offer is about to come to you or that it recently has and you are being encouraged to let another help you with your career goals. It might also mean that you would benefit from such help, in which case you ask through unconditional love, that you be given the help that you need to succeed! That's a good request for anyone to make, at any time.

8 with 3
(e.g. 8.38)

The combination of 8 and 3 is very encouraging. It speaks of something creatively coming together very successfully, usually after a period of hard work or inner toil. The 3 usually relates to an artistic endeavour of some kind, so it could be that your path as an artist, musician, writer, dancer, and so forth, will be successful. The 8 and 3 in combination speak of recognition and acknowledgement for creative works, for the success that may seem overnight, but has probably felt like anything but that for the person birthing the idea.

These numbers also indicate that you need to take responsibility for your own personal acknowledgement of your creativity. Sometimes when developing an idea, or even finishing one, others will not get what you are trying to communicate through your creative work. Sometimes they will of course, but at other times you might be challenged to still believe in yourself even in the face of criticism, rejection or apathetic responses from others. We might need to realise that a work can have value even if it is not commercially accepted. We might also need to realise that in acknowledging and respecting ourselves we will be more likely to gain commercial success. Whatever our truth is in this situation, we will find it through listening to our hearts and learning to give ourselves the validation and recognition that we deserve. Whatever happens beyond that is in the hands of the Universe according to what is useful and beneficial for our life path.

Part of taking responsibility for our creativity is not only in honouring our creations, but in setting aside the time and discipline to actually put in effort to create in the first place. So if you are a musician, you need to play music! If you are a writer, you need to write! A dancer needs to dance and so on. The 8 and 3 remind us to take our art seriously enough to put time, energy, effort and love into it. No matter what we may hope or fear will come from it later on, we need to honour our choice to create by acting on it.

The 8 and 3 also speak of an increase in responsibility, recognition and authority as the result of a creation of some kind. Now that could be that you are suddenly recognised and gain a higher public profile because of something that has been created through you – a song, a work of art, a book, and so on. It could also be on a more biological level, so to speak, in that having a child will be bringing a chance for you to experience more empowerment, responsibility and authority in your life.

8 with 4
(e.g. 8.48)

The 8 and 4 is a very powerful combination that speaks of absolute success in the material or physical world. It talks of building foundations and growing wealth. These numbers indicate that laying a plan for success, or a strong foundation for it, will be helpful. They speak of dressing for success, preparing for success, expecting success.

Sometimes we hear in the self-empowerment movement of the approach of acting 'as if'. This means acting as if you already are successful, for example, as a way to attract what it is that you are seeking, through being it first.

This brings a huge change in attitude. To be in a position to be able to pick and choose the projects you want to work on, based on what feels resonant in your heart, and to be in a state where you know rather than hope that what you intend to create will reach many people and be helpful is a very empowering state of mind.

Think of it like the difference between begging for scraps at the table and expecting that there be a place at the table set in your honour. It is not about being better than another, it is about feeling worthy and dignified (whilst retaining a sense of humour if you trip over on your way to sit at the table) so that you can accept your place in the world.

The 8 and 4 together remind you that you do have a place in this world. My grandmother used to say that "every dog has its day," and I have often heard from people the expression, "it's your time to shine." These expressions relate to the 8 and 4. This is not a vibration about ideas and inspirations, it is a message about real, earthly manifestation and divine timing coming to fruition in the physical world.

It is also about choosing where you place your energy, so that what you invest your time and money in–whether that be fiscally or in friendships, for example–is going to be a wise investment. Spending time with those that you love and who love you, and who are able to uplift you, to bring out the best in you, and you in them, is a wise relationship investment. Spending time and energy with those that drain you, deplete you, say all the right words perhaps but don't follow up with actions, leading to chronic and debilitating disappointment is not such a wise investment of your time and energy.

With the 8 and 4 you are being asked to tend to your foundations, to keep yourself surrounded by those that support you and how you want to feel about yourself. This is sensible. You wouldn't try to build a house on shaky foundations. It isn't wise to attempt to build a successful life with a basis of relationships that undermine, drain or challenge you constantly.

This doesn't mean that we can't ever have disagreements or challenges in healthy relationships – of course we will! Rather the health and wisdom of the relationship is indicated by how those situations are dealt with. Can conflict be approached in a way that is affirming to both parties, that brings energy rather than drains it from one or both of the parties? Learning to say no to depletion and yes to enhancement in our relationships is part of how we prepare for success and part of the message of the 8 and 4.

This is something that I have gone through many times in my life. As my self-esteem grows so too does my realisation that certain behaviours in relationships are actually not healthy or acceptable to me anymore. As I change and grow within myself, any relationships that are unhealthy and cannot grow healthier along with me (it takes two to tango and to relate!) reach a crisis point. I have to then make a choice. Can I continue in that relationship and be true to myself and how I choose to live in the world or not? Often the answer is no and I have to walk away. Sometimes it is yes and that is wonderful. Either way, the results are always that in the long term I am far happier and more fulfilled, although the process of letting go can sometimes be very painful and sad. What makes it bearable is that I realise when I let go of a relationship or other situation or habit that can't really support me anymore, I am always going to attract in more love and be able to be more loving and giving of myself too. This leads us to the 8 and 5.

8 with 5
(e.g. 8.58)

The 8 and 5 combine to bring success through change. No matter what upheaval or chaos or uncertainty or uncontrollable situations there seem to be in your life at the moment, the 8 and 5 come together with guidance that you will be led into a more stable, empowering and successful situation because of all that.

The 5 relates to shifting and change rather than stable foundations. The change that is coming for us will be ultimately beneficial, perhaps a change of status in a positive way, or increased wealth or acknowledgment in our profession. With the 8 and 5, we are being reminded that change is good and necessary for growth. We are encouraged to embrace it. We are encouraged to take radical steps and to remember that if we keep doing the same things, we'll get the same results. Having the courage to do something different brings us different results and those results will be successful. You could consider it the divine hand of the Universe reaching in and messing things up so that a new and more successful outcome can take place.

The way to cope with the 8 and 5 vibration is to remember that we are always responsible for how we respond to life. Even if things appear to be going haywire or not according to our plans, it doesn't mean that appearance is true. There is a saying that you have to break a few eggs to make a cake. With the 8 and 5 we are being reminded that for an old order to end, and a new order to come into being–one that is in this case more successful–there has to be some messing about with the old order. Sometimes things have to fall apart to come back together in a better form more aligned with what we truly want or need to feel fulfilled and reach our destiny this lifetime.

Sometimes we can feel that we are the least in control when we are becoming most powerful. This is because true power and control are not the same thing. Being genuinely powerful means being open to life so that it can happen through you with increasingly less interference or restraint on your part. Then we become capable of great things happening through us – miracles of guidance and healing, being just some of those things. We will see this more in the 8 and 9 vibration. However for now we can acknowledge that if we are feeling as though control and certainty has been wrested from our hands, with the 5 vibration, that is because we are being moved by life into a more empowered and empowering situation. Once we stop identifying our personal sense of control as being power, and start realising that what can happen through us is a better indication of power, we will be able to flow with any changes with more trust in the process.

8 with 6
(e.g. 8.06, 68)

This is a message about leadership from the heart. If you are uncertain about accepting the teachings of a spiritual teacher, for example, trying to ascertain if that teacher is trustworthy or deserving of your time, devotion and attention (congratulations on being so discerning!), then this vibration comes with reassurance that you can trust your heart. If you feel that there is genuine love there, then this person can help you, at least for however long that relationship feels loving to you. If the teacher in question has all the right words and seems to be powerful, but you don't get a feeling of love around that person, it might be wiser to move on.

The 8 and 6 together also speak of a method of attaining success. In a world we were are often taught to take and accumulate from a place of fear rather than to give and offer from a place of love, this vibration brings us a more healing approach to success. Give. And give freely. Give of your knowledge, your love, your wisdom and your power to support others. Give freely and the Universe will bless you many times over in return. I have experienced this in my own life over and over again.

This doesn't mean that you become a doormat to the individual needs of those around you who might be more interested in demanding and taking from you (and draining you), than in receiving that which you offer, with gratitude (which enhances you both).

This is important. Giving freely doesn't mean you stop valuing yourself or what you offer. It doesn't mean that anyone who demands something from you for free should be gifted with your time and energy. The wisdom of not casting pearls before swine, or giving even an inch to those who would take a mile, still applies! Be discerning. The rule that I work to in this is if my heart urges me to give; if I say yes to something that is asked of me without even thinking about payment or any practical issue, then I do it. If I notice myself stopping to wonder if I will be paid, or feeling in any way used, exploited or abused by the person or situation that is expecting my time and expertise for free, then it is not of the soul and heart and I either withdraw from it immediately or refuse to get involved in the first place if I realise it early enough. I have undoubtedly ruffled some feathers using this approach, but what other way is there? I cannot make everybody happy and I have no intention of even trying. What I will try to do is live in integrity with my own heart. Then when I give freely, it is powerful and it flows and I am happy to do it. That is my yardstick.

If you are feeling that you are giving and you feel any sort of resentment or like you are being used – then stop it. It is not the right thing, or the right time, or the right way. Give back to yourself instead. When something genuine is flowing from the heart, you can give greatly and feel no sense of being taken advantage of, or short changed. You'll just give without thought of return and even though your intention is not in what you can receive for that giving, you will actually attract much benefit to yourself also. That is the message of the 8 and 6 – love leading to success.

It is a beautiful antidote to the more typically accepted methods of obtaining 'success' which are fear-based grabbing and stomping over people that leave us feeling so unsatisfied at a heart level, even if we seem to be obtaining temporary successes at an ego level. The 6 and 8 teach us that true success is experienced not only in reaching a certain destination, but in how we take the journey as well.

Finally this number combination also speaks of the power of love. No matter what situation is taking place, and how impossible it might seem to heal it or change it, love has the power to move mountains, or at least, turn them into molehills. We ask for help and healing, through unconditional love, in whatever issue may be causing us distress and through that daily request for help, we can trust that healing will come. Stay in your heart and believe. Although practical action is essential, there is something really incredible about the power of prayer. I once used to work for a management consultant who understood this particularly well. She used to send requests to the Carmelite nuns to include her business meetings on their prayer list. I was somewhat appalled! I understood the usefulness of prayer but I wasn't so sure about asking those devoted to God to pray that one's business meeting went well.

Eventually I found some peace in my heart in trusting that the Universe knew what it was doing and all things would ultimately work according to love and I didn't have to worry so much. I also found peace by qualifying all my own prayers and requests for help with the preface, "through unconditional love" and ending my prayers with, "for the greatest good and with harm to none." With those conditions I was sure my prayers, no matter what they related to, would not be egocentric or harmful, and so I learned to pray with conviction and simply to ask from my heart, for what I wanted. The responsiveness to those requests can be so sudden, sweet and accurate that I knew the power of love was more powerful than anything else, and I could trust that even if our prayers or requests for help weren't 'perfect', love was the ultimate authority and really had everything sorted.

8 with 7
(e.g. 78. 878)

The 8 combining with the 7 is a powerful wisdom number. It brings the energy of unconditional love and insight that flows from the heart. It is a combination that encourages us to share our healing abilities, whether as a teacher, a healer, a good friend or a shoulder to cry upon, with confidence and trust.

When you are attracting in this number pattern, it is confirmation that you are truly a big soul with access to spiritual power and healing ability. Even if you don't think of yourself as a particularly spiritual person, you have the potential within you to be a leading light in helping others find the freedom to be themselves. This can happen simply through first giving yourself permission to be yourself, no matter what, then living your life with as much personal authenticity as you can muster. Others can draw inspiration and confidence from you to learn to give the same permission to themselves. And you can hold that sense of permission to be oneself for others too, encouraging their self-acceptance. What a beautiful gift to offer to yourself and to others!

The 8 and 7 also bring us a message that we are in our integrity. Perhaps we have found ourselves in what seems to be an unexpectedly difficult or challenging situation and we are concerned about how we are handling it. The 8 and 7 let us know that yes, it is a challenge to our personal power but that yes, we are in our integrity in that challenge also, and that we can best find a way through it through listening to our intuition and inner knowing.

It has been my experience that it is often those that are most in their integrity who question this about themselves the most, whilst others who have not nearly so much integrity are far more self-assured! It is within our power to change this irony that so many heart-centred people are crippled with self-doubt. This issue can often arise at times when they are letting others get away with behaving very poorly indeed simply because they are willing to 'see all sides' of the story and then allow that open-mindedness to lead them to question their own motives and rights.

The 7 is certainly about being open-minded and realising that there are three sides to every story–as the expression goes–yours, mine and the truth! However, this doesn't mean that we need to deny our side; we can still hold onto our experience of the events and honour it and learn and grow through it. That is the point of having a 'side' in the first place, to learn to grow through our own life experience whether others agree with it, validate it, understand it or not.

It takes a big mind to be able to accept that the other person can do this too and we will both grow in our own ways according to our own experiences. Remaining in your integrity means that you'll need to stay true to your version of events and grow through that. In time, as you do so, your version of events may become much more detached, compassionate and objective, and that is wonderful. But to attempt to get to that place before you go through your own process and honour your own feelings will not place you in integrity with your heart. Most heart-centred people really don't want to be in confrontation with another. They can crave harmony and yearn for peace. This is part of their gift but they also have to be careful not to allow it to become undermining of their truths either.

The 8 and 7 bring the message to really empower your insights, feelings, intuitions and experiences, even if they are uncomfortable for you because they lead you into feelings of conflict or dislike or even rage. Those feelings will pass. But you must honour them to allow for the passing to happen naturally. If you try to avoid them, you'll end up suppressing them and this will cause you greater pain in the long run. The more sensitive you are, the more this will be obvious to you. The 8 and 7 urge you to empower and trust in your own personal responsibility and give yourself permission to process any situation you are in through your own intuition and insights.

If you are uncertain if you have enough spiritual ability to do this, the appearance of the 8 and 7 confirm that you do hold within you a great deal of spiritual and healing energy and you can heal any situation if you ask for help (through unconditional love) and trust yourself and life.

On a more everyday sort of note, the 8 and 7 can indicate successes in study and learning, that you are perhaps mastering a belief system, philosophy or spiritual course of study and that this study will help you grow in confidence, authority and power. More than likely study will feature prominently in your spiritual and personal growth at this time.

8 with 8
(e.g. 888, 88)

I love this vibration! It is ultra-feminine and abundant. It is the energy of the Divine Feminine, of abundance, prosperity and success. I dedicated the title of a book to it, *Crystal Goddesses 888*, because it is such an amazing number vibration to work with and so deeply satisfying.

I had an experience recently which I have referred to earlier on in this book were I moved house and left a five-year-long relationship in order to start afresh. I was honouring my heart in doing so, but it wasn't an easy process for some very painful months as I went through the necessary grief to really say goodbye to all that had been. During that time, I drew into my life some supportive feminine energy, the sort of nurturing and kindness that I needed to support me as I claimed back my self-confidence and independence again, for that had taken a few knocks in the process of breaking up and moving house.

One day, not long after I had moved and I was attempting to settle into my new life whilst processing my grief at the loss of my relationship and old life, a new friend invited me to attend some nearby markets with her.

I agreed to meet her there, asking the angels to help me find them (for oftentimes the angelic GPS is more reliable than the regular kind on my iPhone!). When I arrived, it was around lunchtime and I was famished. So I ordered some food from a market stall, and my ticket came back with the number 88. It felt like a good omen.

Soon after my friend turned up with a gift of peach-coloured roses for me. It was a sweet gift in its own right, and although my favourite flowers are actually stargazer lilies, roses have a special meaning for me, relating to the energy of the Divine Feminine. Whenever I receive a gift of roses, I always feel somehow that the Divine Mother is closer to me, that the gift has come from her too. So I felt very nurtured indeed.

As I sat down with my new friend to eat my lucky 88 lunch, and settled her gift of roses on the table, I felt a tap on the arm. I turned to find a woman called Tricia next to me, someone whom I had met over a year earlier and not seen for some time. She is a beautiful soul sister who was involved with the project *Women of the Wise Earth* with me and a number of other women. That project is now a book published by Balboa Press and collated by Nicole Gruel, and includes comments by me and the other women involved, on our journeys through the chakras.

During that chakra journey process, we all met at seven sacred sites on the beautiful Northern Beaches on the outskirts of Sydney, and at each site, performed rituals, chanted and engaged in discussion about the chakra that related most to that site. We were in tribal birthing grounds of pink rocks for the base chakra, near a cave and flowing ocean waves for the sacral chakra, hot, sunny sand dunes for the solar plexus chakra, green, rainy, tree-lined bushland for the heart chakra and so on. We created altars, sang, talked, danced, shared our wisdom with each other and it was a very special seven or so weeks of my life.

During that time, my relationship to the Divine Mother Earth deepened considerably and to see this beloved friend in the market that day, reminded me of that connection. It was also the time when I was 'shown' the Northern Beaches by the locals who gathered there for our sacred meetings. I was initiated into that whole culture of earth, nature, spirituality and femininity. It also ended up being the area to which I moved after my relationship break-up, and I felt continually nurtured into new life whilst living in that space.

Mother Earth was involved in the process of *Women of the Wise Earth* from the very beginning. I had travelled interstate to attend a writers' conference. I was urged at the time by a woman who ran the local new age bookstore to go. I wasn't sure about it, but I went anyway. I had some insights during the day, but mostly I wondered why I was there.

On my way to the bathroom during a break a woman stopped me and said, "I love your dress!", and we struck up a conversation. I promised to stay in touch. A week or so after my return to Sydney, my best friend who runs a conscious dance community dedicated to exploring the chakras and healing the soul, told me of a woman she had met and this amazing project based on the chakras and the Earth that she was pulling together. It was called Women of the Wise Earth and she thought I should be involved. I loved the idea! I also felt a nudge from Mother Earth because the woman my friend was speaking of was the same woman who had approached me at the writers' seminar in Melbourne not so long before that, Nicole Gruel.

I emailed her and we laughed at the connection and she invited me to join the group. I told her that I would love to offer voice healing at the beginning of each gathering, which is what happened. During that time I felt a return to feminine energy and nurturing that I had not felt for sometime. So seeing the Wise Earth sister, Tricia, on that day, some time later and out of the blue, felt encouraging to me – it felt like Mother Earth had called me home to the Northern Beaches where I felt so close to her and everything was proceeding according to her greater wisdom and so I shouldn't worry.

Later that day I dropped into a grocery store that I typically did not attend. I just felt to stop there and purchase my groceries. As I walked through the door I had another tap on the shoulder. Yet another sister from the Women of the Wise Earth was there, Nicki. As we chatted, I felt that sense of something significant again, a connection with Mother Earth and a reminder to trust.

On my way home from that nurturing, feminine day, I realised that the Divine Mother was in conscious connection with me, letting me know that everything was OK, that I was in harmony with the flow of her energy in making this move and in letting go of the relationship, and I would be looked after and supported by her energy. I just had to trust in the power of that energy to be able to do so.

When we see multiple 8 number patterns we are being reminded of this. Time and time again the supportive, helpful, guiding, creative and manifesting energy of the Divine Mother has caught me when I needed it.

In trusting her, I have lived some amazing adventures that have taken me around the world and into parts of myself that I hoped but never dared believe actually existed. She is still unfolding her grace in my life and I love her dearly, enough to brave the challenges that life asks of me because I trust that it is her way that is being shown and that way is love. Her wisdom message of power is that it isn't won by force but by love. In the Tarot, the number 8 is usually represented by the Strength card, which is usually depicted as a woman gently holding open the jaws of a lion. It has meaning, that image. It is feminine gentleness that can soothe the savage beast, the fear, the doubt, the aggression within us. Love is the greatest power.

The Divine Mother brings grace to anyone who puts their trust and love in her. I feel so deeply about this that I wrote *Crystal Goddesses 888: Manifesting with the Power of Heaven and Earth* (part of my Crystal

Spirituality series published through Blue Angel Publishing) to guide and help others to access her grace, that spirit of 888, in the same way that I have been fortunate enough to do.

8 with 9
(e.g. 89. 8.09)

The 8 with a 9 brings a message of endings and new beginnings all around money, power, abundance, authority and love. It also brings a blessing of spiritual leadership and grace, and an ability to heal similar to the 8 and 7 pattern but with an added quality of surrender into divine power. What that means is that we are able to 'get out of the way' with our opinions, thoughts, attitudes and fears, and instead allow the Divine to happen.

What that looks like is more acceptance and relaxation as life sorts itself out in apparently miraculous ways. We meet the right people at the right time, and doorways and opportunities just open up for us at the right time. If you are feeling that you have to really bang on a door to gain entry, it's either not the right door for you, or more likely, just not the right timing. When we are in the flow with the understanding that the 8 and 9 bring to us, we realise that what is needed and rightfully ours is delivered to us at the right time and the right way – according to the greatest grace. Imagine as a budding singer, being delivered an opportunity to perform, for example, when there was no one ready to hear you. That would be rather a case of the right thing at the not-quite-ripe-or-right time. The Universe knows right timing. The 8 and 9 promise is that every soul shall have its time to shine (and it's much more than the 15 minutes of fame suggested by Andy Warhol, but rather lifetimes upon lifetimes of radiance bestowed), but we have to trust in the timing of our own awakening. It is a part of a great system of other human beings and life itself. We look after our inner world, but our dreams and own light manifest at the right time according to a larger flowing plan of love.

The 8 and 9 together ask us to recognise the power of love, of divine love, of unconditional love, and to allow it to work its magic. When we do this we surrender doubt in ourselves because we believe in what is flowing through us. We can align with a greater power – whatever we imagine that might be, and in doing so, our own actions become infused with that power. It is said in the Bible that faith the size of a mustard seed can move a mountain. The message of 8 and 9 in combination brings us the same sort of message. The higher authority of divine love is the greatest power that there is – and we can tap into that power through trust and surrender.

The 8 and 9 together also bring us a more everyday sort of message. If we have been involved in a power-game of some sort or other–perhaps a nasty divorce or custody dispute–then we are asked to hand it over to a greater power of unconditional love through asking for help and then taking only the steps that we feel guided to take from our hearts. The guidance is that a resolution will be possible soon, so ask for help and trust and act on your instincts, so that the situation can finally draw to a close.

Finally if you are on a spiritual path and have been really working at surrender, trying to hand over your smaller will to the right workings of a larger plan, then this number pattern brings you encouragement – you are going well! You are becoming an instrument of divine will and power. Keep going. Keep surrendering. Keep trusting. The heavens are moving through you, as you. You are blessed.

8 with 0
(e.g. 808, 80)

When a 0 features along with an 8, either in pattern with additional numbers or just as a pair, the energy of wild divine grace is added to the mix. So not only are you going to be stepping into more power or authority or money or potency, but it is divinely orchestrated that you do so – it is your time in the Sun, so to speak, your time to step up and to be responsible, powerful, recognised. So you will do so and that is in alignment with the greater order of life, as mysterious as that can seem to us at times.

Healing Process

This healing process will help you receive and integrate the guidance of the 8 discussed above and in any other ways that are beneficial for you.

Gaze at the image below for at least eight slow breaths in and out. When you are ready, say quietly in your mind, or aloud, "Through unconditional love, may I surrender into true heart-felt power that I may fulfil my divine destiny. So be it!" Then keep gazing at the image below, and continue for another eight slow breaths in and out.

CHAPTER NINE

Because the 9 ends a numerical sequence, it is often considered the number that indicates endings. However because numbers can continue on indefinitely, the ending of a 9 is also a doorway into a new chapter. This is summed up in the expression, "When God closes a door, somewhere he opens a window." When the 9 appears on its own or in combination, you can be sure that something is ending. You can also be sure that something is soon to be beginning! The 9 lets us know that whenever we are asked to release something, it is because life wants to deliver something greater to us and we'll just need to have open arms ready to receive it.

The 9 brings to us guidance to surrender into that process. It can be easy to resist and fight against life without realising that we are doing it. Of course we always have that choice, but sometimes we can unintentionally make life harder for ourselves through our resistance, preventing the easy flow of what would actually be beneficial for us.

It's my personal belief that if we don't receive from life what is gently offered with open hand, life will politely tap upon our front door to deliver what is rightfully ours. If we ignore that, the polite knock will turn into a furious banging of fists or eventually, that door will just get kicked in. It might be quite a shock if we have been oblivious to the more gentle signs and invitations.

When the 9 appears to you, it's a bit like you have received a notice of delivery from the cosmic post office. Something sacred, helpful or necessary for your life journey is heading your way and you are being asked to be ready to receive it. In the same way that perhaps you might be resting on the couch, curled up for a few precious moments of relaxation, absorbed in a good book when the postman knocks at your door, interrupting you, but delivering something exciting to you.

At first you may begrudge the interruption, but once you unwrap your precious parcel with relish, interruptions to your previous activities will be forgiven. When life is delivering a new cycle to us, it will necessarily entail the ending of something that is currently happening. When we are in the new cycle, we will be happy for it, but we can be reluctant to pull away from what we are used to doing or how we are used to being. Sometimes it is hard to let go of what we have known or become accustomed to, even when we are happy about what is coming to us in a new chapter in our lives.

Now that process can be even more difficult to trust in if we aren't sure what is coming to us in a new chapter. We might be eternal optimists but we could easily be generally more anxious or fearful about change, uncertain as to whether we will 'like more' what is coming to us rather than what currently is. Personally I have found that even the most painful changes in my life have led me into situations that I ended up being very grateful for – but that doesn't necessarily mean that all change has become easy for me. Sometimes it is downright difficult and I wish I didn't have to go through it even though I am excited at another level for what I can sense is coming as a result of all the growth.

There is an energy of compassion in the 9. The Universe recognises that change can be difficult and the presence of the 9 brings us the support of divine assistance and blessing. It's a bit like the Universe saying to you, "We've got your back!" The 9 lets us know that there is unconditional love for us, no matter what is happening in our lives. Whether that love is immediately obvious to us or we find it hard to recognise it amidst whatever challenge is happening for us at the time, it is there nonetheless, helping us.

The 9 holds the energy of the highest levels of spiritual attainment, of unconditional love, compassion and surrender into the greater unfoldment of life. When the 9 comes to us, it is also an urging to trust in our spiritual beliefs, whatever they may be, and in the kindness of love at the heart of all genuine spirituality. The 9 brings us a message that everything is going to work out. I came across a picture online recently. It had a simple statement on it that I just loved. It said, "Not to spoil the ending for you, but everything is going to be OK." It asks us to put our faith in a greater plan, a higher power, something more vast than our own immediate anxieties or hopes. That is the message of the 9. The Universe has got it sorted. Don't worry, let life happen. It's all going to work out.

If you don't consider yourself to be a particularly spiritual or religious person, that is just fine. The 9 comes to you with a message just the same as for anyone else. You are loved. You are meant to be here on this planet, at this time, just as you are. Things are happening in your life according to an inner blueprint or plan, much like the acorn holding the natural intelligence within to become an oak tree. You don't have to think about it, or understand it, but you are here to grow into yourself this lifetime, to become what you are destined to be. Within you, just as within all of nature, is the invisible blueprint for this to occur. It is happening now, the 9 says, and you can trust in it.

The guidance of the 9 is that no matter what appearances are, there is love behind all things, we just have to be open to see it.

I remember a healer once describing an experience that she had with a friend. She could see that he was going to struggle in a situation in his life. She loved this man very deeply and yet as she spoke of her premonition of his struggle in a particular life situation, tears rolled down her face, not in grief but in joy. She understood not only what was going to happen, but that even in the struggle it was so utterly beautiful because she could also see the benefit of great love that was going to come to him as a result of what he went through.

I knew exactly what she was speaking of, having seen it in my own healing work with clients and students–and even in my own life–over the years. I would describe it as the light entering through the wound; it is in diving into and through our pain that we are healed.

This doesn't mean that every time a 9 appears we are going to be wounded or in pain necessarily. It does mean that when we are in those painful or wounded moments in our life, and the 9 is appearing to us on its own or in combination, then the Universe is letting us know that we are going through this experience in order to reach something far more beautiful – sort of like wandering through the desert before reaching the Promised Land. The 9 is letting us know that our Promised Land does exist and our reaching it is only a matter of time.

On a practical level, if you are thinking of releasing something in your life – letting something go, whether it be through a wardrobe clean out, a garage sale, donating books or food, or even something like ending a relationship or leaving behind the life that you have known and moving to a new place to start afresh, the appearance of the 9 lets you know that those impulses are in accord with your life plan and if you ask for help through unconditional love, the Universe will indeed assist you.

The 9 can also just as much indicate that part of the new cycle is coming to you now, and it will be through divine grace that it happens. By that I mean that it is truly meant for you and you might even feel as though the hand of destiny is bringing something into your life, so utterly perfect as it is for you. That leads us into the 9 with 1.

9 with 1
(e.g. 919, 9.19, 09/01)

The 9 with a 1 is a potent sign of new beginnings. I mentioned in the first chapter about the story of 9.11 and how the woman in that example realised that the message was about going beyond the initial impulse to just panic. It was about being able to bring in compassion and a new interpretation of old fear-driven messages.

I remember a spiritual story that circulated around the time of 9/11 and the year or so following, in which it was said that a wise man sat with his grandson and taught him that there are always two wolves baying at us: one wolf is fearful and one is loving. Both are fighting for victory in us. The child asked his grandfather which wolf would win that battle. The wise man replied, "The one that we choose to feed the most."

With the 9 and 1, we are being asked to feed that which we want to prosper in our lives. These two numbers in combination bring us the stark unity of endings and simultaneous beginnings. Sometimes, following an ending, there is a transitional period during which the seeds of the new are still incubating. We might feel as though we are waiting during such times. However with the 9 and 1, this is not one of those times! This is the energy of immediate endings and new beginnings and as such we have to hit the ground running, so to speak – there will not be much time to transition, we will just be in the new cycle. It is guidance to gird our loins and prepare ourselves to simultaneously release the old ways and begin the new.

If you have been asking for help with something in your life, then this number pattern brings you the message that your prayer has been received and is being answered now. Expect things to happen quickly.

This number combination also brings you guidance that your spiritual growth and personal development is going through an 'upgrade'. It means that at some level you have outgrown a cycle of development, having mastered it enough to be able to progress to the next level of growth. Now on a spiritual level, that's exciting stuff. For us on a human level however, it can mean that we find ourselves in situations that test or stretch us and we might feel less than masterful for a while. That's good! It's not necessarily comfortable, but it's good. It means that you are growing into a new zone of ability. The 9 and 1 together affirm that you will get through it and find your mastery – it is part of your personal journey this lifetime to do so.

Finally if you are going through a loss of some kind, a death, a divorce, some sad ending or even an inner crisis of some type that is truly causing you depression or despair, the 9 and 1 brings you the message that there will soon be light at the end of the tunnel, so to speak. Ask for help through unconditional love to have courage and be shown the way through the darkness towards the light, and know that this number combination is an offering of hope – something is going to happen which will help you move through this grief or loss and find your way into a new start. All will be well, especially if you take the hint the numbers are giving you and take the action to initiate requests for help or prayer through unconditional love.

9 with 2
(e.g. 9.29)

The 9 and 2 together speak of the soul mate. Usually we think of a love or romantic relationship when we think of soul mates. These terms tend to describe a sort of bond that is felt at a deep level that we usually consider to be romantic. With a soul mate, whether it is a friend, a lover or a child, there is a sense that the connection between you goes far beyond what the time you have spent together would warrant. So even if you have only been speaking to them for five minutes, you might feel as if you have known them forever. You might equally feel an instant and deep rapport to another that ends up in a long-term connection in a more earthly way – in a friendship, a business partnership that really nourishes your heart-felt plans, or even in a romance.

This kind of connection is not always felt in family, although that may seem surprising. Sometimes particular family members, especially a child, might hold a particular sense of soul bonding with you, but it is more often not the case that all family members will feel so connected at a soul level. Certainly you might love your family all the same, but the 9 and 2 soul connection is about a deeper and more unusual love and bond.

Some people believe that if you have found a soul mate–whether that be a lover, a child, a friend, a 'partner in crime' for whatever escapades you want to get up to in life–that it will be all hearts and flowers and smooth sailing. The thing with a soul mate is that although you will definitely feel your life is enriched for their presence in it–and they will feel the same about you–the path you travel together may or may not be an easy one.

Sometimes it is through our soul mates that we have the really big challenges in our lives, because if we didn't love them as much as we do, we wouldn't stick around to deal with the issues that can come up in our relationship. Those issues are sometimes very painful, but in dealing with them by going through the pain and not avoiding it, we can release them once and for all and grow in the process.

If you have been asking for deeper and more meaningful connections in your life, the presence of the 9 and 2 in pattern is confirmation that your soul mates are either in your midst or soon will be. Although the 9 and 2 relates to one-on-one relationships, you can still have numerous soul mates in a lifetime. You'll feel them as being the family of your heart, even if they are not the biological family of your upbringing (though sometimes they will be that too). So ask for help, through unconditional love, and open your heart to those that are in your life or soon will be.

9 with 3
(e.g. 9.39)

The 9 and 3 speak of divinely inspired birth. Now this can be anything from a sacred child who brings a healing grace into your family to a book that you are inspired to write. I have had dreams that have opened up entire new teaching philosophies to me. My book *Crystal Goddesses 888* actually came about because of a dream of a sassy black Madonna grabbing my hand, stomping around an underground night club in her short white dress and clumpy practical black shoes, before dragging me up some stairs, messing up all the neat and perfect spiritual work I had done with her clumpy shoes in the process, before sashaying off up a further set of stairs whilst I looked on at the strange disarray she had caused.

My life journey and eventually my spiritual work, which always flows on from my personal journey, branched out into new terrain of working with the Divine Feminine during that time, in a completely different way. It turned my world upside down and it was a very rich, though challenging time for me. I speak of that journey in the *Crystal Goddesses 888* book, but for now it is enough to say that our inspirations can come from the Universe in many ways. The author of the popular *Twilight* series of books said that her characters came to her in a dream, so vividly that it was as though they already existed. We can be inspired in many ways.

The 9 with the 3 brings us inspiration from a higher plane. When we receive divine inspiration to create something, to want to live or be in a certain way, it can feel so exciting and liberating and thrilling to imagine at first. Then we can have a fit of anxiety or doubt as we begin to imagine bringing that inspiration to life. How can it work? Will it work? What if it doesn't work? The human mind is capable of a lot of (often unnecessary) angst.

What we need to remember is when something is divinely inspired, we are being asked to co-create with a pretty impressive team of helpers. We don't need to know how it is all going to work out, we just need to do our part. The details and doors opening, when needs be, will be the work of the rest of the divine team. What you are being told when you receive a 9 and 3 message is that the Divine has a vested interest in this particular creation taking place. So pay attention to whatever inspiration is in your heart, or soon appears, once you start receiving 9 and 3 messages. Then pray or ask for help, trust and surrender, do your part, and then just believe that success is possible, for it is.

On a practical note, the 9 relates to prayer and requests for spiritual help. If you have a child in your life that you are worried about, it is within your power to pray for assistance on their behalf. You can do this for them whether you are a blood relation or not – the only authority you need to pray on behalf of another person is enough love for them that you wish them wellbeing. You simply say, "Through unconditional love, and on behalf of [*insert their name*], I call upon the beings that love [*insert name*] unconditionally and ask for help in all matters of concern in his/her life. Thank you."

9 with 4
(e.g. 9.49)

The 9 and 4 let you know that somehow, somewhere in your life, heaven is coming down to Earth. What this means is that your divine plan, your life journey, is going to be made manifest this lifetime. It is an assurance of divine success in the physical world.

I have a client who is very funny. When we speak on Skype to do some spiritual counselling and intuitive guidance together, I am laughing more than usual. And I tend to laugh a lot already! One thing that she often says is that if only her guides would provide her with a map, with clear signs pointing "go this way," she would do it! I know of others who feel the same way.

In a way though, the map actually does exist and we already have a working internal compass to follow it faithfully. That internal compass exists in our hearts. Sometimes it is going to feel as though our heart is leading us into some rather challenging territory and we might prefer to ignore its yearnings because our fears get the better of us, at least for a while, or we doubt that what it speaks of can really manifest, or we believe our desires to be impractical or unsafe, so we try to ignore them.

At some point however, the pull of our destiny–which is to become fully who we are–is going to be so strong that we can't resist it, even if it seems a bit nuts to follow such wild dreams or visions. No more can we pretend that working in a particular job is OK for us (when in fact, it might be killing off our will to live!). No more can we go along with a relationship that demands that most of who we are be left outside the front door when we come home at night! No more living amongst people who want to moan and complain and gossip, leading miserable lives that feed on the misery of others!

When you feel the call of the wildness of life in your heart–even if it scares the wits out of you for a (possibly very long) moment–you cannot turn back. You will at that moment know that there is another life that exists for you outside of what you have known. You'll not be able to forget that. It might take you days, months or years to step forward, but you will do so eventually. The presence of 9 and 4 is letting you know that life is urging you to respond to that call towards greater life, towards more genuine and authentic being of yourself. It is also letting you know that you'll be supported by life in taking steps towards that authenticity. When something is meant to be, it happens – usually far more easily than we imagine. The struggle is often more in us learning to allow it to happen, to get out of our own way, out of our fears and into surrender. With the 9 and 4 you are being asked to surrender and to allow something genuinely divine to take shape in your physical world, according to the greater plan of your own destiny this lifetime.

If you have been praying for help with a matter of physical wellbeing, healing or financial assistance, or in any particularly physical matter such as housing, this number combination also brings you the message that your prayers are heard and being answered. If you are struggling with any of those issues and haven't asked for help through unconditional love yet, please do so. Especially it is suggested that you ask the angels and unconditional love to assist you in whatever matter is troubling you.

If you need confirmation that the angels are assisting you, then this number combination is telling you that angels are real, are helping you, and are hearing your prayers and encouraging you to continue to pray so that they can continue to assist you.

9 with 5
(e.g. 9.59)

The 9 and 5 together can speak of the final upheaval that happens at a moment of great change. We can be preparing for a change for some time internally–readying ourselves to take a step or questioning our beliefs that would have once held us back from taking steps outside of what we have known–but it is often at the moment of transition that everything comes to a head. No matter how prepared we thought we were, we might feel very challenged at that moment indeed! So much so that we might not realise that it is the final convulsion of a dying pattern or belief or relationship, for example. We might think it is alive and more powerful than ever, but it is not. It is the final release of life from a form that has run its course. So even though in that moment we might feel suddenly more challenged by every issue we thought we had finally come to terms with, what is happening is that an end is taking place. It might be uncomfortable, messy, emotional, confusing (because of the 5 vibration which doesn't tend towards neatness and order so much as abrupt, exciting, radical change) but it will be an ending and a shift into a new reality nonetheless.

What you need to remember when the 9 and 5 visit you is that whatever is going on in your life, whether it seems to be the heralding of an ending, or absolute chaos, or even just a subtle internal shift that has you feeling a bit on edge, a bit restless or in need of something (but perhaps not knowing clearly what that 'something' is), there is a divine intercession happening on your behalf.

Sometimes we just need to be moved because what is reaching for us is beyond our comprehension at the time. Life wants us to grow. Life nurtures life. When we are in danger of getting stuck or not finding our way, life intervenes to give us a nudge. That nudge in this case is through change, internal or external or both. The nudge has love behind it. Trust it and take the leap, make the change, surf the waves of transformation that are rippling through your life. If they are not yet doing so, the 9 and 5 urge us to ask for help, and the change and intervention that we need will happen according to perfect divine timing. Remember that no one that genuinely asks for help will be denied. All prayers and requests for help are answered.

9 with 6
(e.g. 9/06, 9.06)

The 9 and 6 together talk of a deep and spiritual love connection. This can be on a human level in terms of your sense of love and deep connection from the heart with family, friends or a soul tribe (a group of people that you just relate to as a family even though you may not be a family in the more typical and biological sense of the word). This sort of love connection is more unconditional and open, with less fear, possessiveness and sense of 'ownership'. It is more about belonging than about holding another to your expectations, for example.

This deeper love connection with the 9 and 6 is also about transcendent spiritual love that exists between you and any spiritual being, whether that is a spiritual teacher that you connect with at a heart level from a place of genuine purity, or your own relationship to the Divine in some way – angels, or God, your spiritual guides, or the Goddess in the form of the Earth and Mother Nature, for example. The appearance of the 9 and 6 together brings you a message to be nurtured from the heart, to realise that the love that you are feeling is real – let it come to you.

The 9 and 6 bring a special blessing of healing to the heart. If you have endured loss of any kind – whether that is conscious or just a sense of abandonment or yearning for connection that you cannot consciously justify or explain, this number pattern is letting you know that healing is going to happen and your heart is sometimes broken open on the spiritual path of healing growth, rather than just broken! Making a decision to allow love into your life–spiritually and in other ways–will be so very helpful for you.

If you have been praying for relationship or other healing that relates to the 6 such as financial healing, or healing around food, weight and body issues, this number combination is a confirmation that your prayers have been received and are being answered. If you are struggling with such matters and haven't asked for help, this number pattern is requesting that you do so, so that help can come to you.

9 with 7
(e.g. 9.07. 9/7. 7.09)

This spiritual number combination is the ultimate request that we have trust and faith in the greater unfolding of a scheme or plan or situation in our life.

We need the most trust when we feel like we would probably be crazy to trust – at least based on appearances. Yet it is often when the wheels are falling off our plans that the Divine is finally getting a chance to break through what we think should be, so that what needs to be can actually be!

For us, although we may question it at times, this is actually a good thing. We can always choose to keep our fantasies in our mind rather than attempting to bring them to life in the physical world. Yet there is so much energy, magic and joy in actually experiencing dreams brought to life! There will be less-than-perfect moments as our dream leaves the realm of fantasy where abstract perfection is possible, in order to come to life in the physical world. But the joy of living the dream, even without all the shiny gloss of a fantasy, makes the inevitable mundane moments bearable. We might fear that actually bringing our dreams to life will shatter our fantasy of what they could be, and in a way this is true, sometimes our version of a dream has to be shredded to pieces in order for it to manifest! This isn't because life possesses some sort of sadistic streak. It is because sometimes our ideas and movements towards creating something in a particular way is just not in harmony with what it can actually be. Sometimes we think too small or miss the point of a creative project or group endeavour. Sometimes we have to think bigger or grow more before our dreams can really get a grip in physical reality and manifest. At other times there is such a small adjustment to be made and great success can flow easily from that adjustment.

There is a fine art to being open to life and sensing its currents and signs, whilst still taking action when we feel to do so – it is a gentle balancing of dynamic action and receptiveness, responsiveness, and intuition. The 9 and the 7 together bring you a message that you are capable of this fine art of co-creation through deepest trust and surrender. That's rather a compliment from the Universe. It is also a message that if you trust, the Universe will do the heavy lifting and your dreams can manifest in the physical world.

The 9 and 7 also bring through confirmation that you have a gift of healing ability. That might be to channel divine love through your hands, through words, through your body in dance or in many other ways such as through trusting in your own individuality and your own perceptions, intuitions and instincts, thereby empowering others with permission to do the same. There are many talented musicians in the world but there are some rather unique ones that lift their listeners to another dimension, open them up to worlds of possibility, healing and truth. In such moments, those musicians are demonstrating the power of 9 and 7 together. When this number pattern appears to you it doesn't necessarily mean that you have to dedicate yourself to a musical career that moves people (although it's a possibility!). It can simply mean that you are being asked to express your own view of the world and know that in doing so, you actually help people access more love and healing in their lives. Your truth can have an uplifting, inspiring and even divine effect on others.

If you have had an intuition that something is coming to an end, this number pattern is clear confirmation of that. If you have a feeling that you are healing an issue, even though you are yet to feel that really concretely, this number pattern is confirmation that healing is taking place and soon will be complete.

If you are feeling that you want to be more free spiritually, more open-minded and really grow on your spiritual path, this number combination brings you a blessing that this can, will and is happening for you now (otherwise you wouldn't be feeling that way in the first place).

If you have been asking for help on some matter, you are being told through this number message that your request has been heard and that the answer is coming to you – and you are most likely to sense or feel it from within your own heart or intuition, so listen to your inner voice, your inner impressions and trust yourself.

If you have been in a crisis of trust or faith, in doubt or conflict over a religious or philosophical issue, or belief system, this number combination asks you to pray for help if you have not already. Ask for assistance through unconditional love because the resolution of that dilemma can come to you with great healing and liberation from your pain into new levels of trust and understanding.

9 with 8
(e.g. 9.08, 9/8)

The 9 and 8 together speak of divine authority. This is about as authoritative as it can get! I have a saying that "God is more powerful than real estate." What I mean by that is that no matter how powerful a system or reality seems to be – such as the rather extraordinarily high costs of real estate in Sydney, Australia, compared to much of the rest of the world, if you are meant to be somewhere, you'll be there. Mother Earth will have her way, no matter what every real estate agency in the city might have to say about it!

I was once given an opportunity to live in a very beautiful (and very expensive) part of Sydney for several years with very little financial strain in the process. It was a situation that was so helpful and supportive, and so ridiculously lucky (from another perspective) that I couldn't have fathomed it before it actually happened.

However when it fell into place, I just knew it was the workings of life through willing and supportive friends at the time. It gave me an opportunity to heal and dedicate myself less to having to earn my daily crust and more to being able to write and produce a lot of material for my publisher during that time. I felt a freedom to surrender more into life that boosted my spiritual growth and opened me up to even more faith and trust in the workings of the Universe not just on a spiritual level, where I had always trusted it, but on a very physical level where even my material needs for housing and food would be met with loving circumstance. I felt extremely blessed and grateful. That experience is what prompted that little expression of mine about real estate. No matter that everyone would have said that the financial obligation should have been about five times what it was, the situation was what it was, and it was because of what needed to happen in that situation that it took place. When the Universe wants something to happen, it will happen, no matter how impossible it may seem or how many people say that it just won't or can't be so.

Our part in the 9 and 8 vibration however is to not become too attached to the situation once it has come about. We have to be willing to let it go when the time is right, trusting that whatever else is needed will come. During the process of surrendering my attachment to living in that house, I realised that it no longer served my needs and I was finding it ever more difficult to live in the energy which at first had been so nurturing to me. The place I moved felt easier to be in, even in a physical way because there were less electronic items, less Wi-Fi operated machines running in the house and less electro-magnetic frequencies because of that. With an abundance of nature all around me, the house situated in a quiet cul-de-sac street elevated on a plateau with expansive views over the surrounding district, including the beach and lush, tree-covered hillsides, I felt more open, held in nature and unconstrained than I had in years. I also felt more peaceful and clear in that quiet bushland, surrounded by clean coastal beaches on either side of the peninsula. My wellbeing was easier to maintain on all levels. It was further away from many events and the airport for my travels, but I had so much more energy living there that I could bear those distances rather more easily than the shorter trips I had taken when living closer to the city in more densely populated areas. I didn't know all that at the time however. I just knew I needed to let go of the place that I had loved; it was time to do so.

When you are connecting with the guidance of the 9 and 8, you are being given a message that divine authority, a higher power, the movement of life itself, is responsible for what is happening in your life right now. Not only can you trust in this; you can be curious, loving, excited and open about it. It's like waiting for the mysterious plot to reveal itself, in a way. It also means that if you have something that is bothering you, an issue that needs resolving for example, the divine authority is what will resolve it. In such instances, it's actually pointless to worry. It's best to let it go and see what happens, but if that is hard for you, then ask for help. You can say, "Through unconditional love, I ask for the highest spiritual authority possible to take care of this situation … Thank you."

The 9 and 8 in combination also bring a message that you are being urged by your own spiritual growth to step more fully into your power and confidence.

I remember hearing a story about one of the most famous and accomplished female singers of modern times saying that she was in a fit of nerves before every single performance and she had to have a stool to sit on rather than standing up on stage, not because it looked good as a performance posture, but because she was too nervous to be able to stand up and sing.

I remember thinking at the time that if she, with all her talent, had those nerves, then what hope was there for the rest of us?! However, the point of the story is that even those with a wealth of talent and experience still have nerves at times, so it isn't nerves that are the issue, it's how we deal with them. Although performance might not be a part of what is involved in you stepping into your power–at least not on centre stage (or perhaps it is)–you may feel that stepping into your power involves becoming visible or more responsible in some way, and you may question whether or not you have what it takes to handle it.

This number pattern says that you have to trust in the higher power that brings you to that place of increased empowerment. When life is offering you something, there's a reason for it. Believe not only in yourself but in life that is bringing you the opportunity or lesson or situation through which you can grow into more of your potential.

If you have been involved in any situation with authority–for better or worse–and you have been praying, this number combination is also an indication that your prayer is going to be answered. If you have been asking for help in a financial matter, or in stepping forward successfully in your work or career, or spiritual vocation, then this number pattern indicates that the answer to your prayer is on its way or happening right now. If you are having such issues but have not asked for help, or are not doing so as a regular habit, this number pattern suggests that you do so – so that you can be more easily assisted.

9 with 9
(e.g. 99, 999)

This beautiful, deeply loving and spiritual number combination speaks of the ending of a struggle and the rebirth into light. It can also indicate a time of genuine maturity within us, irrespective of age, on all levels including spiritually.

In the Tarot, the number 9 relates to the Hermit. This card often depicts a cloaked, solitary old wise man with a bird, an owl or a crow, perched above his shoulder, holding up a lantern. The lantern symbolises the light to find our way. His solitary nature indicates that we need to go within, to find our own truths, to listen to the voice of nature and life (symbolised by the bird) but ultimately, all our choices must be our own. This is maturity. When we learn to make choices based on our heart, and learning from our experiences in life, this is wisdom.

The 9 on its own or in repeating sequence indicates that we have within us power, knowledge and wisdom. We must rely upon it. We are a part of this Universe and all its glory. Accepting this gives us a sense of greatness but also humility.

There is a beautiful prayer called the Desiderata. My mother hung a copy of it in the kitchen of my childhood home, a tradition that I have continued with ever since. When I was young, I used to read it and it would bring me comfort. It holds within it the wisdom of the 9.

I share it with you here; perhaps it is an old favourite of yours, or you are reading it for the first time. Know that when the multiple 9s are appearing, the Universe is reminding you of the teachings of this simple prayer.

Desiderata

Go placidly amid the noise and haste,
and remember what peace there may be in silence.
As far as possible without surrender
be on good terms with all persons.
Speak your truth quietly and clearly;
and listen to others,
even the dull and the ignorant;

they too have their story.
Avoid loud and aggressive persons,
they are vexations to the spirit.
If you compare yourself with others,
you may become vain and bitter;
for always there will be greater and lesser persons than yourself.
Enjoy your achievements as well as your plans.
Keep interested in your own career, however humble;
it is a real possession in the changing fortunes of time.
Exercise caution in your business affairs;
for the world is full of trickery.
But let this not blind you to what virtue there is;
many persons strive for high ideals;
and everywhere life is full of heroism.
Be yourself.
Especially, do not feign affection.
Neither be cynical about love;
for in the face of all aridity and disenchantment
it is as perennial as the grass.
Take kindly the counsel of the years,
gracefully surrendering the things of youth.
Nurture strength of spirit to shield you in sudden misfortune.
But do not distress yourself with dark imaginings.
Many fears are born of fatigue and loneliness.
Beyond a wholesome discipline,
be gentle with yourself.
You are a child of the universe,
no less than the trees and the stars;
you have a right to be here.
And whether or not it is clear to you,
no doubt the universe is unfolding as it should.
Therefore be at peace with God,
whatever you conceive Him to be,
and whatever your labors and aspirations,
in the noisy confusion of life keep peace with your soul.
With all its sham, drudgery, and broken dreams,
it is still a beautiful world.
Be cheerful.
Strive to be happy.

– Max Ehrmann

9 with 0
(e.g. 9.09, 9.00)

The 9 and 0 together bring an absolute completion. There are smaller stops and starts within a cycle, something like climbing a mountain range and reaching a smaller peak on that range, or a plateau upon which to rest before moving on to the rest of the mountain. There will be that moment though when you really are as far as you can go with that climb – you are at the top! The only way to go further is to seek out a whole other mountain to ascend. The 9 and 0 are letting you know that you are at the completion of a process, of an entire cycle, not a small respite before soldiering on with yet another battle to win the war – the war itself is drawing to a close.

This is very special guidance and it typically doesn't happen often, but when it does, pay attention because you can be sure that divinely orchestrated changes are ahead for you and they will not be subtle ones. When you go through a change like this it can feel as though you are starting an entirely new lifetime within your current life. You might feel like a completely different person–perhaps still yourself underneath it all–but more yourself than you've ever felt before.

The 9 and 0 can also come into our lives like a kind of rescue mission. There are times in our lives when we are at our end – emotionally, physically, spiritually. We have just run dry. Again, this is not the typical fatigue that we might have after a busy day or week or year. This is the sort of reaching the end of the proverbial tether that comes during an intense experience of what mystics might call a Dark Night of the Soul. That is a time when everything that we have relied upon fails us. We cannot summon trust of anything or anyone; we cannot summon anything at all, actually. We cannot think our way out of the situation with positive thoughts or affirmations, we cannot find the bright side, or the silver lining, or any type of hope. We are stripped bare by life situations or circumstances, or even more subtly but just as powerfully, by an inescapable inner process that we may not even really be able to describe, nonetheless it has held us in thrall and we are lost.

It is at those times that we are truly the most open and receptive to grace. We might think that we are broken. In truth we have been broken open. The healing that can be given to us from life, from the Universe that can flow into us at such times is immense. That is the 9 and the 0. It is the Divine coming to the rescue, as it were. It is the divine intelligence righting the order from the chaos, restoring that which seemed beyond repair, and lifting us to safety when we no longer have the strength to do so ourselves.

You might wonder why. It teaches us humility certainly, but that is not my sense of the underlying purpose of grace. I believe it is kindness. We have within us so much potential. It is extraordinary what one human being, let alone a group of us working together, can achieve. Yet we also have our limits, the times when we need to be tended to as a fragile being, in order to move forward on the journey. This is the other message of the 9 and 0. Your tending, the love and care that you need, will come to you. You are not ever forgotten or left behind. You shall not fade away or cease to exist, for your heart beats within the heart of life itself and its every beat is felt in the loving heart of this great Universe. You are loved. And you shall be cared for.

This combination also brings you special answers to a prayer that you may have made or want to make – if you want to know the Divine this lifetime, to live an enlightened life where you see the Divine as living and breathing in all beings, then this is within your reach if you ask for it. Grace will come to you and you will be lifted into intimate experience of the divine presence. This is a gift of grace. No matter how much we work, our efforts can only ever get us to a certain point on the path; it is grace of the Divine that lifts us beyond where even the greatest human effort can lead us. If you have been wanting spirituality to become more real for you, then accept this number message that the Universe hears you and is responding. Trust and open your heart to life.

Healing Process

This healing process will help you integrate all the guidance of the 9 messages above, plus anything else that the Universe wants you to know!

Say the following statement aloud, 9 times, whilst placing one or both hands upon your heart:

"Through unconditional love may I be blessed with tender grace and merciful love. May I honour the truest path for me and receive all the support and nurturing love that I need to fulfil my highest destiny. So be it."

Rest for a moment, gazing at the image below, continuing to rest one or both hands at your heart. Breathe in and out slowly for at least nine breaths.

When you have finished your nine breaths, or however many feels right for you, simply place your hands down and become aware of your surroundings, coming back to this present moment in the here and now. You have finished your healing process.

CHAPTER ZERO

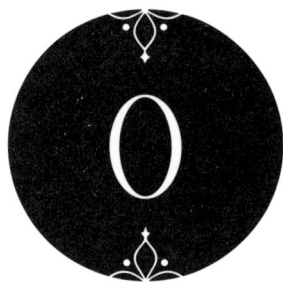

Although I won't repeat the number combinations for 0 as they are in each of the previous chapters and the meaning would remain the same, I do want to make a special mention of it in its own right.

The presence of the 0 catching your attention—even if there has been a blackout and your alarm clock is blinking 00:00 at you—is letting you know the Divine is near, and so therefore is the kindness, magical sense of possibility, and perfect resolution that you are seeking. You are being re-started, given a pardon (if you feel you need it) from your past, and an opportunity to let go of all that has been, to start anew.

The addition of 0 to any number combination, or even just the appearance of zero on its own, to me is like the ultimate stamp of divine presence. The 0 represents the infinite – it is everything and it is nothing. It is a wild card, because when the divine presence is strong, absolutely anything can happen. I feel it represents the energy of the miraculous, because of that.

It is a sort of re-boot, a chance to allow for life to completely take over and start afresh. It's something of a wild card because anything can happen with the energy of 0! Life can start afresh in any direction, unfettered by the past, by expectations or what 'should typically' happen. It might seem utterly random to us, though personally I do believe in a higher plan beyond even the most chaotic and unscripted of appearances. The presence of a 0 lets us know that there is something far greater than our immediate understanding at play. To me, that is the Divine. But to you it could simply be the mystery of life itself letting you know it's happening according to an innate wisdom, even if we cannot fathom how or why things seem to be proceeding the way they are in that moment.

When I see a 0 in combination with other numbers I know that the Divine, life, the Universe, is letting me know that something bold or brilliant is in store, that the Divine is 'up to something'. I have to say it's been my personal experience that although I get thrown some real challenges as I grow, my experience of the Divine being 'up to something' has always been marvellous in the final analysis. Any fear that I have had to conquer, or any emotional pain I've had to confront in order to free myself of resistance to life has always been worthwhile, though there were times when the pain was so great I wondered how that could be possible, of course.

When 0 appears, and the Divine is close up and personal with you—well it always is, but let's say that it feels more like that for us than usual—grace is happening. Grace is the help that is given when we need it, whether we know it or not at the time. It's help that is about keeping us on our path and ultimately away from harm.

Sometimes you won't even realise that you've asked for help, not having done so consciously anyway. In your heart, however, you will have done. And it is what is said in our hearts that life hears the most and responds to instantly, intuitively, compassionately and frequently with great humour.

Grace is always beneficial and compassionate, however when it is a dark grace, its workings can be experienced as destructive, disruptive, even distressing. I would describe dark grace like this. You are eating a yummy chocolate bar. You are happy eating it. Then suddenly it is snatched away from you. You are shocked and upset. You want it back! You might try to fight the hand that took it away. You might feel angry and wonder why it had to happen. What did you do? You just want what you had before. It isn't fair!

The grace in that darkness is that there is a nourishing—and actually rather more delicious—feast that has been prepared for us. To be motivated to get to it, we have to get a little hungry. Cue intervention of the dark–chocolate-grabbing–hand of grace. I say this with humour, but of course when it isn't a sugary snack, but perhaps a loving relationship, a high-status job, financial security, healthy body or comforting sense of familiar identity that is whisked away from us by circumstances beyond our control, the pain evoked by that dark grace can be almost unbearable.

The best way to deal with this gift of dark grace is to trust in what is happening even when it is painful or you don't understand it. Trust in the value of trying different ways to be and don't try to hold on to how things are. The more you allow change—startling and abrupt as it may be at the time—the more you are saying to the Universe, "I know you've got my back, I know you believe in me and I trust you. Show me the best way to fulfilment, to manifest my divine destiny!"

Typically we won't know what the bigger plan is at the time dark grace hits us. We'll just know that change is happening. We can only bear witness to the workings of grace in our lives as we take the journey, mourn what has been lost, grow into what is meant to be, and realise how our destiny is unfolding all the while. It can take time and commitment to see the journey through even whilst satisfaction is not immediate – especially for deeper work that can take years to bear fruit. This is why we need trust to get anywhere on the path without being in a state of constant anxiety, depression or doubt. Faith is the fuel we need to continue to take the journey.

If you feel like you are being asked to let go of many things, perhaps more than others, then know it's because there's a bigger pull to new life for you. The more cosmic re-ordering that wants and needs to happen for you to grow, the more disorder, chaos and divine destruction will come trampling through your life. Try not to fear it though! The Divine Mother can create an almighty mess in her kitchen of the soul, but what she eventually dishes up is nothing short of mouth-wateringly delicious.

And there is always another side of destructiveness – divine as it may be. That is the light of new life, of creation.

Healing Process

If you want to work with the 0 energy on its own, that is a great idea. Here is a healing process to help you absorb its energy.

Gaze at the following image and use either your left or right hand—whatever feels good to you—to gently trace the outside edges of the image from left to right, whilst breathing slowly in and out. Just let your gaze soak up the image. Don't worry about whether or not it makes sense, just stay with the process for as long as feels good, but preferably at least ten breaths in and out.

Once you have finished, rub the palms of your hands together vigorously and gently place them over your eyes and on your head, giving your scalp a little massage, just to ground you again in case you went off into an altered state during this process. If you feel a bit light-headed or find that you are becoming forgetful or accident-prone, bumping into door frames and that sort of thing, you need to ground more. A bit of careful jogging on the spot if possible, or some deep belly singing of your favourite song should help you to ground and come back into the here and now.

You have finished your healing process.

AFTERWORD

The more you work with the numbers, the more they will work with you. Take your time. Use this book as a guide, but also trust in what you notice in your own life or journey when certain numbers appear. Trust yourself. Get to know the numbers as you would any new friends. They'll reveal deeper and truer guidance to you over time and with attention. You are an intuitive being and you can trust in your responses. Just remember this Universe is love and any message you are given that is genuine, and not born of your fears or the fears of others, is going to be helpful and insightful, encouraging and supportive of you taking your life journey with an open heart.

May the numbers be a way for you to feel the love and wisdom that the Universe offers you daily, in pursuit of your spiritual destiny this lifetime. May you live your beautiful soul with all its magnificence and may you remember yourself to be that divine soul.

With love and blessings,
Alana and your Higher Guidance